PEARSON   ALWAYS LEARNING

Rapid Visualization and Drawing Techniques

Custom Edition

Taken from:
Sketching and Visualization, Preliminary Edition
by James M. Kirkpatrick

Design Graphics: Drawing Techniques for Design Professionals, Third Edition
by Peter A. Koenig

Cover illustration by Diana HajAhmad.

Taken from:

Sketching and Visualization, Preliminary Edition
by James M. Kirkpatrick
Copyright © 2012 by Pearson Education, Inc.
To be published by Prentice Hall
Upper Saddle River, New Jersey 07458

Design Graphics: Drawing Techniques for Design Professionals, Third Edition
by Peter A. Koenig
Copyright © 2012, 2006, 2000 by Pearson Education, Inc.
Published by Prentice Hall

This special edition published in cooperation with Pearson Learning Solutions.

All trademarks, service marks, registered trademarks, and registered service marks are the property of their respective owners and are used herein for identification purposes only.

Pearson Learning Solutions, 501 Boylston Street, Suite 900, Boston, MA 02116
A Pearson Education Company
www.pearsoned.com

Printed in the United States of America

17 18 19 20 21 V0UD 19 18 17 16 15

000200010270794877

RG

ISBN 10: 1-256-35789-8
ISBN 13: 978-1-256-35789-6

CONTENTS

Section 1 taken from *Design Graphics: Drawing Techniques for Design Professionals*, Third Edition by Peter A. Koenig

Section 2 taken from *Sketching and Visualization* by James M. Kirkpatrick

Section One

Introduction

....

DRAWING

Why do we draw?

The most simplistic answer to this question, clearly, is to communicate. Designers can try to communicate ideas verbally or with the written word, although we should not choose to emulate the poet or the novelist because ours is a visual art form.

Design graphics incorporates sections on sketching, design drawing, and the drawing process. Can these drawing skills be learned? The answer is a definitive YES. Artistic ability is a plus but not a necessity. Rather, a desire to learn and a willingness to practice, practice, practice are the keys to success.

In many cases, an awareness of reality or simply "learning to see" can be our guide. The average person is happy to process seeing into simply not bumping into anything during the course of a day. This, however, is not the level of seeing one expects from a designer. Special concern for relationships, elements, and details is critical to the designer as observer.

In general, the mere act of drawing—physically putting lines and media on a surface—has survived through the ages. Clearly this skill is being threatened in the age of computer-aided drawing. Fortunately, drawing educators across the country believe not only that the skill must be maintained, but also that it is a necessary foundation for the development of design to complement computer-aided activities.

DRAWING FOR FUN

Sometimes designers draw or sketch just for the sheer emotional and physical pleasure of the experience, utilizing the skill of hand/eye coordination.

DRAWING FOR DESIGN

In the preliminary or schematic phase of design, we are able to think through the use of our visual shorthand, drawing conceptual/doodle diagrams to examine potential solutions on paper. We draw to:

- *Record our ideas, rather than relying on our memory.*
- *Keep track of the evolution of ideas.*
- *Transfer ideas from our **mind's eye** that do not currently exist in a way that can represent future reality.*
- *Express creativity.*
- *Allow for change before change becomes both costly and prohibitive.*
- *Acquire preliminary and then final client approval.*

DRAWING FOR COMMUNICATION

This is the skill of presenting design ideas, concepts, and solutions to a client. These drawings may vary in scope from sketch—napkin art over lunch—to a full-blown presentation. The design process section of this text examines several presentation alternatives including the overlay method. These methods vary and are always affected by time and budgetary constraints.

Part One

S K E T C H I N G

How do we define sketching?

The art of **sketching** is an expression of a style or technique of freehand drawing. It is a skill generally learned by drawing what you see, relying on the development of hand/eye coordination.

A sketch may be:

- **tight** or **loose** (Figure P1.1),
- **line drawing only** (Figures P1.2 and P1.3), or
- any combination of line, tone/shadow, or texture (Figure P1.4A, B, C, D). (Color is not covered in this text.)

Sketching as a technique is taught through exercises that improve the ability to "see" while practicing and improving hand/eye coordination.

For the designer, the primary benefit of sketching is truly realized in the schematic or preliminary phase of the design process. This phase includes conceptual/doodle diagrams and image drawings. At this point, fast, loose, sketch-style drawings are a real time-saver.

Sketching as a technique knows no media restrictions; you can use whatever works or is at hand. However, a variety of pencils, pens, and felt-tip pens are still the most popular tools today.

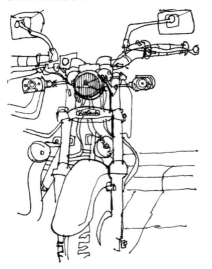

Faced with communication in the computer age, you should still carry a sketchbook with you at all times because design ideas can come to you in any place and at any time. A good designer's creative process never sleeps. Since it is impossible to remember all of your ideas during a busy day, putting them on paper is a safe way to prevent you from losing a potentially great one. Sizes and types of sketchbooks vary greatly. Choose one that works for you and that you will actually use.

When practicing sketching, draw things that already exist and that you can clearly see rather than using your imagination. Select things you want to improve on, and work and concentrate on them exclusively.

Sketches are pieces of information; they don't have to be considered works of art. They have their own innate beauty and should not be compared with more time-consuming types of drawings.

Often sketches have a level of simplicity that allows the viewer's eye to finish the picture. This type of sketch is referred to as a vignette and can save a lot of rendering time.

Sketching is clearly a very valuable design tool that is well worth developing. It can be done in any place and at any time with a minimum amount of equipment and can be used throughout your design career. Often a

Figure P1.2

LINE WEIGHT VARIATION FROM
ITALY SKETCHBOOK

Figure P1.3

LINE WEIGHT VARIATION APPALACHICOLA, FL

thumbnail *sketch drawn in a matter of minutes is actually very representative of what the more finished drawing or design turns out to be (see Figures P1.5– P1.7). Quick sketches done right in front of the client are one of the most helpful means of getting a point across. Once this valuable skill is learned, it becomes part of your design drawing vocabulary.*

Figure P1.4A

LOOSE ON SITE
COMBINATION OF LINE AND
TEXTURE

Figure P1.4B

LAKE ELLA, TALLAHASSEE, FL

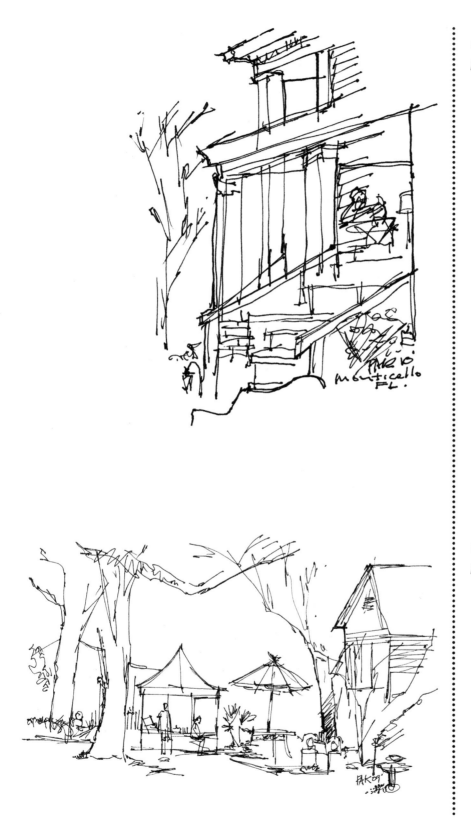

Figure P1.4D
LINE WEIGHT VARIATION

9   SKETCHING

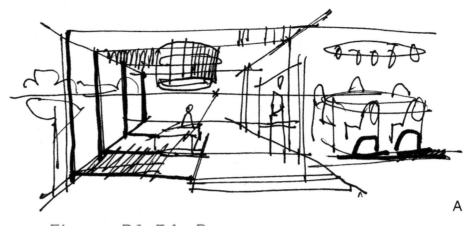

Figure P1.5A, B
THUMBNAIL SKETCHES, LESS THAN 3 MINUTES EACH

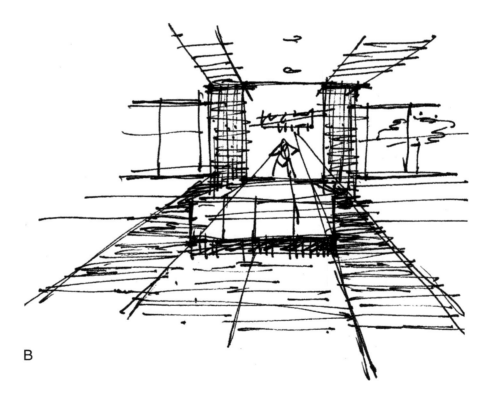

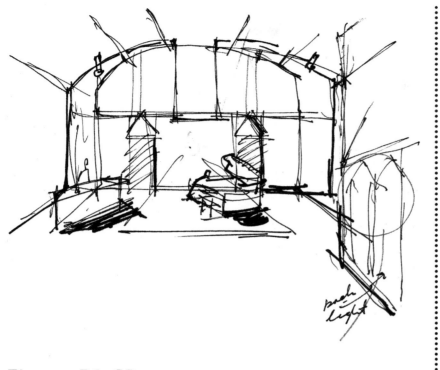

Figure P1.6B

THUMBNAIL

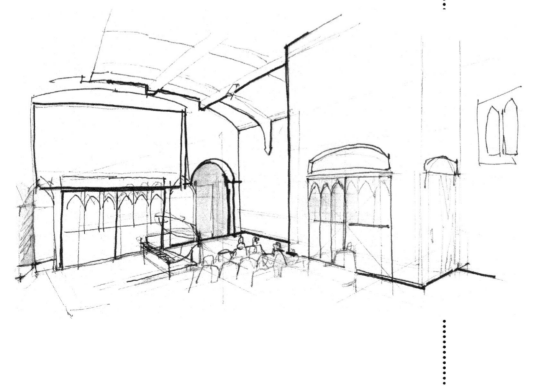

Figure P1.6C
THUMBNAIL

Figure P1.6D
MORE FINISHED

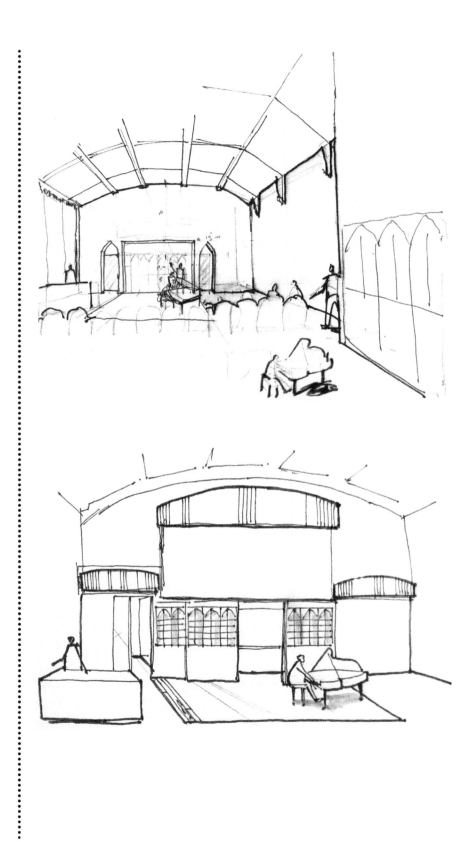

Figure P1.6E

MORE FINISHED

Figure P1.7A
STUDY FOR PEGASUS RECORDING STUDIO

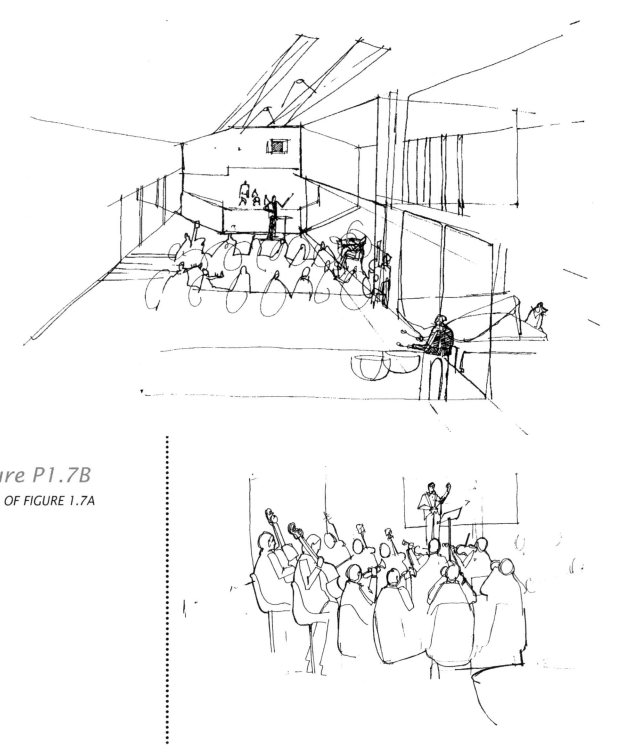

Figure P1.7B
DETAIL OF FIGURE 1.7A

PEGASUS STUDIOS

Figure P1.7C
FINAL PEN-AND-INK RENDERING FOR PEGASUS RECORDING STUDIO

THE BASICS

right
1

What materials do I need?

Basic texts often spend much time and effort listing and visually illustrating presentation tools and materials, even going so far as to carefully render a mundane drawing pencil (Figure 1.1). Since even a brief foray through a good art supply store will provide access to all your needs, the following information is offered simply as a starting point.

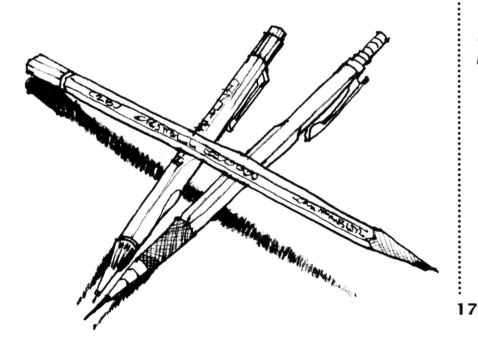

Figure 1.1

PENCIL SKETCH OF PENCILS

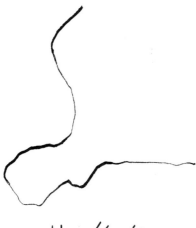

Figure 1.2

ACHIEVING A CHISEL POINT

DRAWING TOOLS

Pencils

*A pencil is one of the most versatile tools and is often ignored. The typical drawing pencil is a nonmechanical wood and graphite tool without an eraser. Mechanical, adjustable-lead pencils can be used, but the type of lead they use cannot be **chiseled**. The lead is generally brittle and breaks easily. Keeping a proper point on a pencil is essential to good sketch quality, so keep a pencil sharpener handy or carry a small portable one with you. A chiseled point opens the range of line quality that can be achieved by simply turning the pencil point. The chisel point is achieved by rubbing a sharpened pencil point against a sandpaper block or even just a piece of paper (Figure 1.2).*

As mentioned earlier, the typical drawing pencil does not have an eraser. There is a specific reason for this, and it may be more psychological than actual. The rationale is that because a sketch is a fast, personal expression of an idea or a method of recording what you see, you do not need to fix or correct it, thus eliminating the need for an eraser.

Pencils come in a variety of lead weights, the hardest being 6H and the softest, 6B. The softer leads are more suitable to sketching, while the harder ones were more appropriate for drafting. Today, hand drafting has been replaced by the use of CAD.

Black Felt-, Fiber-, or Nylon-Tip Pens

These pens are very popular sketching tools. Many of the drawings in this book were drawn with Pilot, Pentel, and Sanford brands of pens (Figure 1.3).

These pens come in a variety of points from microfine to broad tip. The basic broad-tip marker is now offered with several point sizes on the same tool. This is meant to make changes in line simpler to accomplish, although the basic chisel-shaped broad tip is extremely versatile when used sensitively. Versatility is extremely important since we must consider consistency, weight, and character of lines as they affect all of our drawings.

Figure 1.3

VARIETY OF FELT-, FIBER-, AND
NYLON-TIP LINE WEIGHTS

MISCELLANEOUS For sketching or rendering, any tool at hand or whatever works for you is acceptable (Figure 1.4)

Design Markers

The design marker is a fast, economical, and easy-to-maintain medium. I have been rendering with design markers for more than 40 years, and they have remained

Figure 1.4

BASIC TOOLS—PENCIL, FELT-TIP, AND DESIGN MARKER—AND THEIR USES effectively the same over time with some minor variations in the container and variety of tips. These tips vary from fine to broad, with some markers offering three or more choices on the same marker. It is my contention that the basic broad-tip marker is by far the most versatile and easy to use. Effective use of markers often depends on some simple choices, such as the paper you use. Parchment tracing paper and sketchbook paper are good for preliminary drawings. But the marker sits on parchment paper and dries slowly, whereas bleeding is a problem with sketchbook paper. Graphics paper is a tracing medium designed for final marker drawing. Following are some suggestions for the use of markers.

LINE.   With the broad-tip marker, turn to the narrow edge for the finest line, the medium edge for mid-range stroke, and the broad side for broadest stroke (see Figure 1.5). For finer lines, I prefer the basic felt-tip pen, but few tools offer the flexibility and versatility of the standard design marker. All brand-name markers are basically the same. I make my selection based on color range and comfort of the form of the marker.

TONE/SHADOW.   The design marker is especially effective for defining form and space with tone and shadow using the fast-sketch technique. Broad areas of

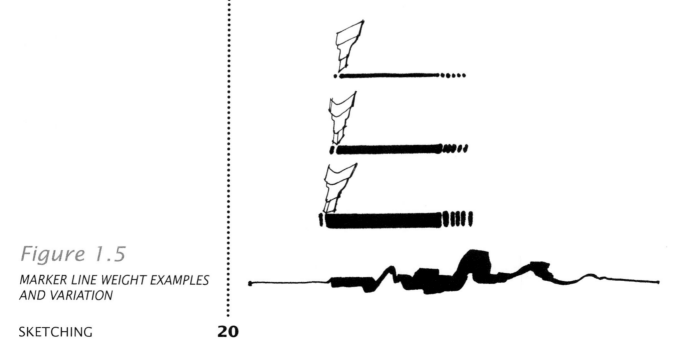

Figure 1.5

MARKER LINE WEIGHT EXAMPLES AND VARIATION

a sketch or the final level in a drawing can be covered in a very short time. Here again, we find certain marker characteristics that can be particularly frustrating for the beginner. For example, when covering a plane with vertical or horizontal strokes that are not perfectly aligned, you get a linear effect from the overlapping strokes (Figure 1.6). When the effect is controlled, however, it can enhance the vertical movement on a vanishing plane. In addition, overlapping the marker stroke in the same or opposite direction will enable you to get several different values from the same marker. To achieve a **wash,** or more even effect, move the marker stroke in a circular motion (Figure 1.6A, B). Various markers are available that allow you to render in the standard value scale of 0–10. Usually, white paper provides the 0 value, with 10 being black.

It is critical to remember that markers are a light-to-dark medium. Lay on the lighter values first and build up. For example, if you put a 7 value on paper, you cannot bring it back to a lower value using this medium. If you choose to mix media, such as markers and colored pencils, some lightening of value can be achieved.

Figure 1.6A, B

MARKER STROKE EFFECTS CAN BE USED TO MOVE A VANISHING PLANE

A

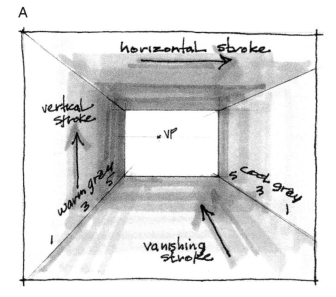

B

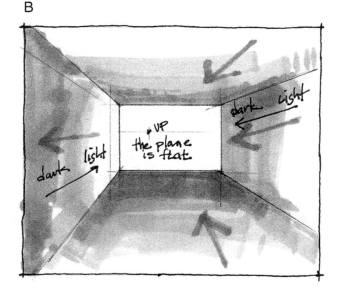

Figure 1.6C

TEXTURE WITH MARKER.MARKER STROKE IN CIRCULAR MANNER (WASH) PRODUCES A SMOOTHER EFFECT; AVOID OVERLAPS

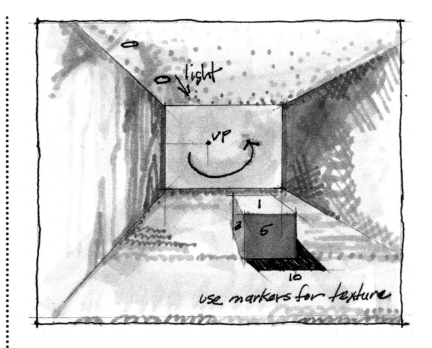

TEXTURE/MATERIALS. By using the different edges of the marker and different strokes, you can create a variety of textures. The T-square and triangle although antiquated tools can help control your strokes while not creating too tight an effect in the drawing (Figure 1.6C).

In this book, we are concerned only with warm and cool values of gray and the role they play in monochromatic studies and drawings. Obviously markers come in a complete range of colors that continue to make this medium one of the most popular for designers in both sketching and final-level drawings for client-oriented presentation.

DRAWING PAPER

The Sketchbook

Choosing a sketchbook is very simple since the media it is suitable for is usually described on the cover.

The key to getting the right effect from your paper is its **tooth**—the coarseness or smoothness of the surface. Any good-quality, medium-tooth paper works with pencil. It allows you to develop rich values and textures. Coarser papers are more absorbent and may cause felt-tips or markers to bleed, a frustrating and often negative factor in controlling the media in a drawing.

So usually it is simply the size that determines the selection of a sketchbook, based on ease of use, rather than the paper, which tends to be relatively standard.

Tracing Paper

There are three basic types of tracing paper: parchment (mentioned previously), vellum, and graphics paper. The latter two are high-quality papers suitable for a variety of media and are durable enough for commercial reproduction. Tracing paper, as we will see later in this text, is a crucial element in the overlay method.

YELLOW OR WHITE PARCHMENT TRACING PAPER.
This is the least expensive tracing paper and comes in rolls or pads of varying widths and sizes. The paper is very fragile and is suitable only for preliminary types of sketches and studies. It is meant to be used, abused, and inevitably thrown away. Designers historically refer to it as trash or bumwad. Psychologically, this paper is seen as a preliminary medium for fast, loose drawings that are clearly subject to change. Soft pencils and felt-tip pens are ideal on this surface, since anything harder will easily tear the paper. White tracing paper is far more popular today.

VELLUM AND GRAPHICS PAPER.
Generally vellum is recommended for drafting, while graphics paper is used for presentation purposes. Graphics paper is a good surface for graphite, inks, and markers. Drawings on vellum and graphics paper can be saved as originals using a variety of reproduction methods or used in final presentations or scanned for use with computer software programs or PowerPoint presentations.

Miscellaneous Papers

A tremendous selection of drawing papers may be purchased by the sheet. I suggest, once again, visiting the art supply store to see and to sample them.

BASIC DRAWING ADVICE

The very first step to success in drawing is to **loosen up**. Drawing, like many athletic activities, is a connection among mind, eye, and hand. Thus, as with all physical activity or exercise, a warm-up phase is suggested. Simple movement of the arms, wrists, and fingers can be effective. When drawing, having tight muscles and joints will have an adverse effect, so remember to be loose, free, and relaxed. This will allow you to enjoy and enhance your drawing experience.

LINE

What is line?

Line is the basic element common to all drawings. To the beginner, simply making the first mark that destroys the purity and perfection of the white sheet of paper can instill fear. Remember that this fear is irrational, so be bold and draw away!

In the sketching phase, although most students still have a T-square and triangles even in the CAD age, these tools are not allowed to be used.

A beginner who does not feel that he or she is artistic often exclaims, "I can't even draw a straight line!" We deal with this by stressing that design drawing and sketching can be learned. In fact, in freehand drawing it is the acceptance of the illusion that the line is straight that really counts. Of course, with practice you can achieve relatively straight lines by improving your hand/eye coordination. In the final analysis, the ability to draw a line from point A to point B (Figure 2.1) does not an artist make!

When attempting to draw a straight line, rest your hand firmly on a steady surface and move only your hand

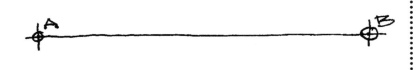

Figure 2.1

DRAW A STRAIGHT LINE IN ONE STROKE

Figure 2.2

DON'T SHAKE OUT THE LINE

Figure 2.3

EXAMPLE OF ARCHITECTURAL
OVERLAP

and forearm across the paper. Avoid what I refer to as shaking out the line (Figure 2.2). Try to draw the line with one bold, confident stroke, rather than stopping and starting to correct for direction. An architectural effect can be achieved by overlapping the line at the corners of a shape or form (Figure 2.3).

ELEMENTS OF A LINE

The three basic **elements of a line** are consistency, line weight variation, and quality.

Consistency

Practice this effect in a drawing by keeping the lines the same weight (thickness) or character no matter what the subject (Figure 2.4). This is an interesting but limited technique that is more of an exercise of control. It is often used more effectively in technical or mechanical drawing (see Figure 2.4B).

Figure 2.4

LINE CONSISTENCY

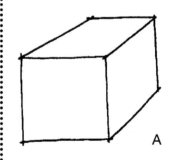

Weight Variation

Line weight variation adds to the illusion of three-dimensional form. Visually, **line weight** is the thickness of a line. The thinner the line, the lighter is the weight. These weight differences help us to distinguish between architectural elements and to define individual forms (Figure 2.5). Lightweight lines usually are internal and help to complete the form. Medium-weight or profile lines define the form and help place it spatially. Heavyweight lines define architectural features or act as base plane lines that help to ground the form (Figure 2.6). The two sketches in Figure 2.7A, B show line weight variation on sketchbook paper. See Figure 2.7C that shows line weight variation on grey board.

Quality (Character)

Quality is the most expressive use of line, and it truly enhances a sketch's style. Good line quality helps define and make the illusion of curved or round shapes or forms more believable (Figure 2.8A, B, C, D). Most often, however, the quality of line is best utilized in freeform objects such as plants, clothing, window coverings, and many other elements typically found in residential or commercial interior or exterior sketches.

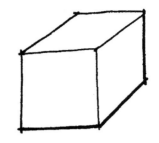

Figure 2.5

LINE WEIGHT VARIATION

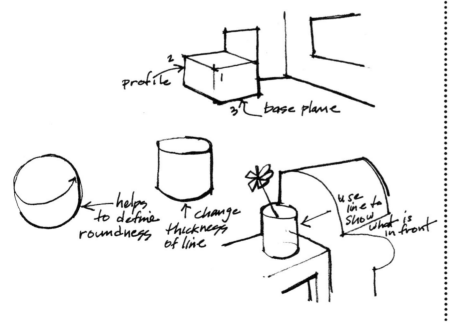

Figure 2.6

LINE WEIGHT VARIATION USED TO DEFINE SPACE AND OBJECTS

Figure 2.7A, B

SKETCHES WITH LINE WEIGHT
VARIATION ON SKETCHBOOK
PAPER

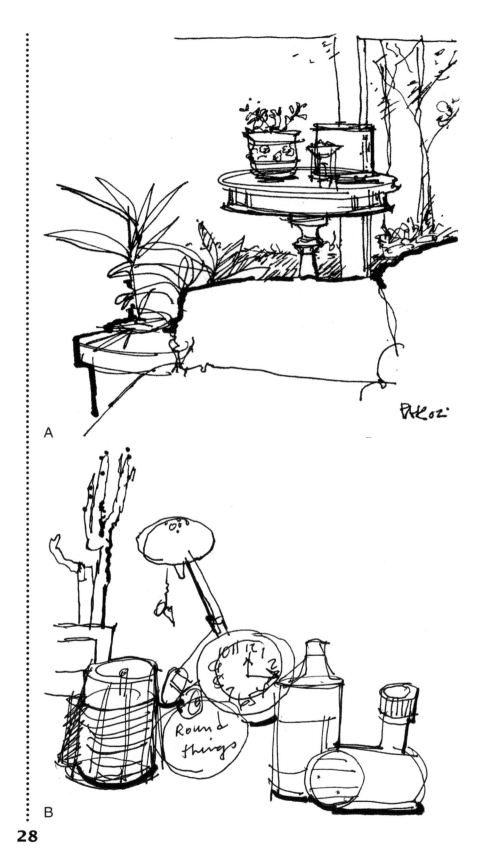

A

B

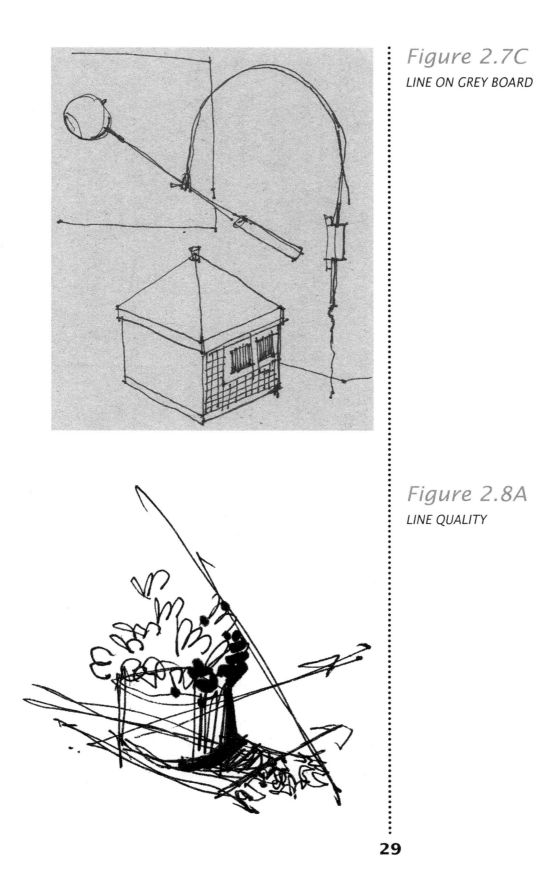

Figure 2.7C
LINE ON GREY BOARD

Figure 2.8A
LINE QUALITY

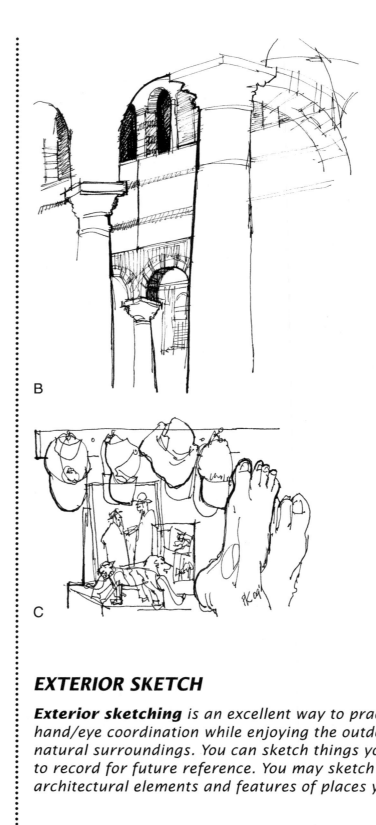

B

C

EXTERIOR SKETCH

Exterior sketching is an excellent way to practice hand/eye coordination while enjoying the outdoors and natural surroundings. You can sketch things you want to record for future reference. You may sketch the architectural elements and features of places you visit,

Figure 2.8D
(CONTINUED)

*or you can sketch in nature just for the sheer pleasure
of doing it.*

*Whether sketching natural or man-made elements, it
is important to remember the basics: line, tone/shadow,
and texture/materials.*

*When sketching trees and plants, look carefully at—
"learn to see"—their form, growth patterns, shapes, and
textures. Natural sunlight is the strongest source of light
and will strongly affect the elements and the impact of*

your drawing. Sunny days usually produce the shadows that make the boldest sketches.

Select your subject matter carefully and compose your sketchbook page with the eye of a camera. Composition remains a consideration whether you are drawing a major landscape or cityscape, a single element, or even the smallest detail.

As a beginner, you should limit the scope of what you choose to draw and keep track of the time it takes you to accomplish what you set out to achieve. Over time, with practice, you will be able to increase the pace and shorten the time it takes to do these sketches. Your knowledge of basic one-point and two-point perspective is important. While drawing outdoors, look for and identify the ground line, horizon line, and vanishing points and establish a picture plane that will increase the illusion of a believable perspective view (Figure 2.9).

Always note the goals you wish to achieve in your sketch exercises; this allows you to measure your success. For example, I sometimes study a building's form using line only. Or I may study the leaf growth pattern of a particular tree.

Set time limits for these sketches from a few minutes to an hour (see Figure 2.10A, B, C).

INTERIOR SKETCH

Interior sketch subjects are always available and are not affected by weather conditions. You can study entire rooms in residential and nonresidential situations. You can study furniture relationships; usually a grouping of three objects works well. You can study any interior detail.

You can actually set up a still life to practice drawing specific items that express the shapes, forms, and textures that will offer a challenge. Or go out and look for things that are interesting to practice on.

Figure 2.10A

EXTERIOR VIGNETTES

Figure 2.10B
EXTERIOR VIGNETTES

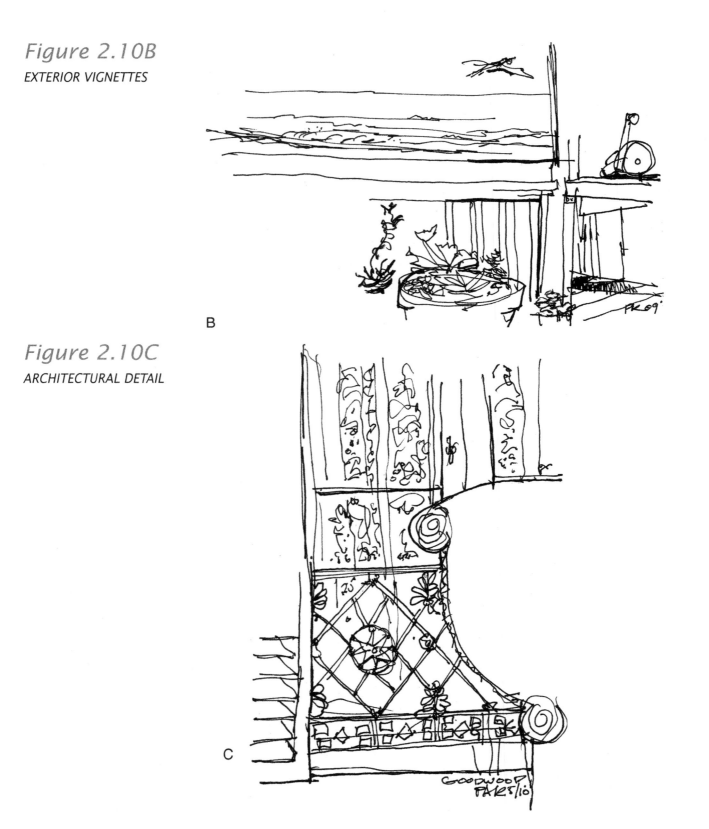

B

Figure 2.10C
ARCHITECTURAL DETAIL

C

Line Exercises

I. "LOOSEN-UP" EXERCISE

The most informal of the "loosen-up" exercises involves the use of line in a variety of movements across the page. These exercises should be fast paced and should serve only as a warm-up.

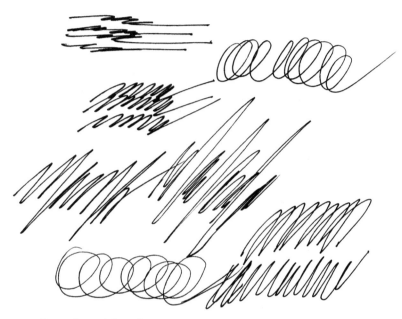

Media: sketchbook
          all pencil, pen, felt-tip, etc.

II. LINE CONTROL EXERCISES

1. Basic Line Consistency

Use a variety of vertical, horizontal, and diagonal line directions or vary the spacing while keeping the line a consistent thickness. Control is the key to this exercise.

  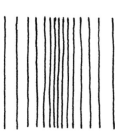 

2. Line Consistency with Variety

Use your imagination to draw loops, swirls, or any other interesting line movements.

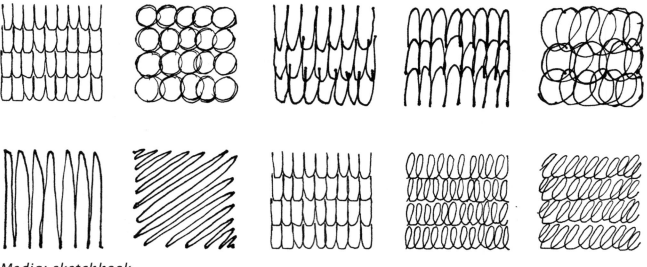

Media: sketchbook
pencil, felt-tip
One or two pages
Size: 1½" x 1½" squares

III. HAND/EYE COORDINATION EXERCISES: STILL LIFE STUDY

This study may be a single object or a complex composition. In the classroom, a good variety of shapes, forms, and textures works best. They may include cans, bottles, purses, jackets, drafting tools, plants, and various found objects. Still lifes improve hand/eye coordination.

1. Line

Study the subject in line weight only.

2. Texture/Materials

Study texture and materials only; disregard line and light. It is not necessary to draw the entire still life; be selective within the time limit.

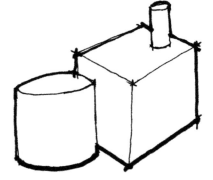

Again time is relative, but a minimum of 10 minutes is effective. This exercise can be done in either interior or exterior locations.

In the classroom, use the same still life for all of these exercises. The still life must include objects that have clearly definable textures or patterns. Wood, glass, coarse fabrics, and plants are just a few things that work well.

Everything has texture, but things with smooth or slick textures don't work as well. You should, however, feel free to use some generic textures such as stippling or cross-hatching.

3. Tone/Shadow

Tone/shadow exercises can be done in either interior or exterior locations. In the classroom specifically, setting up a still life works well. A good source of light is very important.

Study the subject for tone and shadow only. Don't outline objects, but use tone to define form and shadow to reinforce the direction and quantity of light. Remember this rule of thumb: Shadow is darker than shade. Do not consider texture or pattern.

4. Line, Tone/Shadow, and Texture/Material

This exercise is usually the final step after completing the previous two exercises. Having studied the still life for light and texture/material (pattern) separately, you should now put them together selectively with line effects to produce the strongest drawing. As you will learn later in the book, this is the basic concept behind the overlay method.

Once again the time spent is relative to the scope and complexity of the still life.

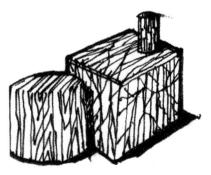

Media: sketchbook
    pencil, felt-tip,
    marker
Size: varies ½ to full page
Time: 10–20 minutes

LIGHT

What is light?

Light is the element of design that defines all that we see and how we see it. Sunlight and artificial light from any man-made source are the primary choices to determine how our drawings read and make a visual impact. We distinguish shapes or forms in space through tone, value, or shade (basically interchangeable terms) and shadows cast by light striking form.

TONE, VALUE, OR SHADE

The terms tone, value, and shade refer to the way light affects a shape, object, or form. **Value** is most often used to grade lightness or darkness. Values range from zero (0), which equals white, to 10, which equals black (Figure 3.1).

A value of 10 is usually reserved for shadow based on the rule of thumb "Shadow is darker than shade." This is an important factor because we can clearly read form relationships only with a lighter value next to a darker one. A value of 10 on a form with shadow value of 10 would blend together and the clarity of the form would be lost.

Changes in value are produced by altering the direction and intensity of the light source.

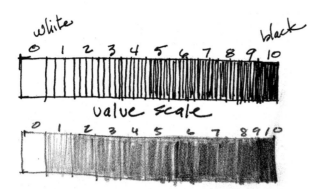

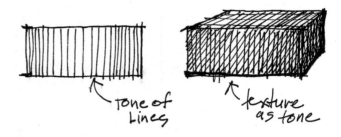

Figure 3.1

VALUE SCALE

SHADOW

There are an almost unlimited number of formulas for casting shadows. The key to understanding the use of shadow in a drawing is to follow the rule, "What you see is what you get." It is no more complicated than that. Reality-based shadows can be created using a simple lamp as a source on objects or models to simulate the scene you want to create.

Shadows often have an **umbra**, a darker aura, and **penumbra**, a lighter aura (Figure 3.2A, B, C, D). Shadows may appear crisp with hard or soft edges and blend more

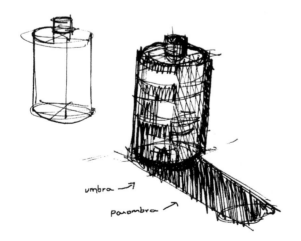

Figure 3.2A

A. SKETCH DONE WITH BLACK
UNIBALL MICRO PEN

Figure 3.2B

B. SHADOW RELIES ON SUN
DIRECTION AND SCALE

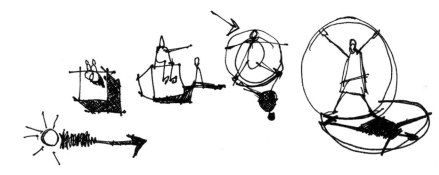

Figure 3.2C

C. SKETCH FIGURES WITH
SHADOWS

Figure 3.2D

MOYA AND MIA CASTING
SHADOWS

*into the drawing. Your drawings should always maintain
a clear and consistent light source.*

*People who view your drawings may not be artistic,
but they are used to seeing the effects of light in their
daily lives. So, if you want them to accept the illusion of
what you have drawn, your use of light will be critical.*

ONE-POINT SHADOW CASTING

1. Select a light source.

2. Apply tone to the form (see Figure 3.3).

3. Select points on the planes of the form that will block light and cast a shadow.

4. Draw consistent angles from these points (typically 30°).

5. From the top shadow-casting points, use 45° angle lines to determine the length of the shadow. In reality, the shadow changes as the angle of the light source changes. When a light source is directly over an object, it produces no shadow.

6. The 45° lines will intersect the 30° lines, then close out the shadow with a parallel line and a line to the vanishing point (VP).

7. The same principles apply to this open-leg table.

TWO-POINT SHADOW CASTING

1. Select a light source.
2. Draw lines through the shadow-casting points in the direction the shadow will fall.
3. Draw a line parallel to the object at point A.

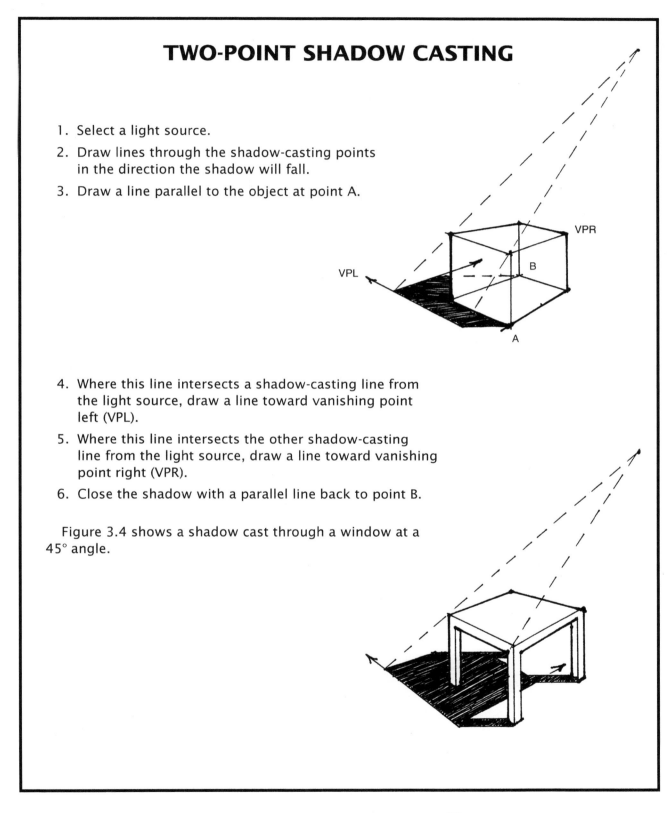

4. Where this line intersects a shadow-casting line from the light source, draw a line toward vanishing point left (VPL).
5. Where this line intersects the other shadow-casting line from the light source, draw a line toward vanishing point right (VPR).
6. Close the shadow with a parallel line back to point B.

Figure 3.4 shows a shadow cast through a window at a 45° angle.

Figure 3.3
TEXTURE OVER TONE

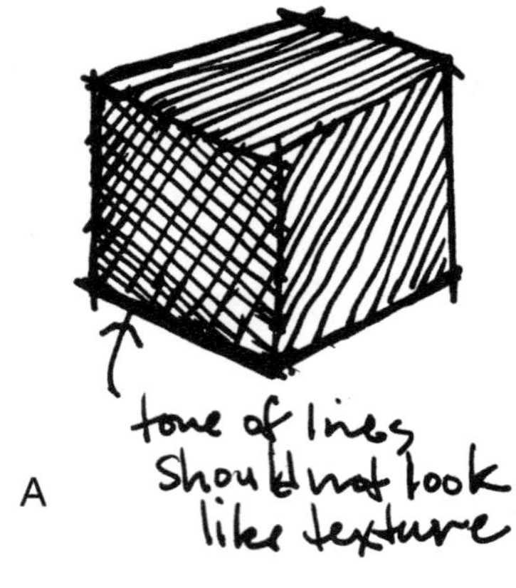

A — tone of lines should not look like texture

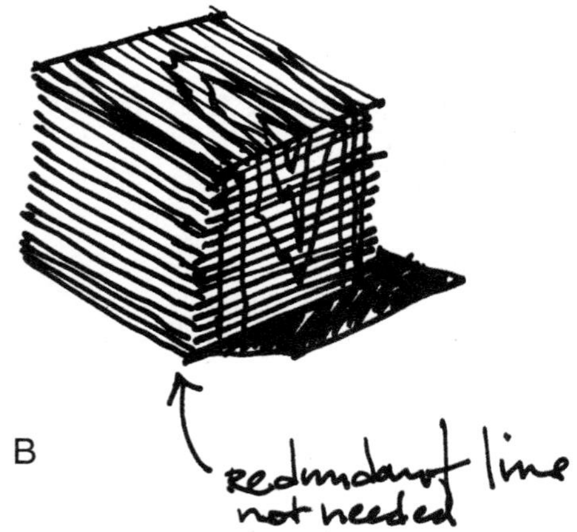

B — redundant line not needed

C

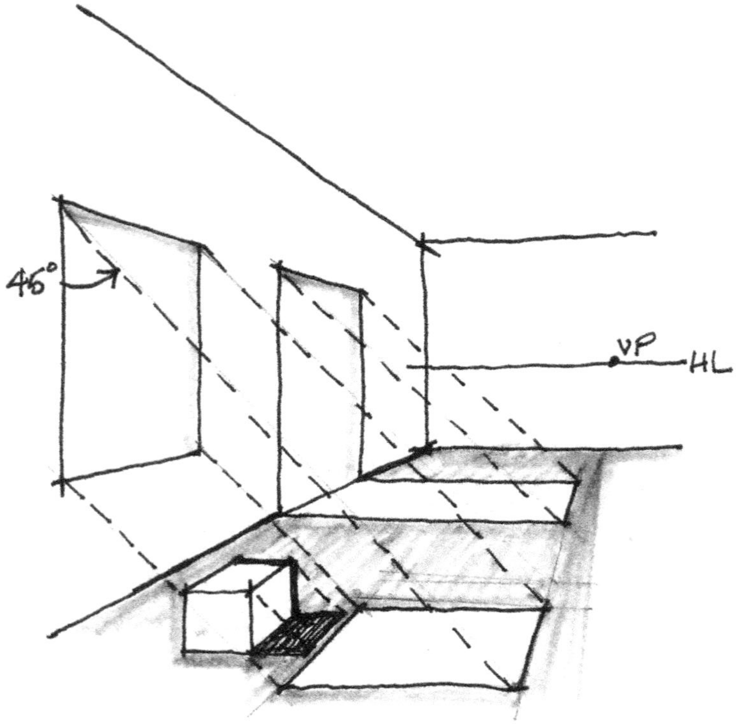

45°

VP HL

Figure 3.4

SHADOW CAST THROUGH A WINDOW, 45° ANGLE

Figure 3.5
ARTIFICIAL LIGHT, PILOT
PRECISE FINE

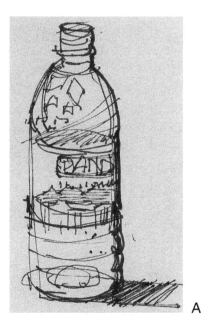

A

B

Figure 3.6

A. GREY PAPER
B. GREY BOARD

Figure 3.7
LINE WEIGHT STUDY

Figure 3.8A
A. INTERIOR LIGHT WITH
CONTRAST STUDY

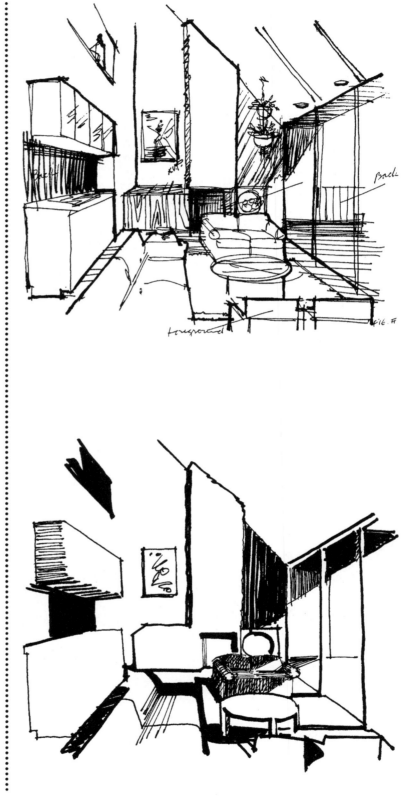

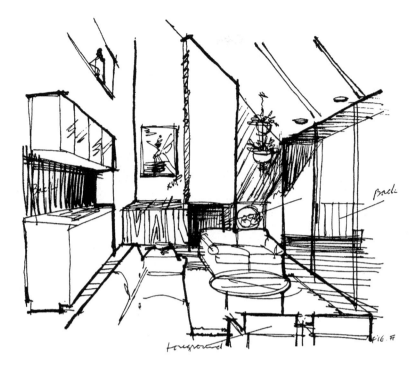

Figure 3.8B

B. TONE/TEXTURE STUDY

Light Study Exercises

1. Value Study

    a. Practice a value study 0–10
    b. Media: sketchbook, pencil, felt-tip, marker

2. Objects in Nature in Sunlight

3. Objects in Interiors in Sunlight and Artificial Light

    a. Concentrate on tone and shadow only
    b. Use shade technique or tone of lines
    c. Media: sketchbook, pencil, felt-tip, marker
    d. Time: 5–20 minutes each

4. Basic Forms (Cube, Cylinder, etc.)

a. Choose typical light source, vary direction from upper left to upper right

b. Work on tone first

c. Shadow

d. Practice umbra and penumbra

e. Media: sketchbook, pencil, felt-tip, marker

TEXTURE

What is texture?

Texture *is the element of design that helps define the character of a space. Everything has texture ranging from rough to smooth. The type and extent of texture used also affect the principle of design: emphasis. Seize the opportunity to express texture since it produces the most interesting, active, sensual, tactile character in the drawing.*

MATERIALS

Both natural and man-made materials are affected by textures and patterns. In exterior sketches we find plant life, water, stone, and a variety of other natural materials. If there are architectural features in the drawing, both natural and man-made materials will come into play. When sketching interior spaces we find wood, stone, brick, glass, wall covering, floor covering, and fabric as popular materials (Figure 4.1 A, B, C).

Obviously, certain materials are much easier to draw than others. It pays to emphasize those, while merely suggesting others. One of the keys to drawing materials is to carefully study and understand them. For example, there are certain distinct grain patterns in trees that are grown and harvested for furniture. The patterns vary in the way the tree is cut and whether hardwood or veneer

Figure 4.1A

TEXTURE STUDY, BOLD
CONTRAST

is used. As mentioned previously, the average person may
not be artistic but he or she has a sense of reality. If your
drawings do not reflect this quality, the viewer will not
accept your illusion.

The way stone, brick, and wood flooring are laid also
creates identifiable characteristics (Figure 4.2). These

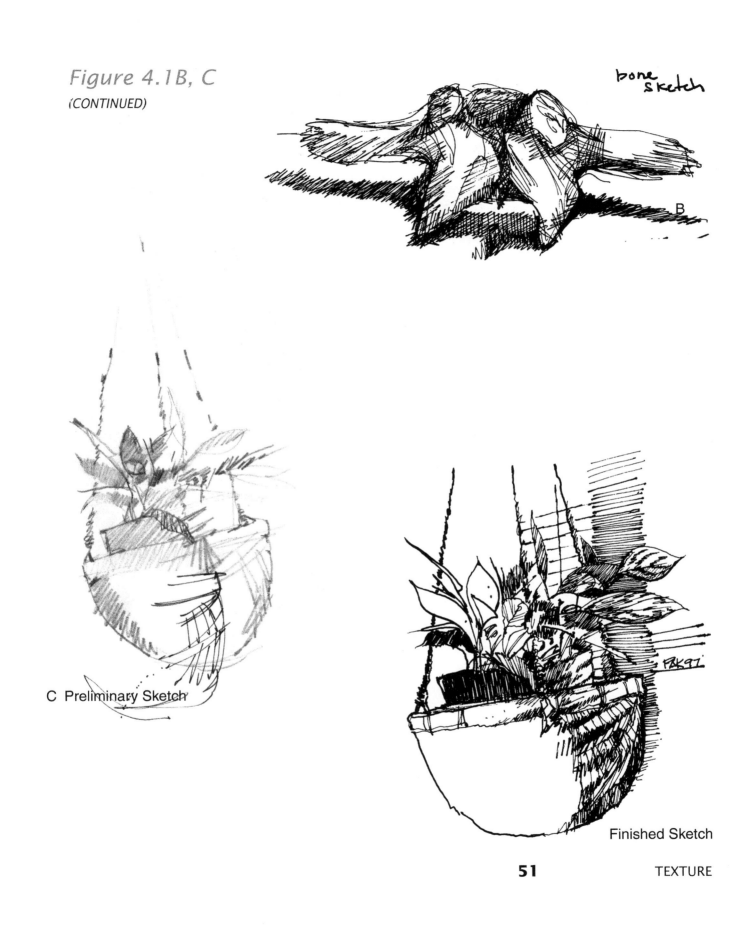

Figure 4.1B, C
(CONTINUED)

bone
sketch

B

C Preliminary Sketch

F&K97

Finished Sketch

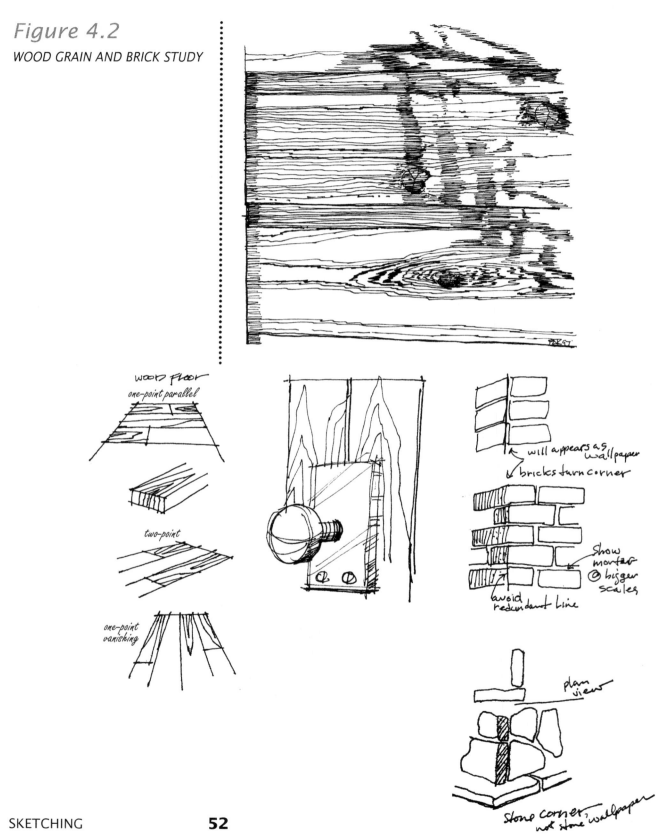

Figure 4.2
WOOD GRAIN AND BRICK STUDY

wood floor
one-point parallel

two-point

one-point
vanishing

will appears as
wallpaper

bricks turn corner

show
mortar
@ bigger
scales

avoid
redundant line

plan
view

stone corner,
not stone wallpaper

characteristics may be especially apparent in materials of standard sizes. The most popular flooring material is carpet, which is an excellent source of textural treatment. Again, you must take care in how you draw carpet since it is a milled product that produces a clear nonrandom linear quality. To keep the floor from appearing to fly up, both pattern and carpet pile must diminish in size in a perspective sketch.

Whether it is a window or part of a piece of furniture, glass is often a difficult material to draw. Changes in the value or clarity of what you see in the room from what you see outside helps the viewer believe the material must be glass. This is also true of drawing what you see through a glass tabletop (Figure 4.3). It is important to use techniques triggering cues and symbols that make it impossible for viewers not to believe what you want them to see.

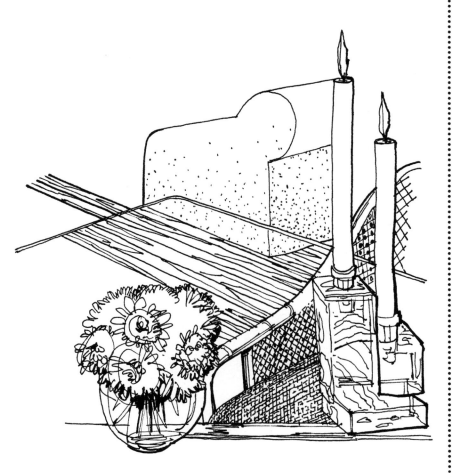

Figure 4.3
TEXTURE STUDY WITH GLASS

Wall coverings and fabrics are materials that can be used to enhance a drawing. Often it is the pattern that brings the material to life. Drawing at a small scale, it is impossible to clearly see all of the detail of a pattern. Simply suggesting the pattern with a convincing use of texture and line will be effective. Basic materials, such as nylon and leather, can be more easily suggested by clearly defining the way the material is used on the furniture—the tufting, the seams, and the skirt, for instance.

Textures and materials may be drawn generically or realistically. There are several types of generic textures: **stippling** (the use of graded dots, Figure 4.4), cross-hatching, loops, and so on. It is important not to use the same generic texture for different materials in the same drawing. If you use stippling for hard-surface materials such as plaster or concrete, you must not use it for a soft fabric. This would only confuse the viewer, who is adjusting his or her eye to the use of your generic texture.

Although realistically capturing the illusion of a specific material on paper often depends on your drawing skills, you must have a working knowledge of its growth patterns, structural characteristics, construction, and basic features or details. With patience and practice, the proper emphasis on textures, materials, and patterns in your drawings will prove to be a source of satisfaction and pleasure while enriching the visual effect through a strong tactile experience.

Figure 4.4

TEXTURE STUDY WITH GENERIC
STIPPLING WITH SHADOW
MOVING UP A VERTICAL PLANE

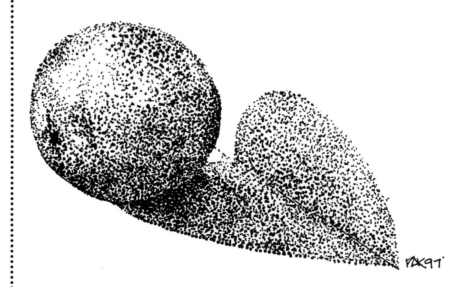

Texture Exercises

I. TEXTURE EXERCISE: REAL AND GENERIC

The first exercise in texture/materials is a simple controlled "learn to see" study. Look at specific textures or materials and draw them in a square or rectangle. Or just have fun playing with texture.

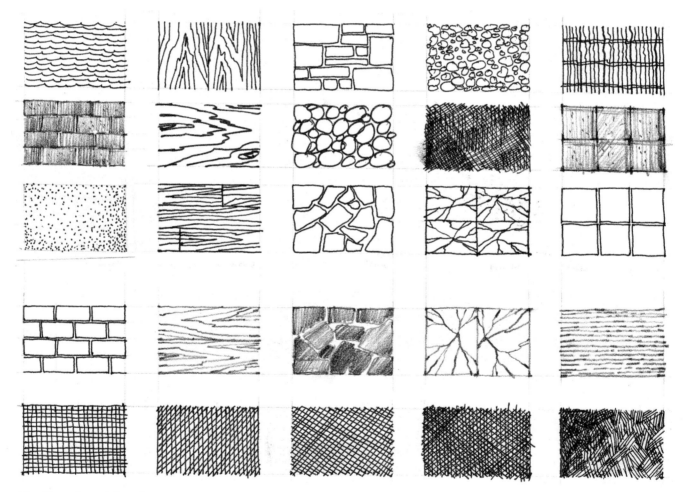

Media: sketchbook
*   pencil, felt-tip*
Size: 1" x 11/2"

II. TEXTURE SHOWING RECEDING EFFECT

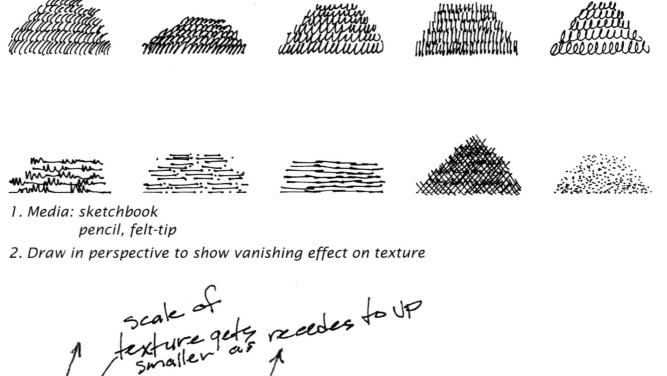

1. Media: sketchbook
pencil, felt-tip

2. Draw in perspective to show vanishing effect on texture

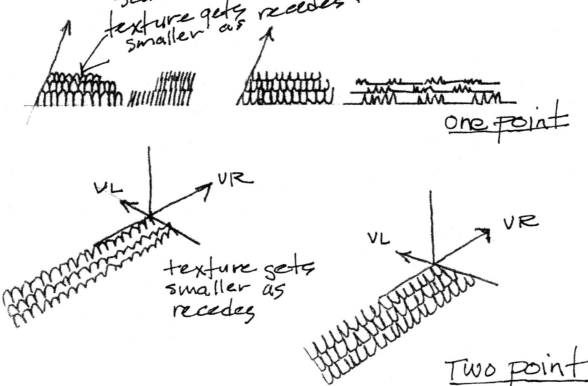

scale of
texture gets
smaller as recedes to UP

one point

VL   VR

texture gets
smaller as
recedes

VL   VR

Two point

Part Two

DESIGN DRAWING

What is design drawing?

Design drawing is a visual language or shorthand used in the schematic or preliminary phase of the design process to help in the search for potential solutions to design problems.

In this section, we will examine bubble flows, conceptual doodle/diagrams, perspectives, and image perspectives that are used for design drawing. These types of drawings are meant to be used in house by the designer while problem solving and are generally not shown to the client. This type of drawing has its own look, style, and integrity, and it should not be judged on rendering skill or artistic merit. In fact, it is the speed with which this style of drawing can be put on paper, not the accuracy, that counts (see Figures P2.1–P2.3).

In certain high-stress situations, these quick drawing skills can be essential. At the student level, whether working on short-term sketch problems or eight-hour sketch problems, these skills may be a deciding factor in examinations for professional licensing.

In certain situations, however, design drawing can be used to create a quick sketch to effectively express an idea to a client. One typical example popularized over the years is referred to as **napkin art**,

57

so-called because a designer sketches an idea on a napkin during a business lunch. This skill impresses most clients and often reinforces the historic phrase, "A picture is worth a thousand words." Most graphic educators consider design drawing to be the most valuable and lasting tool that students carry with them into the design profession.

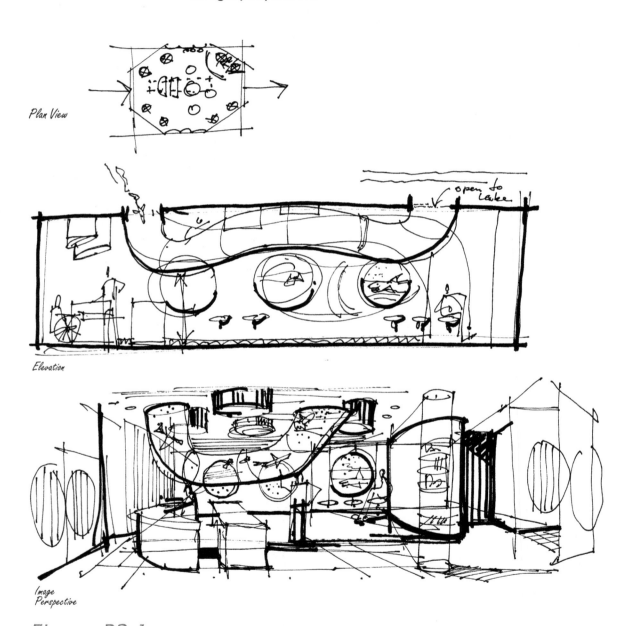

Plan View

Elevation

Image Perspective

Figure P2.1

PLAN VIEW, ELEVATION, AND IMAGE PERSPECTIVE

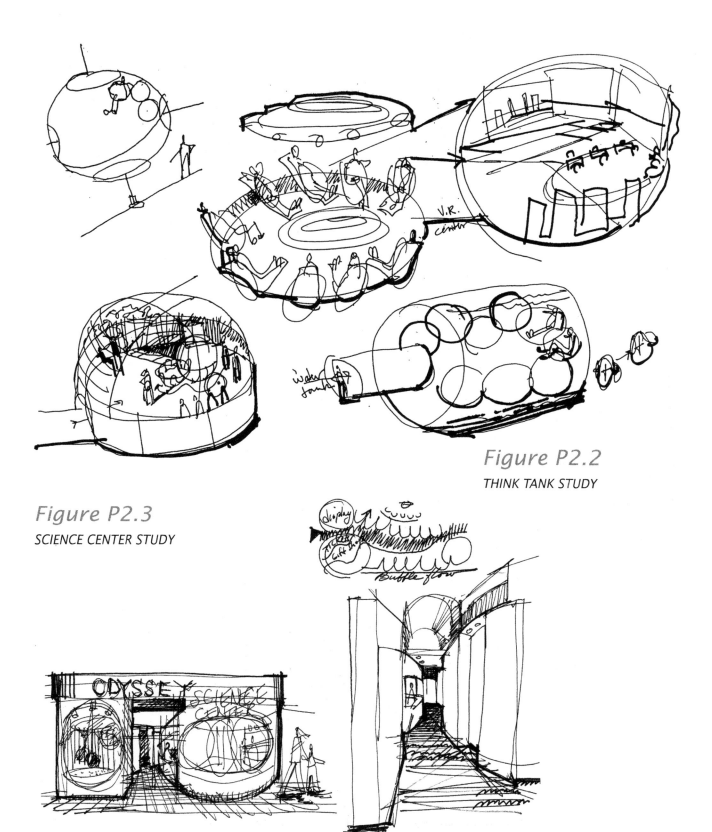

Figure P2.2
THINK TANK STUDY

Figure P2.3
SCIENCE CENTER STUDY

Figure P2.4
INTERIOR SKETCH, MONTICELLO,
FLORIDA

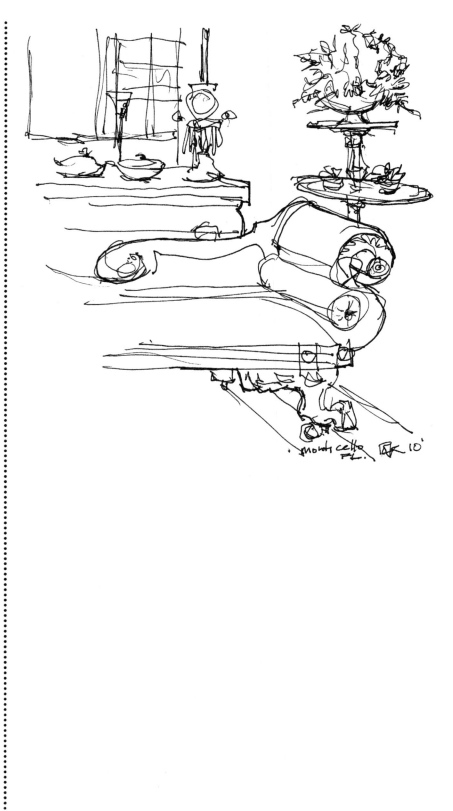

CONCEPTUAL DOODLE/DIAGRAMS

5

What is a conceptual doodle/diagram?

The conceptual doodle/diagram is the heart of the schematic phase of design. It is the designer's first marks on paper after research and programming have taken place. Conceptual doodles are the designer's visual shorthand using drawings that are sketchlike, small, and fast. These diagrams allow the designer to examine many different ideas at this preliminary stage of the design process. Conceptual doodle/diagrams are in-house aids to the designer and, as a general rule, they are not shown to the client. This means they need to be understood only by the designer and are not necessarily a communication tool.

Everyone has doodled at one time or another and it can be a satisfying, if mindless, activity. In our definition, we have added the word conceptual *in front of* doodle *to* remind that this activity is definitely not meant to be mindless. Sketches in Figure 5.1 are not conceptual doodle/diagrams. The pen is simply a sketch of a pen. The lightbulb can be symbolic of a "bright idea," but as you will see, neither of them is a conceptual doodle/diagram. See the doodles from a faculty meeting and seminar in Figure 5.2.

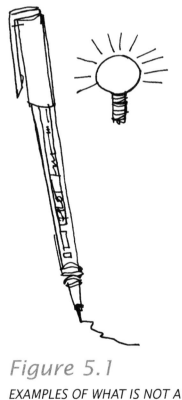

Figure 5.1

EXAMPLES OF WHAT IS NOT A CONCEPTUAL DOODLE/DIAGRAM

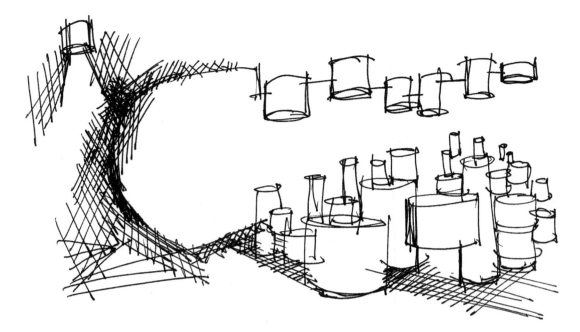

Figure 5.2
FACULTY MEETING DOODLES

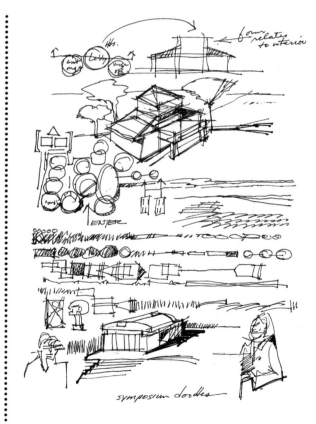

symposium doodles

Figure 5.2

(CONTINUED)

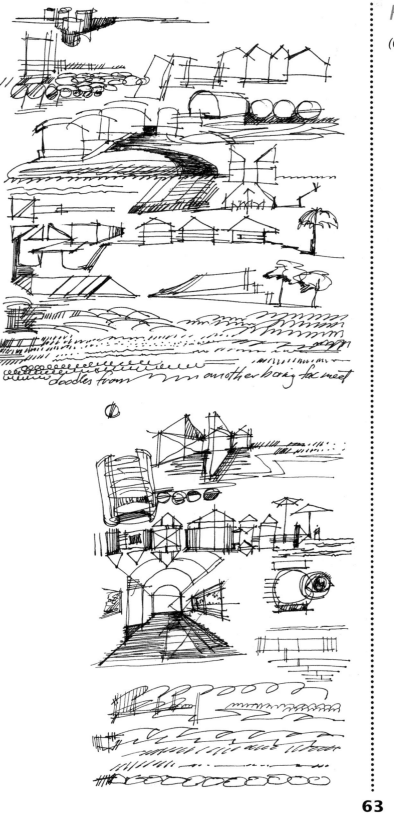

doodles from another boring fac meet

CONCEPTUAL
DOODLE/DIAGRAMS

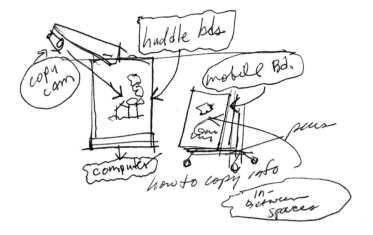

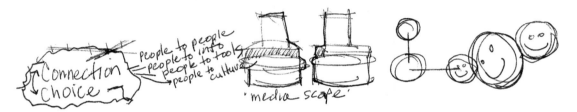

Figure 5.2

(CONTINUED)

Conceptual doodle is defined as a form of design graphics expressing a word, space, or action, to be used to examine potential design solutions in the schematic phase of the design process. The key word is *potential*, since at this time you should look at alternatives that may be further developed (Figures 5.3 and 5.4).

Diagram is defined as an involved series of conceptual doodles. If a conceptual doodle is a shorthand word, then a diagram is a sentence or even a paragraph. From a design standpoint, a lone conceptual doodle is usually meaningless if it is not part of a diagram.

Conceptual doodle/diagrams become the personal shorthand of designers. They may be realistic, symbolic, or abstract.

The vast majority of conceptual doodle/diagrams are symbolic, since realistic drawings tend to be more time-consuming. If they are repeated often enough, abstract drawings that have meaning for us eventually become

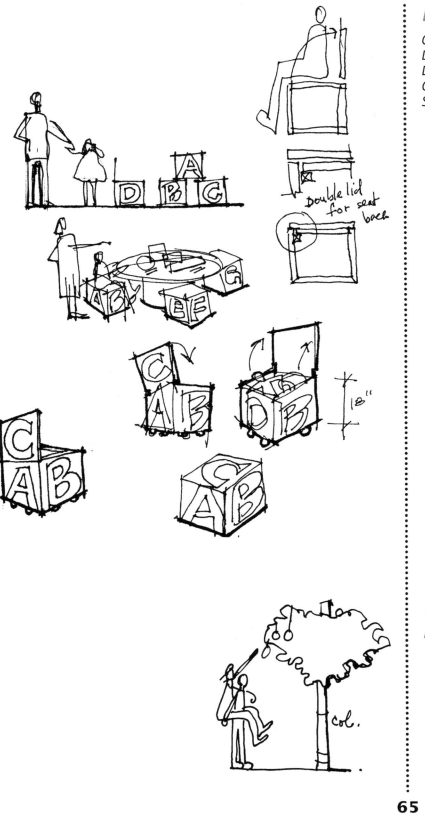

Double lid for seat back

18"

Figure 5.4

DOODLE/DIAGRAM

col.

Figure 5.4

(CONTINUED)

symbolic. For example, if there was one place left on earth where Coca-Cola was not sold, its symbol would be abstract to those people. However, if by some form of magic a Coke machine were installed, the abstract letters would, in a very short time, become symbolic of the soft drink they represent.

The basic design process starts with data collection and programming, identifying client needs, and clarifying their image and character. You begin the preliminary design process with conceptual doodle/diagrams using the elements *and principles* of design. *The following are typical* elements: *form, scale, color, texture, and light. The* principles *are: unity, variety, harmony, balance, emphasis, repetition, and proportion. The design process includes:*

- *project program*
- *research*
- *preliminary design*
  - *a. bubble flow*
  - *b. conceptual doodle/diagrams*
  - *c. image perspectives*
- *final design*

When working on preliminary designs, I recommend moving from the **macrocosm**, *or overview, to the* **microcosm**, *or smallest detail (Figure 5.5). When first*

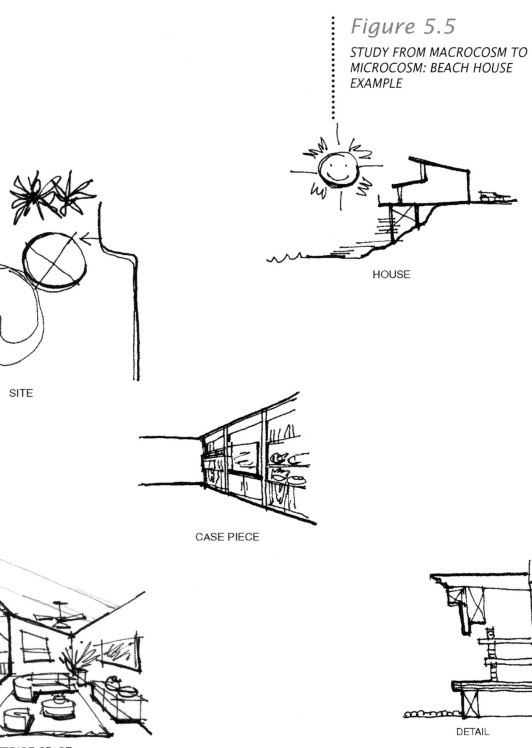

Figure 5.5

STUDY FROM MACROCOSM TO MICROCOSM: BEACH HOUSE EXAMPLE

HOUSE

SITE

CASE PIECE

INTERIOR SPACE

DETAIL

CONCEPTUAL
DOODLE/DIAGRAMS

working with conceptual doodle/diagrams, beginning design students are tempted to jump to preconceived notions for design solutions rather than letting solutions develop through the natural course of design evolution. They often have the tendency to work backwards by coming up with a design decision and then doing conceptual doodle/diagrams to support the end result. This, of course, entirely defeats the purpose of the diagram. The use of conceptual doodle/diagrams is not only critical in the design development phase, but they will serve as proof of a logically conceived and functional preliminary design solution.

Reminder: At this point, it is evident that sketch figures are very important in conceptual doodle/diagrams to help establish a sense of scale and proportion (Figure 5.6).

Figure 5.6

EXAMPLE OF SCALE FIGURE
TYPES FOR USE IN DIAGRAMS

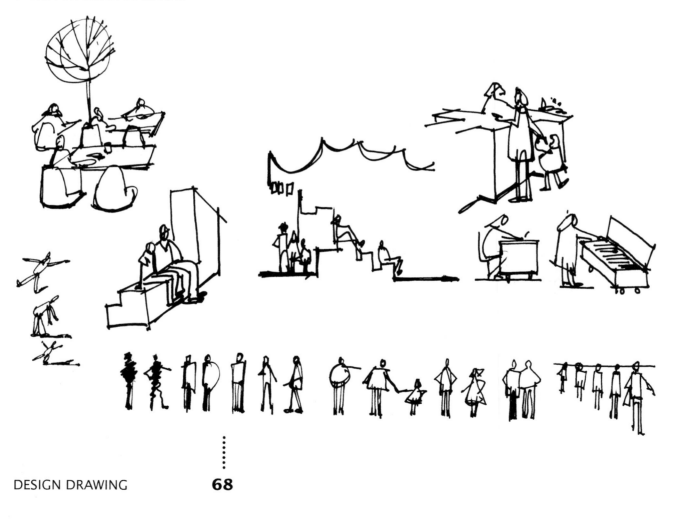

CONCEPTUAL DOODLE/DIAGRAM PERSPECTIVES

Conceptual doodle/diagrams may be plan, elevation, section, or perspective drawings. The conceptual doodle/diagram perspective is freehand, small, fast, and loose. It may or may not be in color. It is not meant to be pretty, but rather it should express action/reaction, showing a particular potential design solution that is best seen and understood in the third dimension (Figure 5.7). Unlike traditional perspectives, it can have notes, arrows, or other symbols drawn all over it to help the designer in the creative process. Remember, conceptual doodle/diagrams are part of the preliminary phase of design and are considered in-house drawings that are not used for client presentation. These perspective sketches are most effective when illustrating things in the design that change, move, or have some flexibility— action/reaction.

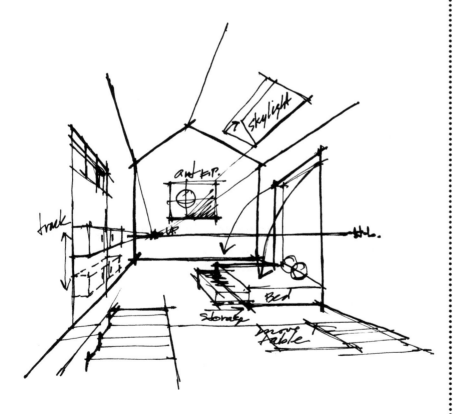

Figure 5.7

CONCEPTUAL DOODLE/DIAGRAM PERSPECTIVE, ILLUSTRATING ACTION/REACTION

BUBBLE FLOW DIAGRAMS

Bubble flow diagrams *are one of the most popular schematic phases of design studies. They are used for space planning and circulation. A five-step bubble flow version that stylistically falls under the umbrella of conceptual doodle/diagrams leads to a preliminary floor plan.*

An unlimited number of bubble flow diagrams may be generated by client information in the facilities program statement. Of course, the number of diagrams the designer pursues will be controlled by contract deadlines—time limitations are always a factor. The bubble flow diagram with the best potential will be developed in the final design phase. As in all conceptual doodle/diagrams, the bubbles are a designer's shorthand; they are often accompanied by a specific and, in some cases, lengthy verbal description.

All of the spaces listed in the client's design program should be represented by an individual bubble. It is advisable to place the name of the space or room in the bubble. The bubbles should be drawn freehand since the use of a circle template is too formal and time-consuming. Color can be used to give a psychological sense of space. Warm colors are active; cool colors are passive.

Following are guidelines for using bubbles as a language:

1. *The size of the bubble relates directly to the size of the space it defines. This is based simply on proportion: a small bubble may represent a 50-square-foot space, while a bubble 4 times its size represents a 200-square-foot area.*

2. *Two bubbles physically touching indicate that two spaces are adjacent to one another. But this step does not clarify what is between the spaces—which may be a wall, partition, or some other form of space divider.*

3. *Overlapping bubbles indicate spaces that interact, share function, or are linked in concept through open-space planning.*

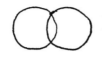

4. *An opening between the bubbles indicates that the spaces do not touch and may be separated by a corridor.*

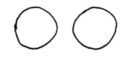

EXAMPLE OF A FIVE-STEP BUBBLE FLOW DIAGRAM

Step 1. This step indicates the *WHERE* or location of each space as communicated to the designer and defined by the client's needs. Name the spaces:

Step 2. This is a vital step in a circulation study. It indicates *HOW* the people are moved through the spaces. A key with strong graphic symbols should be used to indicate major or minor circulation patterns or any other form of movement including site lines or view. You will need a key for this step.

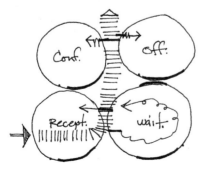

CONCEPTUAL
DOODLE/DIAGRAMS

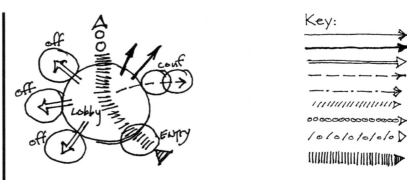

Key:

Step 3. This step converts the bubbles into basic geometric shapes that will become recognizable as a floor plan in Step 4.

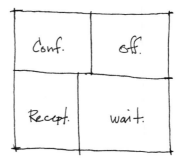

Step 4. This step shows a single-line floor plan with recognizable architectural features such as doors, windows, fireplaces, and so on. Spaces that are separated by walls or some other form of divider are now clear.

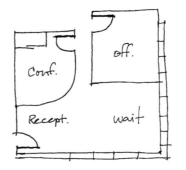

Step 5. The final step is a preliminary layout. It should be to scale or "eyeball" to scale. All wall thicknesses and architectural features are shown. Floor materials with appropriate textures should be shown. It is beneficial at this point in the schematic phase of design to place generic furniture in the plan. Commitment to specific pieces will be made at a later stage in the design process.

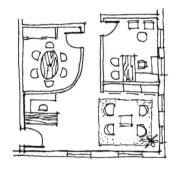

At the completion of a five-step bubble flow, you will see a clear progression of thought and analysis. When placing the steps side by side, you see not only their logical relationships but often you are able to spot a problem that might have been missed or inadequately solved. The preliminary floor plan will meet all the client's functional and circulation needs. Now you are ready to make all modifications to achieve a final floor plan that will be used for specifications and eventual construction. Of course, this potential design solution is in the second dimension, or plan view, only. You must do conceptual doodle/diagrams in elevation, section, and perspective at the same time to truly develop your design in a logical sequence. As a quick sketch-style drawing tool, a five-step bubble flow can play an important role in helping to solve problems in the schematic phase of design development.

CONCEPTUAL
DOODLE/DIAGRAMS

Conceptual Doodle/Diagram Exercises

I. FIVE-STEP BUBBLE FLOW DIAGRAM EXERCISE

Practice the five steps (use an existing class project)

    a. Media: sketchbook or parchment paper, pencil, felt-tip, marker

    b. Freehand drawing (no circle template)

II. CONCEPTUAL DOODLE/DIAGRAM EXERCISE

Choose a problem to solve (use an existing class project) and state it clearly

    a. Work from macrocosm to microcosm

    b. Use the elements and principles of design

    c. Use sketch figures

    d. Media: sketchbook or parchment paper, pencil, felt-tip, marker

    e. Small, fast, freehand

    f. Time: 30 seconds to 10 minutes each

BIBLIOGRAPHY

Arends, Mark. *Interior Presentation Sketching for Architects and Designers.* New York: Van Nostrand Reinhold, 1990.

Ching, Francis D.K. *Architectural Graphics* (2nd Ed.). New York: Van Nostrand Reinhold, 1985.

Ching, Francis D.K. *Drawing: A Creative Process.* New York: Van Nostrand Reinhold, 1990.

Crowe, Norman, and Laseau, Paul. *Visual Notes for Architects and Designers.* New York: Wiley, 1986.

Doyle, Michael E. *Color Drawing: Design Drawing Skills and Techniques for Architects, Landscape Architects and Interior Designers* (2nd Ed.). New York: Wiley, 1999.

Herzberger, Erwin. *Freehand Drawing for Architects and Designers: Watercolor, Colored Pencil and Black and White Techniques.* New York: Watson-Guptill, 1996.

Laseau, Paul. *Graphic Thinking for Architects and Designers* (2nd Ed.). New York: Wiley, 1988.

Leach, Sid. *Techniques of Interior Design Rendering and Presentation.* New York: McGraw-Hill, 1978.

Lin, Mike W. *Drawing and Designing with Confidence.* New York: Wiley, 1997.

Lockard, William Kirby. *Design Drawing.* Eldridge, IA: Crisp Publications, 1993.

Lockard, William Kirby. *Drawing as a Means to Architecture* (2nd Ed.). Eldridge, IA: Crisp Publications, 1995.

Mitton, Maureen. *Interior Design Visual Presentation: A Guide to Graphics Models and Presentation Techniques.* New York: Wiley, 2004.

Oliver, Robert S. *The Complete Sketch.* New York: Van Nostrand Reinhold, 1989.

Wang, Thomas. *Pencil Sketching* (2nd Ed.). New York: Wiley, 2001.

White, Edward T. *Building Meaning: Analysis and Design for Image-Sensitive Projects.* Tucson, AZ: Architectural Media, 1995.

GLOSSARY/INDEX

architectural overlap   A technique of overlapping a line at a corner to create a specific sketch character.

balance   A characteristic of composition; a composition may be symmetrical or asymmetrical.

bubble flow diagram   A diagram that involves five steps that evolve from simple bubbles to a preliminary, sketchy floor plan. It is a popular tool in the schematic phase of the design process and is useful for space planning and circulation.

chisel point   An angled tip on a pencil point achieved by rubbing a sharpened point against a sandpaper block; can be used to draw a variety of line weights and qualities.

coloring book effect   The result of trying to stay inside the lines when rendering and distinctly outlining all of the elements in a rigid manner.

composition study   A series of quick perspective sketches that allow the designer to consider the best way to approach the final drawing of a particular space.

conceptual doodle/diagram   A form of design graphic expressing a word, space, or action to be used to examine potential design solutions in the schematic phase of the design process combined into an involved series.

conceptual doodle/diagram perspective   A quick, sketchy perspective drawing that illustrates action/reaction.

consistency   Use of lines of the same weight or character as an exercise to develop control in drawings.

design drawing   A visual language or shorthand used in the schematic or preliminary phase of the design process to help in the search for potential solutions to design problems.

drawing papers Papers suitable for drawing media, typically pencil.

drawing process Drawing steps used in conjunction with the design process.

drawing tools Various types of pencils, pens, and markers.

elements of a line Consistency, line weight, variation, and quality.

entourage Any and all elements of a drawing that humanize it and bring it to life, including trees, plants, people, and other items that add interest to the space and make the viewer believe that people inhabit it.

exterior sketch A freehand drawing done in open air.

eyeball perspective A sketchy perspective drawing without a mechanical grid that is commonly used for quick sketch-type communication.

figure studies Drawings of the human form.

final perspective A finished drawing that is the end result of the overlay method. Final perspectives may be loose and sketchy or photorealistic. They are often budgeted as an additional expense to the client.

fudge factor Artistic license that allows the artist to change or manipulate a part of a drawing to make it more believable.

full frame A perspective that extends to the full size of the paper.

gesture drawings Quick studies done in a sketchy style that help to develop a sense of the human form.

ground line The place in a perspective drawing where the visual plane meets the ground.

hand rendering Adding color, texture, tone, shadow, and character to a drawing; may be accomplished with marker, colored pencil, or any variety of media.

horizon line The imaginary line in a perspective drawing that is always at eye level.

image perspective An eyeball sketch-style drawing done in the preliminary phase of design that provides the designer the opportunity to explore a wide array of options or ideas pertaining to the said design.

interior sketch   A freehand drawing done in any architectural interior space.

line   The most basic element of a drawing.

line only   A drawing using the qualities of line only: line weight, line variation, and line character.

line quality (character)   The most expressive lines, most commonly used for freeform or organic shapes, such as trees or plants.

line weight   Visually, the thickness of a line: the thinner the line, the lighter is the weight.

line weight variation   The use of lines of different weights or thicknesses to add distinction to a drawing. Light weights are internal, medium weights define the form, and heavy weights define architectural features or establish base planes. A good drawing should contain a minimum of these three line weights.

loose sketch   A fast freehand drawing.

loosening up   Relaxing while drawing; can be done in a number of ways, including doing sketching exercises in a quick, freehand manner or by actually physically stretching.

macrocosm   The big picture or overview; the first thing tackled in a design problem.

mechanical perspective   A perspective drawing that is completed with the use of mechanical tools.

microcosm   The small details; considered last when tackling a design problem.

mind's eye   One's perception of how something will look or turn out; how we see things inside our heads.

napkin art   A quick sketch (eyeball perspective) done on a napkin during a lunch meeting.

no lift   A technique used to create a drawing in which the drawing tool is never lifted from the paper.

no look   A technique used to create a drawing in which the artist never looks down at the paper while drawing.

one-point perspective   A drawing that focuses on one wall as the rear elevation and allows for development of two other walls as well in the drawing.

overlay method   The method by which one completes a final drawing, following the steps from composition study single-line blowup to tone/shadow study to texture/materials study. The final step is to combine the aforementioned three studies into one final drawing.

penumbra   The lighter aura that is part of a shadow.

perspective drawing   The oldest and most popular method of design communication; drawn as if seeing from a particular place in a room. These drawings can appear realistic and believable.

picture plane   In a perspective drawing, the plane in space that frames and defines the perspective that is drawn.

presentation   The method used to display a design, including drawings to a client.

redundant line   A line added to define a surface or plane that may already be defined by tone/shadow or texture.

scale figures   Human figures used in conceptual doodle/diagrams that help to establish a sense of scale and proportion.

shadow casting   A characteristic of light that shows shadow from any form.

sketching   A style or technique of freehand drawing that may be loose, tight, line only, or any combination of line, tone/shadow, or texture.

station point   The point in a perspective drawing from which a person views the space or object.

still life studies   Sketches of a single object or a variety of objects. Techniques include no lift, no look, tone/shadow, texture/materials, or a combination thereof.

stipple   A series of dots, either small or of varying sizes, used in drawing to create tone, shadow, or texture.

support board   A presentation board that facilitates one's design by presenting finish materials, fabrics, furniture, or other features in order to help the client understand the design concept.

texture   The design element that helps define the character of a space. It occurs on every item and ranges from very smooth to very rough.

thumbnail sketch   A small, quick sketch that is usually created at the beginning stages of the design process.

tight sketch A slower freehand drawing created using some mechanical tool(s).

tone and shadow Part of the overlay method, used to study light conditions.

tooth The texture or grain of paper; a paper with a heavier tooth has a more prominent texture.

tracing paper Paper that is translucent, available as parchment, vellum, or graphics paper.

two-point perspective A perspective drawing that focuses on the corner of a room or space, allowing the viewer to see only two walls of the space in a particular drawing; may also be an exterior of a building.

umbra The darker aura that is part of a shadow.

value scale A measure of light to dark, usually ranging from 0 (zero) for white to 10 for black.

vanishing point A point or points in a perspective drawing that are on the horizon line; the point or points at which all parallel lines converge.

vignette A sketch done with a level of simplicity that allows the viewer's eye to finish the picture as the four planes fade out equally on the paper.

wash A loose blend of media to cover a large area; usually associated with watercolor painting.

Section Two

1 Sketching Tools, Supplies, and Their Uses

_____OBJECTIVES

After completing this chapter, you will be able to:

> Correctly identify the tools used for sketching.
> Describe how these tools are used.
> Read architectural scales accurately.
> Sketch lines to scale.
> Use an orthographic grid correctly.

SKETCHING

Sketching well can be very useful for people who are designing and sketching any product. Sketching can be done with nothing more than a pencil, an eraser, and a piece of paper. Sketching can also be done with triangles, a circle template, pencils, eraser, scales, drawing powder, and paper. This book is designed for you to use as elaborate a sketching system as you want.

If you choose not to use triangles and circle templates for manual sketches, be aware that architectural sketches such as the ones that will be assigned in this course must be accurate, neat, and legible. This book will show you how to make manual sketches with or without the aid of triangles and circle templates.

SKETCHING TOOLS

The tools for sketching include pencils, erasers, scales, grid paper, and, if desired, triangles, circle template, and drawing powder. This chapter describes these tools, how to use them, and how to keep them in good working condition.

Pencils

Both thin-lead mechanical pencils and wooden pencils work well for technical sketching.

Mechanical Pencils
Lead for mechanical pencils (Figure 1-1) is made in several degrees of hardness and several widths. Those most commonly used for technical sketching are:
> .5 mm diameter - 2H or H hardness: Used for thinner lines.
> .7 mm diameters - 2H or H hardness: Used for thicker lines.

9H ——— 4H 3H 2H H F HB B ——— 7B
HARD   MEDIUM   SOFT

Figure 1-1
Lead Hardnesses

Mechanical pencils should be held perpendicular to the paper when used with triangles or templates so that you sketch with the full diameter of the lead and avoid breaking the lead (Figure 1-2).

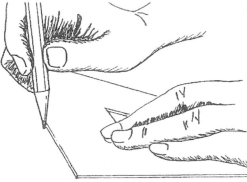

Figure 1-2
Holding a Mechanical Pencil

Wooden Pencils and Lead Holders

Wooden drawing pencils are made in several degrees of hardness from 9H to 7B. 9H is the hardest, 7B is the softest. H, HB, or 2H is a good hardness for sketching. A standard Number 2 yellow pencil with a soft red eraser on the end of it is fine for most sketches. Keep wooden pencils fairly sharp. Crush the end of a finely sharpened pencil or lead holder a little so that sketch lines will not be too fine (Figure 1-3).

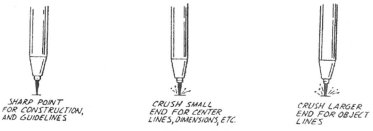

SHARP POINT
FOR CONSTRUCTION,
AND GUIDELINES

CRUSH SMALL
END FOR CENTER
LINES, DIMENSIONS, ETC.

CRUSH LARGER
END FOR OBJECT
LINES

Figure 1-3
Preparing a Sharpened Pencil

When they are used with triangles or templates, wooden pencils and lead holders should be held at about a 60 degree angle to the paper and rolled slightly between the fingers to make lines of uniform width (Figure 1-4).

60° ANGLE TO PAPER

Figure 1-4
Holding a Wooden Pencil or Lead Holder

Erasers

A pink pearl eraser is best for erasing on bond or vellum papers. You will find this eraser on the end of a # 2 yellow pencil as well as in a separate round or rectangular form (Figure 1-5).

Figure 1-5
Erasers

Grid Paper

This book contains pages with grids that will aid you in sketching. Grid paper is also available at most stores that sell architectural, engineering, or drawing supplies. Grids at 1/10", 1/4", or isometric angles are available at these locations.

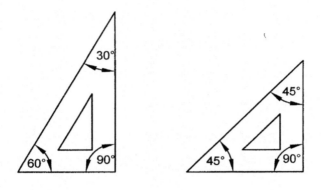

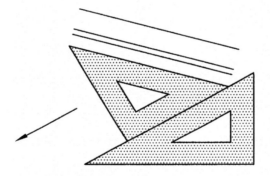

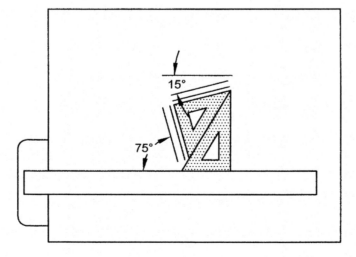

Figure 1-6
Triangles and T-Square

1-4

Triangles

Both 30-60 degree and 45 degree triangles (Figure 1-6) are used for technical sketching. Inexpensive triangles are fine. To sketch vertical lines, place the triangle on a grid line or a straight edge such as a T-square and hold the triangle firmly with one hand as you sketch upward with the other hand. You will soon learn to return downward over a line to improve its density. Notice that the pencil is slanted in the direction of the line (Figure 1-7) but is not tilted in relation to the edge of the triangle. Mechanical pencils are held perpendicular to the paper.

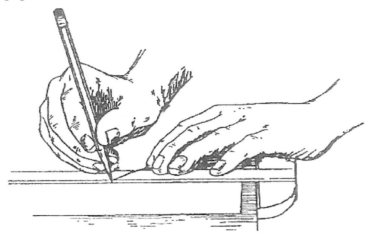

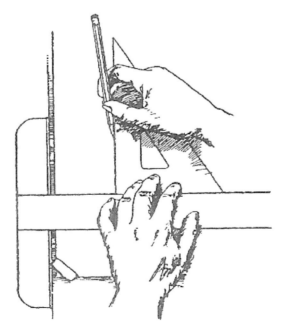

Figure 1-7
Sketching Vertical and Horizontal Lines

Circle Template

Circle templates can be used to sketch most of the circles on the assignments in this book. The template should contain circles from 1/8" to 1-1/2" in diameter. To use the circle template, align the cross hairs of the template on the center lines of where the circle will be drawn. Sketch the circle with the pencil held perpendicular to the paper (Figure 1-8).

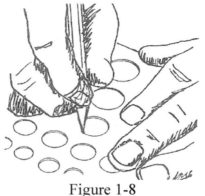

Figure 1-8
Sketching with a Circle Template

Drawing Powder

An excellent aid for keeping drawings clean is the drawing powder bag or can. The bag is made of a coarsely woven material so that the coarse powder falls out of it when the bag is kneaded (Figure 1-9). The powder is sprinkled over the drawing before a drawing is started. When the drawing is completed, the powder is rubbed over the drawing very lightly to pick up the excess graphite. The powder is then brushed off the drawing.

Figure 1-9
Drawing Powder

SCALES

Scales are made in a variety of styles. All scales are designed to be used by selecting the correct scale for the situation and measuring with it. There is no arithmetic involved. You do not have to multiply, divide, add, or subtract to use a scale. Just read it. For example, the 5 mark on a scale can only be .5, 5, 50, 500 or some other number with a 5 and more zeros, or a decimal point with zeros and then a 5 (.005). It cannot be read as 10, 200, or any other number.

Although there are many different types of scales, only the architect's scale is used in most of the exercises in this book.

Architect's Scale

The architect's scale is designed to be used to sketch architectural structures and is, therefore, divided into sections for feet and inches. The six-sided triangular architect's scale has a total of 11 different scales marked on its edges.

Using the architect's scale to represent feet and inches

Figure 1-10 shows the edge of the architect's scale that contains the 1/4 scale on the right end and the 1/8 scale on the left end. Notice that the 1/8 scale uses the smaller divisions marked on the shorter lines and is read from the left 0 on the scale. The 1/4 scale uses the larger divisions marked on the longer lines and is read from the right 0 on the scale.

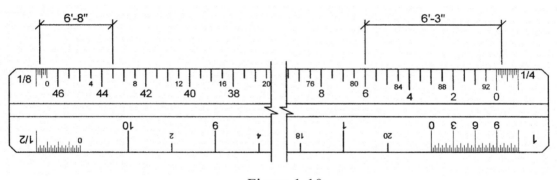

Figure 1-10
Architect's Scale

The section to the left of the left 0 shows a foot on the 1/8 scale divided into inches. There are six spaces in this section, and because there are 12 inches in a foot, each mark represents 2 inches. The section to the right of the right 0 shows a foot on the 1/4 scale divided into inches. There are 12 spaces in this section, so each space represents 1 inch. Notice the labeled measurement closest on the 1/8 scale. The measurement showing 6'-8" starts at the right of the 0 on the 6' mark (two marks to the right of 4) and stops at the fourth space to the left of the 0. These four spaces represent 8 inches since each mark to the left of 0 is 2 inches.

Study the labeled measurements on the 1/4 and 1/8 scales until you are satisfied you know how to read these two scales. After you know how to read these scales, you know how to read all scales on the architect's scale.

Using the architect's scale to represent inches and fractions of an inch

The architect's scale can also be used to represent inches with the section to the right or left of 0 representing fractions of an inch. Figure 1-11 shows the 3/4 scale as it represents inches and fractions of an inch. The labeled measurement closest to the 3/4 scale shows the right end of the measurement stopping on the 3" mark and the left end stopping on 0. The next line up shows the right end on the 4" mark and the left end 1/4 of the distance across the section that in this case shows fractions of an inch. The top line shows the left end 3 marks short of the full inch. Because there are 24 spaces in this inch scale, 3 marks is 1/8 (8/8 − 1/8 = 7/8).

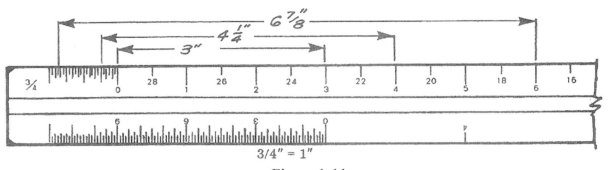

Figure 1-11
Using the Architect's Scale for a Scale of ¾" =1" (inches not feet)

EXERCISE 1-1
Sketching lines to scale. There are four sheets for this exercise: 1-1A, 1-1B, 1-1C, and 1-1D.

Remove the sheet labeled Exercise 1-1A from your book and use the instructions below to sketch lines to scale.

Use the architect's scale to sketch lines to scale:

Step 1. Use the 1/8 scale to represent 1/8"=1' and sketch a line 32'-0" long.

1. Determine which scale is required to fit the drawing on the sheet size you are sketching. In this case, use the 1/8 scale.
2. Align the 0" mark with the start point of the measurement and make a small mark or dot at that point with your pencil on one of the grid lines of your grid paper.
3. Locate the 32' mark and make a small pencil mark or dot at that point.
4. Use a triangle or sketch freehand a line between the marks.

Step 2. On your own:

1. Use the 1/8 scale to represent 1/8"=1' to sketch a line 6'-6" long.
2. Use the 1/8 scale to represent 1/8"=1' to sketch a line 42'-10" long.
3. Use the 1/8 scale to represent 1/8"=1' to sketch a line 60'-8" long.
4. Use the 1/8 scale to represent 1/8"=1' to sketch a line 12'-0" long.

Step 3. On your own:

1. Use the 1/4 scale to represent 1/4"=1' to sketch a line 2'-9" long.
2. Use the 1/4 scale to represent 1/4"=1' to sketch a line 4'-3" long.
3. Use the 1/4 scale to represent 1/4"=1' to sketch a line 20'-6" long.
4. Use the 1/4 scale to represent 1/4"=1' to sketch a line 3'-0" long.
5. Use the 1/4 scale to represent 1/4"=1' to sketch a line 4'-6" long.

Remove the sheet labeled Exercise 1-1B from your book and use the instructions below to sketch lines to scale.

Use the architect's scale to sketch lines to scale:

Step 1. Use the 3/8 scale to represent 3/8"=1' and sketch a line 8'-0" long.

1. Determine which scale is required to fit the drawing on the sheet size you are sketching. In this case, use the 3/8 scale.
2. Align the 3" mark (3 of the small spaces to the left of 0) with the start point of the measurement and make a small mark or dot at that point with your pencil on one of the grid lines of your grid paper.
3. Locate the 8' mark and make a small pencil mark or dot at that point.
4. Use a triangle or sketch freehand a line between the marks.

Step 2. On your own:

1. Use the 3/8 scale to represent 3/8"=1' to sketch a line 10'-3" long.
2. Use the 3/8 scale to represent 3/8"=1' to sketch a line 2'-9" long.
3. Use the 3/8 scale to represent 3/8"=1' to sketch a line 6'-6" long.
4. Use the 3/8 scale to represent 3/8"=1' to sketch a line 4'-0" long.

Step 3. On your own:

1. Use the 3/4 scale to represent 3/4"=1' to sketch a line 4'-2" long.
2. Use the 3/4 scale to represent 3/4"=1' to sketch a line 5'-3" long.
3. Use the 3/4 scale to represent 3/4"=1' to sketch a line 2'-0" long.
4. Use the 3/4 scale to represent 3/4"=1' to sketch a line 6'-6" long.
5. Use the 3/4 scale to represent 3/4"=1' to sketch a line 7'-0" long.

Use the architect's scale to sketch lines to scale:

Step 1. On your own:

Remove the sheet labeled Exercise 1-1C from your book and use the information on that sheet to

sketch lines to scale.
Remove the sheet labeled Exercise 1-1D from your book and use the instructions below to sketch lines to scale.

Use the architect's scale to sketch lines to scale:
    Step 1. Use the 3/4 scale to represent 3/4"=1' and sketch a line 4'-3" long (Figure 1-12).

        1.   Determine which scale is required to fit the drawing on the sheet size you are sketching. In this case, use the 3/4 scale.
        2.   Align the 3" mark (6 of the small spaces to the left of 0) with the start point of the measurement and make a small mark or dot at that point with your pencil on one of the grid lines of your grid paper.
        3.   Locate the 4' mark and make a small pencil mark or dot at that point.
        4.   Use a triangle to sketch a line between the marks.

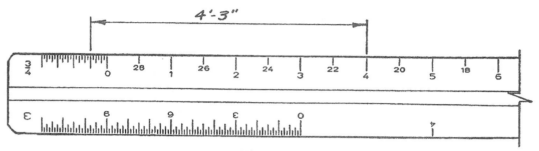

Figure 1-12
4'-3" at a Scale of ¾" = 1'-0"

Step 2. On your own:

        1.   Use the 3/4 scale to represent 3/4"=1' to sketch a line 6'-2" long.
        2.   Use the 1/8 scale to represent 1/8"=1' to sketch a line 15'-6" long.
        3.   Use the 1/2 scale to represent 1/2"=1' to sketch a line 7'-10" long.
        4.   Use the 3/8 scale to represent 3/8"=1" to sketch a line 9'-9" long.

Step 3.   **Use the 3/4 scale to represent 3/4"=1" and sketch a line 5 3/4" long (Figure 1-13).**

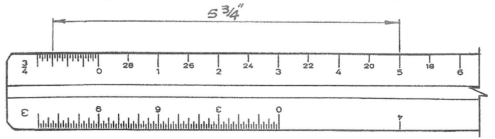

Figure 1-13

5-3/4" at a Scale of ¾"=1" (inches not feet)

1. Determine which scale is required to fit the drawing on the sheet size you are sketching. In this case, use the 3/4 scale.
2. Align the 3/4" mark to the left of the 0 with the start point of the measurement and make a small pencil mark or dot at that point.
3. Locate the 5" mark to the right of 0 and make a small mark or dot at that point with your pencil.
4. Use a triangle to sketch a line between the marks.

Step 4. On your own:

1. Use the 3/4 scale to represent 3/4"=1" to sketch a line 6-3/4" long.
2. Use the 1/8 scale to represent 1/8"=1" to sketch a line 20-1/2" long.
3. Use the 1/2 scale to represent 1/2"=1" to sketch a line 8-1/4" long.
4. Use the 1 scale to represent 1"=1" to sketch a line 4'-2" long.

Step 5. On your own:

Fill in the date, the class, and your name with your best lettering.
You will learn the preferred methods of lettering for technical drawing in Chapter 2.

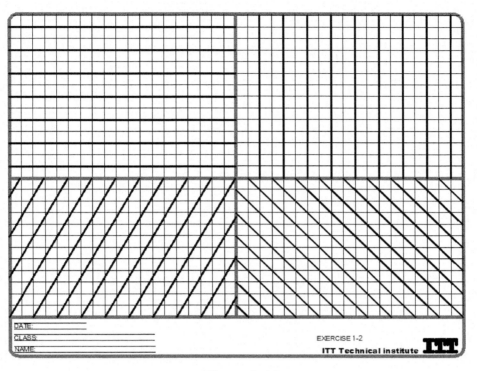

Figure 1-14
Exercise 1-2 Complete

EXERCISE 1-2   Complete Exercise sheet 1-2 by sketching lines parallel to the printed lines. Your final drawing should look like Figure 1-14. Use these steps:

Step 1. Make sure lines are parallel by using your 30-60 and 45 degree triangles in the manner shown in Figure 1-7. Refer to Chapter 5 if necessary for a description of this procedure.

Step 2. Concentrate on making your pencil lines the same thickness and density as the printed lines.

Step 3. The lower left quarter of the drawing will require you to use a 30-60 degree triangle to construct a line perpendicular to the two existing ones. Sketch construction lines perpendicular to the angular lines and make tick marks or dots 1/2" apart so that all lines will be the same distance apart. Refer to Chapter 5 if necessary for a description of this procedure.

Step 4. Use a procedure similar to Step 3 to sketch the lower right quarter using a 45 degree triangle.

Step 5. Fill in the date, the class, and your name with your best lettering.

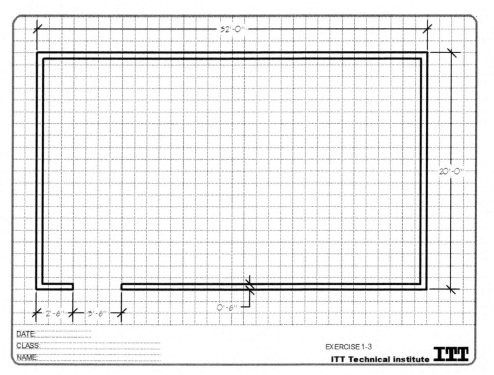

Figure 1-15
Exercise 1-3 Complete

EXERCISE 1-3   Complete Exercise sheet 1-3 by drawing the floor plan shown in Figure 1-15 at a scale of 1/4"=1'. Your final sketching should look like Figure 1-15 without dimensions. Use these steps:

Step 1. Sketch construction lines parallel to the grid lines for the vertical lines so you will know where to stop the horizontal lines.

Step 2. Sketch all horizontal lines dark, making sure they are parallel by using your 30-60 or 45 degree triangles to sketch lines on the grid lines or parallel to them if the measurement falls between grid lines.

Step 3. Concentrate on making your pencil lines the same thickness and density as the printed lines.

Step 3. Sketch the vertical lines solid to complete the drawing.

Step 4. Fill in the date, the class, and your name with your best lettering. You will learn the preferred methods of lettering for technical drawing in Chapter 3.

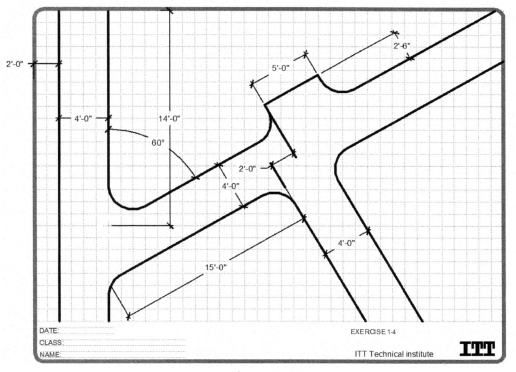

Figure 1-16
Exercise 1-4 Complete

EXERCISE 1-4　　　　Complete Exercise sheet 1-4 by drawing the site plan shown in Figure 1-16 at a scale of 1/4"=1'. Your final drawing should look like Figure 1-16 without dimensions. Use these steps:

Step 1. Sketch construction lines by extending two of the angular lines to the right edge of the border.

Step 2. Sketch a construction line parallel to the other angular line 4' from it using a scale of 1/4"=1'.

Step 3. Sketch all radii in their final form. Concentrate on making your pencil lines the same thickness and density as the printed lines.

Step 4. Sketch the remaining vertical line solid and darken all lines necessary to complete the drawing.

Step 5. Fill in the date, the class, and your name with your best lettering.

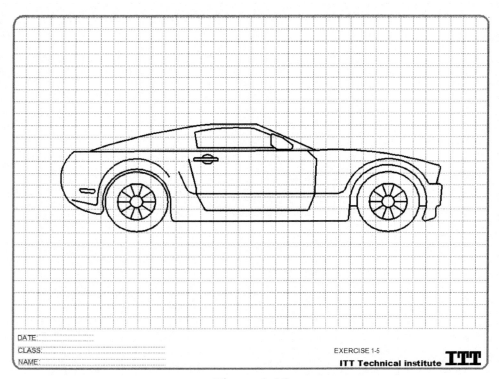

Figure 1-17
Exercise 1-5 Complete

EXERCISE 1-5   Complete Exercise sheet 1-5 by sketching the car shown in Figure 1-17 using the grid marks on your exercise sheet. Your final drawing should look like Figure 1-17. Use these steps:

     Step 1. Sketch as many dots as you think you will need for all sketch lines but the circles.

     Step 2. Sketch lines connecting the dots.

     Step 3. Sketch the circles freehand or with a circle template. Concentrate on making your pencil lines the same thickness and density as the printed lines.

     Step 4. Fill in the date, the class, and your name with your best lettering.

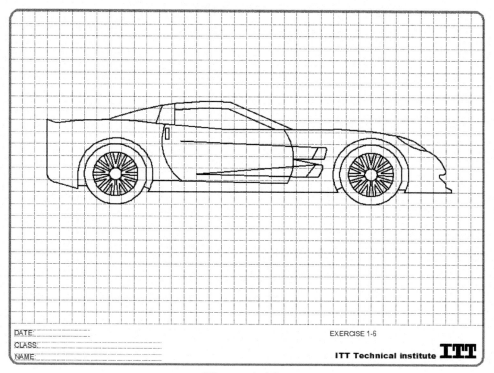

DATE:

CLASS:

NAME:

EXERCISE 1-6

ITT Technical institute **ITT**

Figure 1-18
Exercise 1-6 Complete

EXERCISE 1-6   Complete Exercise sheet 1-6 by sketching the car shown in Figure 1-18
                    using the grid marks on your exercise sheet. Your final drawing should
                    look like Figure 1-18. Use these steps:

    Step 1. Sketch as many dots as you think you will need for all sketch lines
            but the circles.
    Step 2. Sketch lines connecting the dots.
    Step 3. Sketch the circles freehand or with a circle template. Concentrate
            on making your pencil lines the same thickness and density
            as the printed lines.
    Step 4. Fill in the date, the class, and your name with your best lettering.

CHAPTER SUMMARY

This chapter contains the information on the sketching tools, supplies, and their uses. In addition, you have done exercises using these tools. Now you will be able to continue to progress in your ability to use these items to make effective sketches.

REVIEW QUESTIONS

Circle the most correct answer.

1. Which of the following is not a technical sketching tool?

   a. Pencil
   b. Eraser
   c. Compass
   d. Scale

2. Which hardness of lead should be used for technical sketching?

   a. 7B
   b. 2B
   c. H
   d. 4H

3. Which of the following erasers is best for technical sketching?

   a. pink pearl
   b. art gum
   c. gray ink
   d. white

4. Which of the following is found on the same edge of the architect's scale as the 1/4 scale?

   a. 1/16
   b. 1/8
   c. 3/8
   d. 1/2

5. When the architect's scale is used to represent 1/8"=1', each of the small spaces in the area to the left of 0 on the 1/8 scale represents:

   a. one foot
   b. one inch
   c. two feet
   d. two inches

6. Scales are never used for sketching in this course.
   a. True   b. False

7. Orthographic grids are helpful in technical sketching.
   a. True   b. False

8. Dimensions are never shown on technical sketches.
   a. True   b. False

9. Circle templates can be used in technical sketches.
   a. True   b. False

10. Sketches can be made without the use of an orthographic grid.
    a. True   b. False

Matching:
Write the number of the correct answer on the line.

a. A tool that is used to sketch items
   to a specific size   _____   1. Dimensions

b. A tool used to draw round features   _____   2. Scale

c. Features of a sketch that show the
   size of items   _____   3. Grid

d. Lines on paper that are used
   in making a sketch   _____   4. Pencil

e. A tool for drawing sketches   _____   5. Circle
                                                        template

General Questions:
Review the following questions.

1. Why are sketches needed?

2. When would you want to use dimensions on a sketch?

3. What tools are absolutely necessary to draw sketches?

4. How can sketches be used to show features in detail?

5. When can grids be helpful in drawing sketches?

2 Lettering

After completing this chapter, you will be able to:

Develop a legible, uniform lettering style that is pleasing in appearance.

INTRODUCTION

The sketches you draw in this book must have not only correct construction and good line quality and be well arranged in the field of the drawing (that area inside the border where the drawing is placed), but also lettering that is uniform, legible, and pleasing in appearance. A good lettering style is the result of careful planning and a controlled lettering style. The following alphabet is a good model for a legible, uniform lettering style, which you can develop with a little careful practice.

THE SKETCHING ALPHABET

The letters used in the **sketching alphabet** are made with single strokes and are as simple as possible. There are no serifs on the letters, and all strokes are the same width (Figure 2-1). Most companies use all capital (uppercase) letters because lowercase letters are more likely to become illegible when they are copied in a reduced size.

Figure 2-1
The Sketching Alphabet Style

Uppercase Letters

The sequence of strokes for each letter in the vertical alphabet is shown in Figure 2-2. Study each character until you know what it should look like. It may take a while for you to form the letters well. After you have drawn a letter, compare it to the form shown in Figure 2-2. If your letter does not look as good as or better than those in the figure, stop, analyze what is wrong, and correct it. *Go slowly at first and do it right.* You can pick up speed later.

Figure 2-2
The Vertical Alphabet

Fractions

It is important that fractions be large enough to still be legible when reproduced at a reduced size. Fractions should be twice the height of whole numbers if they are vertical (Figure 2-3A). Each number of the fraction should be almost the same size as whole numbers if the fraction must be horizontal to fit a given space (Figure 2-3B). The vertical fraction is preferred. Do not let fraction numbers touch the horizontal bar, because that can make the fraction illegible (Figure 2-3C).

Figure 2-3
Fractions

Slant

Letters can be vertical or inclined; either style is usually acceptable. Which one you use usually depends on your natural ability. The important characteristics of a good lettering style are that all letters are the same height and slant and that they are bold enough to reproduce well. Figure 2-4 shows the inclined alphabet.

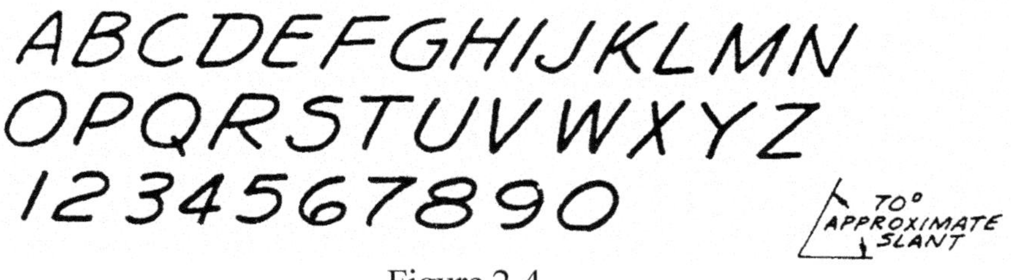

ABCDEFGHIJKLMN
OPQRSTUVWXYZ
1234567890
70°
APPROXIMATE
SLANT

Figure 2-4
The Inclined Alphabet

Guidelines

Use guidelines, ruled paper, or a lettering aid like that shown in Figure 2-5 for all letters and numbers. The lettering aid shown is easy to use (Figure 2-6). Just write the letters inside a slot, "bouncing" all letters off the top and bottom of the slot so that they are all the same height. Guidelines must be very thin and so light that they are barely visible. All lettering should be very dark and thin enough to be easily read.

1/4
3/16
5/32
1/8

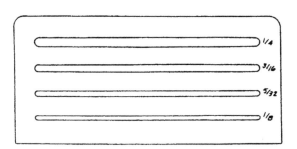

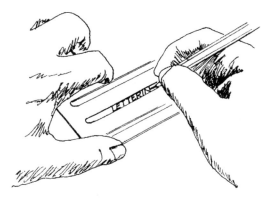

Figure 2-5
A Lettering Guide

Figure 2-6
Using a Lettering Guide

DEVELOPING A GOOD LETTERING STYLE

The most important characteristic of lettering is legibility. Lettering must be consistent and neat, but above all must be easily read so that numbers and values cannot be mistaken. The alphabets shown in Figures 2-2 and 2-4 can be written legibly with a little practice. The rules for developing a good lettering style are as follows:

1. Make sure the form of the letter is right. Do not mix uppercase and lowercase letters. Use all uppercase letters unless your instructor tells you otherwise.
2. Use guidelines, a lettering aid, or ruled paper. When drawing guidelines, make sure they are very light and thin.
3. Keep the slant of the letters the same. Use either a vertical or slanted stroke, but keep the stroke consistent.
4. Put all the letters in words as close together as possible while still making them look good.
5. Concentrate on keeping the characters open and easily read.
6. Do not make letters too tall for the thickness of your stroke. When written with a slightly blunted pencil point, letters 1/8" to 3/16" high look good.
7. Make the space between words approximately big enough for the uppercase letter I. The space between lines of lettering should be one half to two thirds the height of the letter (Figure 2-7).

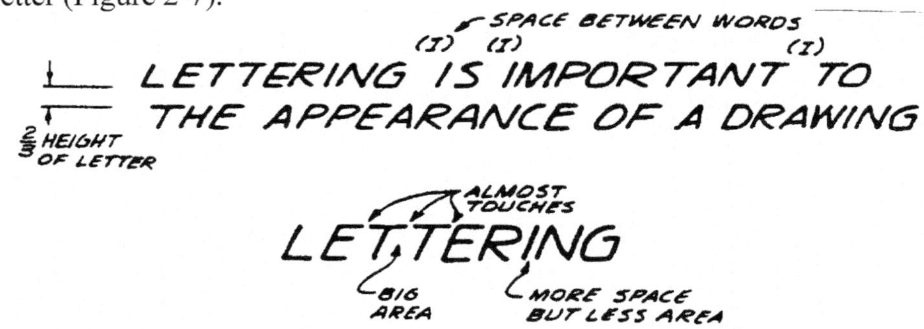

Figure 2-7
Spacing between Words and Lines

8. Do not allow letters or numbers to touch any object line, border, or fraction bar. Letters and numbers should have clear space all around them (sides, top, and bottom).
9. Begin by drawing letters and numbers. *Take your time.*
10. Make all letters very dark. If you must repeat a stroke to improve its density, do so. A number 2 pencil or an H-grade lead is right for most people.
11. Work to improve your speed after you have the form, density, and slant correct.

Two alphabets you can use in this book are shown in Figures 2-8 and 2-9.

Figure 2-8
Vertical Alphabet

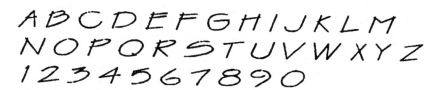

Figure 2-9
Inclined Alphabet

_____**EXERCISES**

EXERCISE 2-1

Using the vertical style of lettering, repeat each of the letters, numbers, fractions, words, and sentences in Figure 2-8 (on the sheet labeled Exercise 2-1 in the back of this book) the stated number of times.
Fill in the date, the class, and your name with your best lettering.

EXERCISE 2-2

Using the inclined style of lettering, repeat each of the letters, numbers, fractions, words, and sentences in Figure 2-9 (on the sheet labeled Exercise 2-2 in the back of this book) the stated number of times.
Fill in the date, the class, and your name with your best lettering.

CHAPTER SUMMARY

This chapter contains information on how to produce legible lettering.   Now you will be able to continually improve your ability to letter legibly and quickly.

REVIEW QUESTIONS

Circle the best answer.

1.   Guidelines for lettering should be drawn

   a.   thin and dark
   b.   thin and light
   c.   thick and dark
   d.   thick and light

2.   Vertical fractions should be

   a.   twice the height of whole numbers
   b.   the same height as whole numbers
   c.   about one and a half times the height of whole numbers
   d.   a little smaller than whole numbers

3.   The most important quality of good lettering is

   a.   consistent height
   b.   consistent slant
   c.   consistent darkness
   d.   legibility

4.   The space between words should be approximately

   a.   the spacing for the letter W
   b.   the spacing for the letter O
   c.   the spacing for the letter I
   d.   twice the height of the letters

5.   The space between lines of lettering should be

   a.   approximately two-thirds the height of the letters
   b.   approximately twice the height of the letters
   c.   invisible (lines of lettering should touch)
   d.   approximately one and a half times the height of the letters

6. Either vertical or inclined lettering is acceptable in most companies.
   a.   True   b.   False

7. A good lead grade for lettering is H.
   a.   True   b.   False

8. It is OK for letters to touch the lines forming the title block of a drawing.
   a.   True   b.   False

9. When you practice lettering, you should letter as fast as you can in the beginning.
   a.   True   b.   False

10. Lettering must be perfect to be acceptable.
    a.   True   b.   False

Matching:
Write the number of the correct answer on the line.

a. _____ A lead hardness for making lettering   1.   9H

b. _____ A lead hardness for making guidelines   2.   Twice the height
        for lettering   of the letter

c. _____ The height of a fraction   3.   H

d. _____ Lines on paper that are used   4.   Grid
        in making a sketch

e. _____ The most important quality of.   5.   Legibility
        lettering

General Questions:
Review the following questions.
1. Why is legible lettering needed?

2. When would you want to use inclined lettering?

3. Why are different lead hardnesses needed in making lettering and guidelines?

4. Why would different companies want a specific type of lettering?

5. Is it really that important to keep all letters the same height?

3 Sketching Line Weights and Drawing Constructions

_____OBJECTIVES

After completing this chapter, you will be able to:

Sketch dense, uniform, dark lines of the correct thickness for object, cutting plane, center, dimension, and extension lines.

Sketch thin, light lines for drawing construction and lettering guidelines for stated problems.

Divide lines, angles, and arcs.

Construct polygons.

Sketch tangents to circles, lines, and arcs.

LINES USED IN TECHNICAL DRAWINGS

Line quality is one of the most important elements of a good drawing. Many different types of lines are commonly used. All lines except construction lines for sketching and guidelines for lettering must be sharp and dark. Some are thicker than others, but all lines must be black and uniformly dark. Lettering guidelines and construction lines must be very thin and light—just barely dark enough to be followed for sketching the final lines.

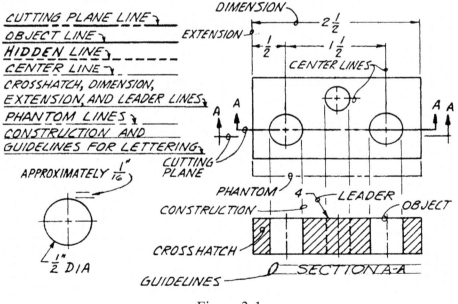

Figure 3-1
The Alphabet of Lines

The alphabet of lines is shown in Figure 3-1. You will use these lines to sketch the exercises in this book. They are described as follows:

Cutting plane lines are the thickest lines. They have a long dash and two short dashes. Another form of the cutting plane line, also shown in Figure 3-1, is used in making sectional views, which will be covered in Chapter 6.

Object lines are approximately half as thick as cutting plane lines and are continuous (no breaks).

Hidden lines are series of short dashes that are the same thickness as or slightly thinner than object lines. Each dash is approximately 1/8" long separated by 1/16" spaces.

Hatch, dimension, extension, and leader lines are continuous and are approximately half as thick as object lines but are just as dark.

Center lines are the same width as dimension lines and consist of a long dash and one short dash. The long dash is approximately 5/8" long, the short dash is approximately 1/16" long, and the space between dashes is approximately 1/16". The center line should extend approximately 1/16" past the feature it is describing. Center lines describe circular features and the centers of some objects.

Phantom lines are used to show some alternate position or feature that differs from the main drawing. They are similar to the center line but have two short dashes instead of one.

Construction lines and guidelines for lettering are continuous and are thin and very light.

SKETCHING GOOD LINES
Using a Wooden Pencil or a Lead Holder
Sketching good lines with a wooden pencil or lead holder requires that the pencil be sharpened often. In sketching thin lines, such as center lines and dimension lines, the lead must be sharpened to a point, as shown in Figure 3-2. For sketching object, hidden, and cutting plane lines, use a blunter point (Figure 3-2). To sketch the line, hold the pencil about one inch from the end, at approximately a 60 degree angle to the paper (Figure 3-3). Roll the pencil in your hand as you sketch the line from left to right. Apply enough pressure to get a solid, dark line. Go back over the lines from right to left if necessary. Use a number 2 pencil or an H or 2H lead for these lines.

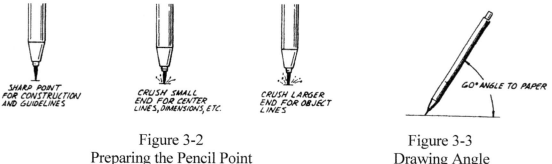

SHARP POINT
FOR CONSTRUCTION
AND GUIDELINES

CRUSH SMALL
END FOR CENTER
LINES, DIMENSIONS, ETC.

CRUSH LARGER
END FOR OBJECT
LINES

60° ANGLE TO PAPER

Figure 3-2
Preparing the Pencil Point

Figure 3-3
Drawing Angle

Using a Mechanical Pencil

The mechanical pencil has a lead of uniform thickness and as a result must be held perpendicular to the paper. To sketch object and hidden lines, use a .7 mm lead of H or 2H softness. To sketch thin lines, such as dimension lines, center lines, and extension lines, use a .5 mm lead of H or 2H softness. Use a firm, even pressure to get a solid line and to avoid breaking the lead. Go back over lines if necessary to get a solid, dark line. Construction lines and lettering guidelines can be drawn with a .3 mm lead of 2H or 4H softness.

CONSTRUCTION TERMS

Many drawing constructions are done repeatedly in technical drawings. Because many of the terms used to describe these constructions are not familiar to everyone, the most common terms are defined as follows:

Radius the distance from the center of a circle or arc to the outside edge or circumference, Figure 3-4. It is the distance halfway across a circle template.

Diameter the distance all the way across a circle, though the center (Figure 3-5). It is the size marked on circles on a circle template.

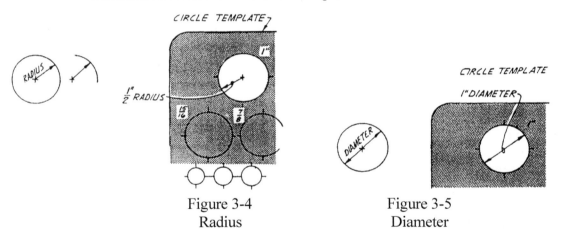

Figure 3-4
Radius

Figure 3-5
Diameter

Circumference the distance around the outside of a circle.

Intersection where two or more lines, circles, or arcs cross (Figure 3-6).

Parallel two lines or curves that are the same distance apart along all parts of the lines or curves (Figure 3-7).

Perpendicular lines at a 90 degree angle to each other (Figure 3-8).

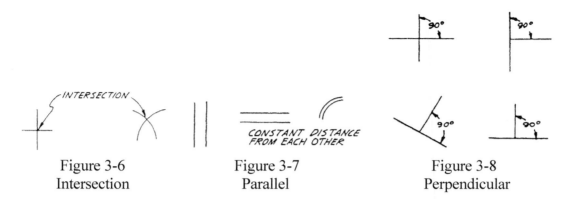

Figure 3-6
Intersection

Figure 3-7
Parallel

Figure 3-8
Perpendicular

Tangent lines or arcs that touch at only one point. When lines or arcs are tangent, they lie exactly on top of each other at one point (Figure 3-9).

Bisected divided in half (Figure 3-10).

Proportional the same ratio or proportions (Figure 3-11).

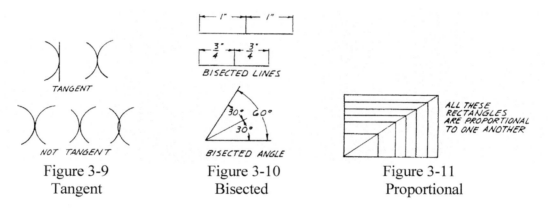

Figure 3-9
Tangent

Figure 3-10
Bisected

Figure 3-11
Proportional

Across corners a measurement made across corners through the center of a feature (Figure 3-12).

Across flats a measurement made across the parallel sides of a feature (Figure 3-13). The measurement is made perpendicular to the sides.

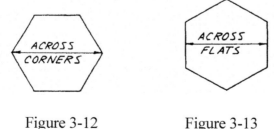

Figure 3-12
Across Corners

Figure 3-13
Across Flats

Right angle a 90 degree angle (Figure 3-14).

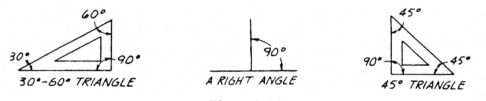

Figure 3-14
Right Angles

Acute angle an angle less than 90 degrees (Figure 3-15).

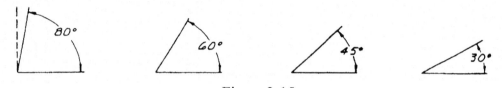

Figure 3-15
Acute Angles

Obtuse angle an angle greater than 90 degrees (Figure 3-16).

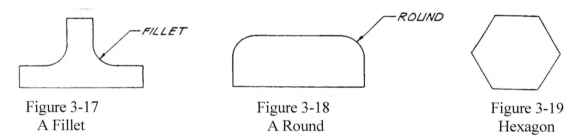

Figure 3-17
A Fillet

Figure 3-18
A Round

Figure 3-19
Hexagon

Fillet an inside radius (Figure 3-17).

Round an outside radius (Figure 3-18).

Hexagon a feature with six equal sides and angles (Figure 3-19).

Polygon   a feature enclosed with straight lines (Figure 3-20). Regular polygons have equal sides and angles. Irregular polygons have unequal sides and/or angles.

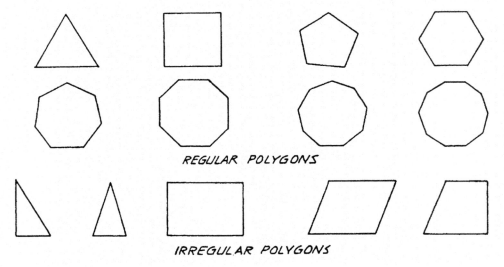

REGULAR POLYGONS

IRREGULAR POLYGONS

Figure 3-20
Regular and Irregular Polygons

SKETCHING CONSTRUCTIONS
Now that the construction terms have been defined, the most common drawing constructions will be described.

Sketching parallel lines
There are several methods for sketching parallel lines. The grid paper in your book allows you to use the grid for sketching parallel vertical and horizontal lines. Figure 3-21 shows the use of a drafting machine or T-square and triangles to sketch parallel lines. This book is designed for you to use triangles to sketch parallel lines. To sketch parallel lines on an angle, follow these steps:

      Step 1. Sketch one line at the desired angle.
      Step 2. Align one edge of a triangle on the newly drawn line.
      Step 3. Place one edge of another triangle at the base of the first triangle as shown in Figure 3-21.
      Step 4. Either tape the second triangle in place or hold it firmly as you slide the first triangle along its edge and sketch the parallel lines.

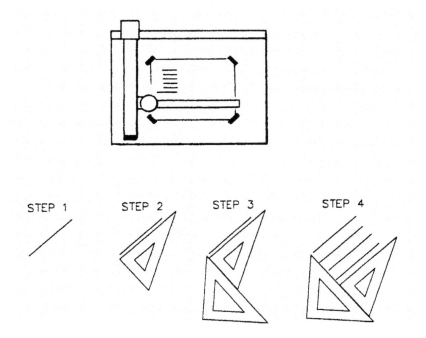

Figure 3-21
Sketching Parallel Lines Using a Drafting Machine and Triangles

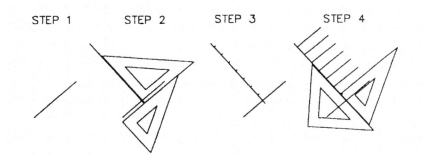

Figure 3-22
Sketching Parallel Lines Using Two Triangles

Figure 3-22 shows the steps for sketching parallel lines a given distance apart (in this case 3/4") by sketching a construction line perpendicular to the first line sketched. The perpendicular ensures that the lines are spaced exactly the distance marked. The steps are as follows:

Step 1. Sketch one line at the desired angle.
Step 2. Construct a perpendicular construction line by aligning one triangle on the line and placing another triangle containing a 90 degree angle on it as shown in Figure 3-22.
Make sure your construction line is very thin and light.
Step 3. Using either a dot or a small light line, mark 3/4" spaces on the perpendicular line.
Step 4. Using the two-triangle method in Figure 3-21, sketch lines through the points.

Sketching perpendicular lines

In addition to the method for sketching perpendicular lines described in Figure 3-22, two methods are shown in Figure 3-23. The first method involves the use of a straight edge and a triangle. The straight edge can be a drafting machine, a T-square, or another triangle. The second method is described as follows:

> Step 1. Start with a line of a specified length (in this case 2 1/2").
> Step 2. Using a radius greater than half the length of the line, sketch arcs from each end of the line.
> Step 3. Connect the intersections of the arcs to form a perpendicular.

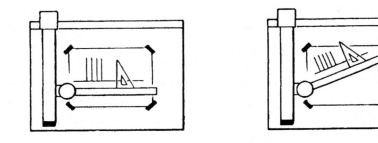

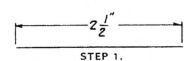

STEP 1.

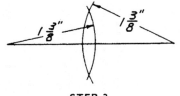

STEP 2.

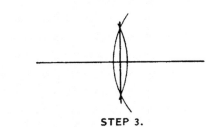

STEP 3.

Figure 3-23
Sketching Perpendicular Lines

Sketching tangents

The following figures show several instances where tangents are used and the methods for sketching them.

Sketching a line tangent to two circles (Figure 3-24)

Step 1. Lay a triangle so that it rests just below the outside edges of both circles. This small space allows your pencil lead to pass exactly through both circles making the line tangent to them.

Step 2. Sketch the line tangent to both circles.

Step 3. Position the triangle differently in Step 1 to achieve an alternate position.

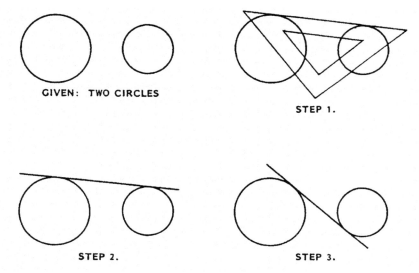

Figure 3-24
Sketching a Line Tangent to Two Circles

Sketching an inside arc tangent to two circles (Figure 3-25)

Although you will not use method 1 in your sketching exercises because it often requires a compass, it is important that you study this method so that you will know how it is done.

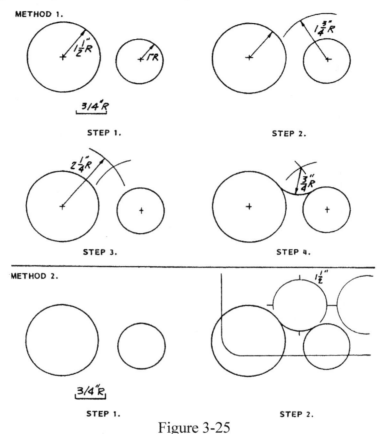

Figure 3-25
Sketching an Inside Arc Tangent to Two Circles

Method 1:

Step 1. Start with two given circles and a given radius (in the example, a larger circle with a 1 1/2" radius, a smaller circle with a 1" radius, and a 3/4" radius for the arc to be sketched tangent). The circles must be close enough together to allow the arc to touch.

Step 2. From the center of the 1" radius circle, sketch an arc with a radius that is 1" (the small circle radius) plus 3/4" (the radius of the arc to be sketched).

Step 3. From the center of the 1 1/2" radius circle, sketch an arc with a radius that is 1 1/2" (large circle radius) plus 3/4" (radius of the arc to be sketched).

Step 4. From the intersection of the two arcs, sketch an arc with a radius of 3/4". This arc will be exactly tangent to both circles.

Method 2:

Step 1. Start with the same given circles and radius used in Method 1.

Step 2. With a circle template, place a circle hole with a 3/4" radius (1 1/2" diameter) tangent to both circles and sketch the radius (allow for the pencil lead width).

Sketching an outside arc tangent to two circles (Figure 3-26)

Although you will not use this technique in your sketching exercises because it requires a compass, it is important that you study this method so that you will know how it is done. You will find it to be useful in understanding constructions in sketching.

Step 1. Start with two given circles and a given radius (in the example, a larger circle with a 1 1/2" radius, a smaller circle with a 1" radius, and a 4" radius for the arc to be sketched tangent). The radius must be large enough to touch the outside edges of both circles.

Step 2. From the center of the 1 1/2" radius circle, sketch an arc with a radius that is 2 1/2" (the 4" radius minus the radius of the 1 1/2" radius circle).

Step 3. From the center of the 1" radius circle, sketch an arc with a radius that is 3" (the 4" radius minus the radius of the 1" radius circle).

Step 4. From the intersection of the two arcs, sketch an arc with a radius of 4". This arc will be exactly tangent to both circles.

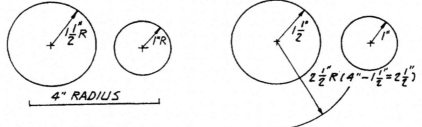

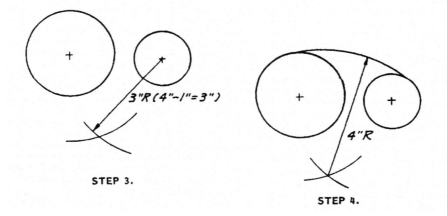

Figure 3-26
Sketching an Outside Arc Tangent to Two Circles

3-11

Sketching an arc (fillet) tangent to lines at right angles (Figure 3-27)

Method 1:
Step 1. Start with given lines AB and CD at right angles and a given radius (1/2" in the example).
Step 2. Sketch construction lines parallel to lines AB and CD 1/2" from the lines.
Step 3. From the intersection of the construction lines, sketch a 1/2" radius arc, which will form the fillet.

Method 2:
Step 1. Start with the same given lines and the radius used in Method 1.
Step 2. With a circle template, place a circle with a 1/2" radius (1" diameter) in the correct position and sketch the radius tangent to lines AB and CD.

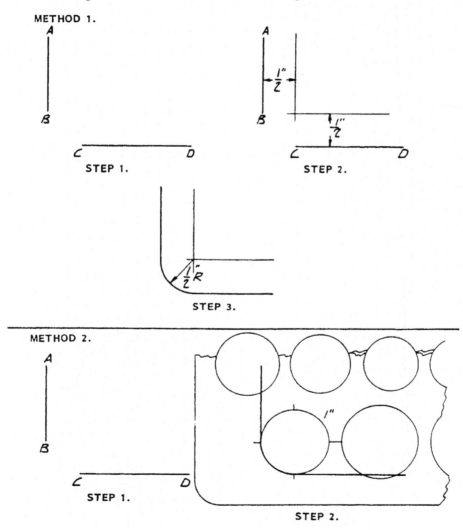

Figure 3-27
Sketching a Fillet Tangent to Two Lines at Right Angles

Sketching an arc (fillet) tangent to lines at any angle (Figure 3-28)

Method 1:
Step 1. Start with given lines AB and CD, which will intersect if extended, and a given radius (1/2" in the example).
Step 2. Sketch construction lines parallel to lines AB and CD 1/2" from the lines.
Step 3. From the intersection of the construction lines, sketch a 1/2" radius arc, which will form the fillet.

Method 2:
Step 1. Start with the same given lines and the radius used in Method 1.
Step 2. With a circle template, place a circle with a 1/2" radius (1" diameter) in the correct position and sketch the radius tangent to lines AB and CD.

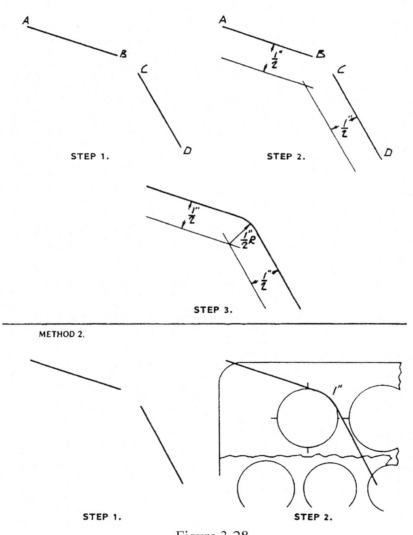

Figure 3-28
Sketching a Fillet Tangent to Lines at Any Angle

Sketching an arc of a given radius tangent to a straight line and a circle (Figure 3-29)

Method 1:
Step 1. Start with a given circle (1 1/2" radius in the example), a straight line, and a given radius (3/4" in the example).
Step 2. From the center of the circle, sketch an arc that has a radius of 1 1/2" (the radius of the circle) plus 3/4" (the radius of the arc to be drawn).
Step 3. Sketch a line parallel to line AB 3/4" away from it to intersect the arc.
Step 4. From the intersection, sketch the 3/4" radius tangent to the line and the circle.

Method 2:
Step 1. Start with the same given circle, line, and radius used in Method 1.
Step 2. With a circle template, place a circle with a 3/4" radius (1 1/2" diameter) tangent to the circle and the line and sketch the 3/4" radius.

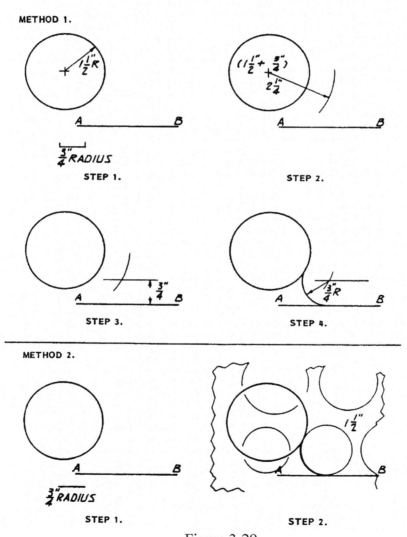

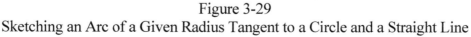

Figure 3-29
Sketching an Arc of a Given Radius Tangent to a Circle and a Straight Line

Sketching an arc tangent to two parallel lines (Figure 3-30)

Method 1:
Step 1. Start with two given parallel lines (2 1/2" apart in the example).
Step 2. Sketch a perpendicular that crosses both lines.
Step 3. From each intersection, sketch an arc with a radius greater than half the distance between the two lines.
Step 4. Sketch a line through the intersection of the two arcs. Then, using the distance AB as a radius and point A as the center, sketch the arc tangent to the two parallel lines.

Method 2:
Step 1. Start with the same given parallel lines used in Method 1.
Step 2. With a circle template, place a circle with a 2 1/2" diameter between the lines to sketch the arc tangent to the two lines.

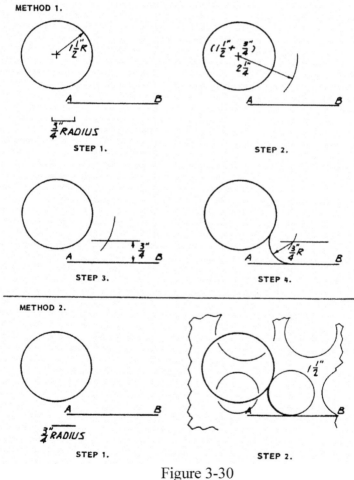

Figure 3-30
Sketching an Arc Tangent to Two Parallel Lines

3-15

Dividing lines and angles

When you are sketching, it is sometimes necessary to divide a line into a specified number of parts or to bisect an angle into two equal parts. AutoCAD makes this very easy with the Divide command; but when you are sketching, the following methods can be used:

Dividing a line into any number of equal parts (Figure 3-31)

Method 1:

Step 1. Start with a line of any length, AB.

Step 2. Sketch a line perpendicular to one end of line AB.

Step 3. On a scale, select any convenient length that has equal units (six in the example) and place it so that one end is at point A and the other end lies on the perpendicular line. Make marks on the paper at the six unit points.

Step 4. Sketch perpendicular lines through the six marks to intersect line AB and divide it into six equal parts.

Method 2:

Step 1. Start with a line of any length, AB.

Step 2. Place a scale with six equal units on it at a convenient angle to point A. Make marks on the paper at the six unit points.

Step 3. Connect the last unit (0 in the example) with point B and sketch lines parallel to line OB to divide line AB into six equal parts.

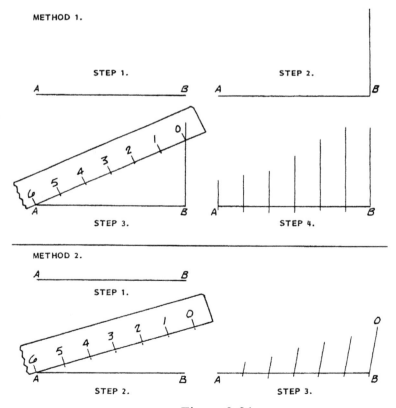

Figure 3-31
Dividing a Line into Any Number of Equal Parts

3-16

Dividing a line into proportional parts (Figure 3-32)

Step 1. Start with a line of any length, AB.
Step 2. Place a scale with six equal units on it at a convenient angle to point A. Make marks on the paper at the specified unit points (5 units, 3 units, 2 units, and 1 unit in the example).
Step 3. Connect the last unit (0 in the example) with point B and sketch lines parallel to line OB to divide line AB into parts proportional to 5, 3, 2, and 1.

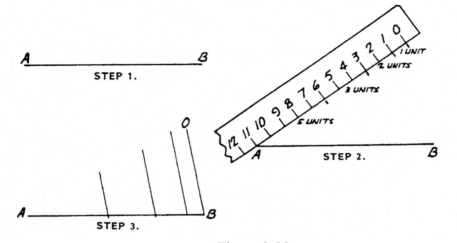

Figure 3-32
Dividing a Line into Proportional Parts

Bisecting an angle (Figure 3-33)

Step 1. Start with a given angle (52 degrees in the example).
Step 2. Sketch a radius from the start point of the angle (A) to intersect the sides of the angle.
Step 3. Using the intersections B and C as centers, sketch arcs of equal radius.
Step 4. Sketch a line from the intersection of the arcs to point A to bisect the angle.

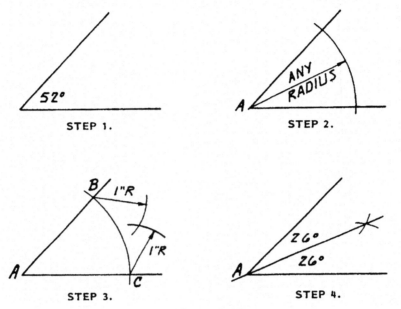

Figure 3-33
Bisecting an Angle

Sketching polygons

Sketching polygons requires considerable construction. The sketching technique is described below:

Inscribing a hexagon in a circle (Figure 3-34) (Inscribing means sketching the hexagon inside the circle.)

      Step 1. Start with a given circle.
      Step 2. Sketch a horizontal line through the center of the circle to the outside edge.
      Step 3. Using a 30-60 triangle as shown, sketch lines from the points at which the horizontal line intersects the circle.
      Step 4. Complete the hexagon by sketching horizontal lines at top and bottom.

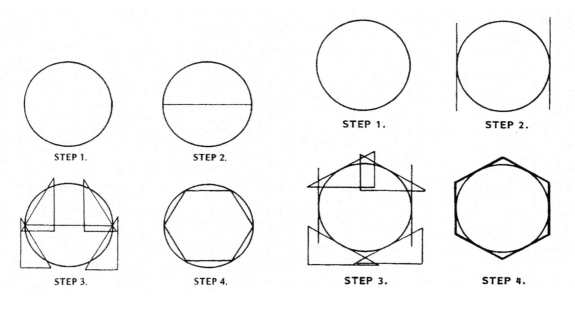

Figure 3-34
Inscribing a Hexagon in a Circle

Figure 3-35
Circumscribing a Hexagon around a Circle

Circumscribing a hexagon around a circle (Figure 3-35) (Circumscribing means sketching the hexagon outside the circle and tangent to it.)

      Step 1. Start with a given circle.
      Step 2. Sketch vertical lines tangent to the circle.
      Step 3. Using a 30-60 triangle as shown, sketch lines tangent to the circle.
      Step 4. Darken the lines to complete the hexagon.

Inscribing an octagon in a circle (Figure 3-36)

Step 1. Start with a given circle and sketch perpendicular construction lines through the center for reference.

Step 2. Sketch a 22 1/2 degree line through the center (bisect a 45 degree angle).

Step 3. Where the 22 1/2 degree line intersects the circle, sketch 90 degree and 45 degree angles. (Use 45 degree triangles as shown.)

Step 4. Sketch horizontal lines at top and bottom to complete the octagon.

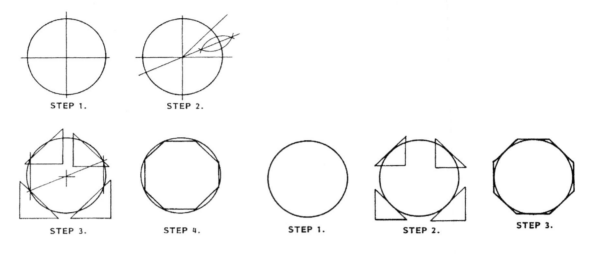

Figure 3-36
Inscribing an Octagon in a Circle

Figure 3-37
Circumscribing an Octagon around a Circle

Circumscribing an octagon around a circle (Figure 3-37)

Step 1. Start with a given circle.

Step 2. Use the 45 degree triangle in the position shown to sketch 45 degree and 90 degree angles tangent to the circle.

Step 3. Sketch horizontal lines at top and bottom to complete the octagon.

_____EXERCISES

EXERCISE 3-1

Use the sheet in your book marked Exercise 3-1 for this exercise.

Sketch Exercise 3-1 on the sheet in your book using the dimensions shown in Figure 3-38. Make sure that your lines are the correct weight and are of even width and darkness. Use guidelines for lettering and use your best lettering. Sketch and letter everything shown in Figure 3-38. Refer to Figure 3-1 for correct line weights. Fill in the date, the class, and your name with your best lettering.

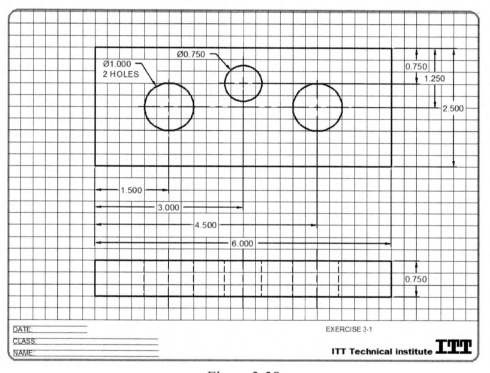

Figure 3-38
Dimensions for Exercise 3-1

EXERCISE 3-2

Use the sheet in your book marked Exercise 3-2 for this exercise. Divide the drawing area into four equal parts as shown in Figure 3-39 and make the required constructions. Center your construction in the areas. Darken the object lines and the division marks. Leave very light construction lines. Fill in the date, the class, and your name with your best lettering.

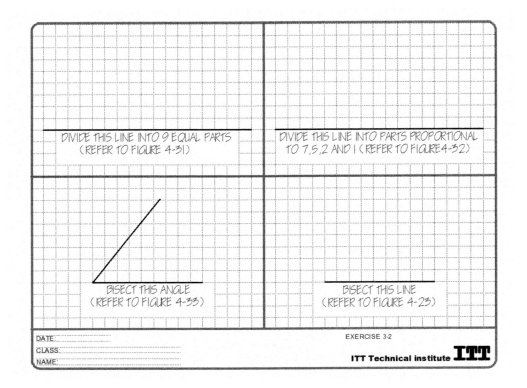

Figure 3-39
Instructions for Exercise 3-2

EXERCISE 3-3

Use the sheet in your book marked Exercise 3-3 for this exercise. Divide the sketching area into four equal parts as shown in Figure 3-40 and sketch the polygons described in that figure. Center your construction in the areas. Darken the object lines and leave very light construction lines. Fill in the date, the class, and your name with your best lettering.

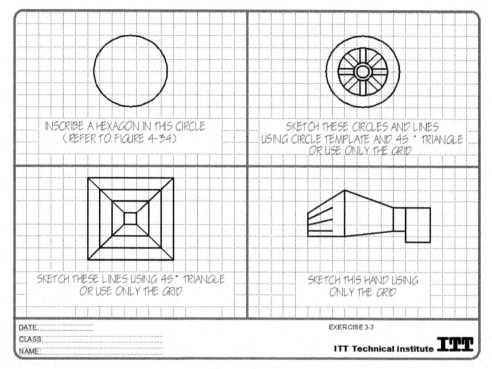

Figure 3-40
Instructions for Exercise 3-3

EXERCISE 3-4

Sketch Exercise 3-4 on the corresponding sheet in your book using the dimensions shown in Figure 3-41. Make sure that your lines are the correct weight and are of even width and darkness. **Do not show any dimensions or other lettering on the drawing itself.** Fill in the date, the class, and your name with your best lettering. Use the construction methods shown in Figures 3-24 through 3-30.

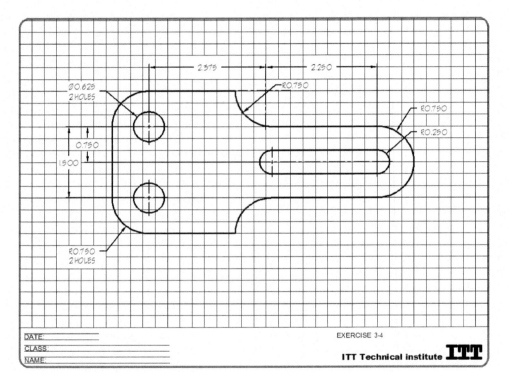

Figure 3-41
Dimensions for Exercise 3-4

EXERCISE 3-5

Sketch Exercise 3-5 on the corresponding sheet in your book using half scale of the dimensions shown in Figure 3-42. Make sure that your lines are the correct weight and are of even width and darkness. **Do not show any dimensions or other lettering on the drawing itself.** Fill in the date, the class, and your name with your best lettering. Use the construction methods shown in Figures 3-24 through 3-30.

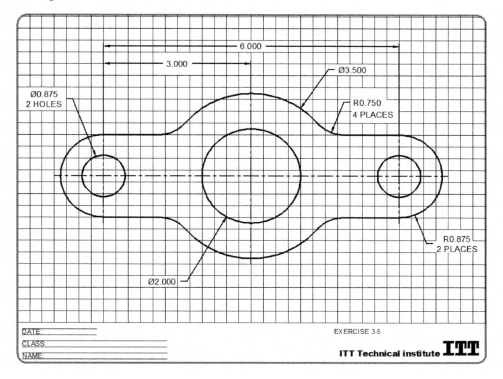

Figure 3-42
Dimensions for Exercise 3-5

This chapter contains information on sketching line weights and drawing constructions. You have sketched lines, circles, and arcs with solid lines, hidden lines, and center lines. Now you will be able to continually improve your ability to use these items to make effective sketches.

_____**REVIEW QUESTIONS**

Circle the best answer.

1.   Construction lines and guidelines for lettering should be
        a.   thin and very dark
        b.   thick and very dark
        c.   thin and very light
        d.   thick and very light

2.   Hidden lines are shown with
        a.   a series of short dashes
        b.   a long dash followed by a short dash
        c.   solid lines
        d.   two short dashes and a long dash

3.   A good lead softness to use for object lines is
        a.   H
        b.   B
        c.   4H
        d.   6H

4.   A good lead thickness for object lines is
        a.   .25 mm
        b.   .35 mm
        c.   .5 mm
        d.   .7 mm

5.   The distance from the center of a circle to the outside edge is called
        a.   a diameter
        b.   a radius
        c.   a circumference
        d.   an arc

6.   Lines that are the same distance apart along all parts of the lines are
        a.   parallel
        b.   perpendicular

c. tangent
d. proportional

7. Lines that are at 90 degrees to each other are
   a. parallel
   b. perpendicular
   c. tangent
   d. proportional

8. Lines that are tangent
   a. lie very close to each other
   b. just touch at the edges
   c. lie exactly on top of each other at one point
   d. do not touch

9. A 90 degree angle that is bisected will result in
   a. two angles greater than 90 degrees
   b. two 45 degree angles
   c. no angle at all
   d. two 90 degree angles
   e. two 30 degree angles

10. A right angle is
   a. 90 degrees
   b. greater than 90 degrees
   c. less than 90 degrees
   d. any angle correctly drawn

11. Center lines, hatch lines, extension lines, and dimension lines are drawn thin and very dark.
   a. True   b. False

12. An obtuse angle is 90 degrees.
   a. True   b. False

13. An acute angle is less than 90 degrees.
   a. True   b. False

14. A circumference is the distance from the center of a circle to the outside edge.
   a. True   b. False

15. A hexagon has 6 sides.
   a. True   b. False

Matching:
Write the number of the correct answer on the line.

a._____ The distance from the center of a
circle to the outside edge _____ 1. Parallel

b._____ 90 degrees _____ 2. Perpendicular

c._____ A 6-sided figure _____ 3. A right angle

d.____ Lines that are at 90 degrees to each
other _____ 4. Hexagon

e. _____Lines that are the same distance apart
along all parts of the lines _____ 5. Radius

General Questions:
Review the following questions.

1. Why are different line weights needed?

2. When would you want to sketch obtuse or acute angles?

3. What types of lines are absolutely necessary to make sketches?

4. How can knowing drawing constructions help to make sketches?

5. Where should center lines be used on sketches?

4   Reading and Sketching Orthographic Views

_____OBJECTIVES

After completing this chapter, you will be able to:

Correctly identify surfaces in two-dimensional views from given three-dimensional views.

Correctly sketch two-dimensional views from given three-dimensional views.

Correctly answer questions regarding the orthographic projection method of drawing.

ORTHOGRAPHIC PROJECTION

Orthographic projection is a system of drawing that is used throughout the world. Orthographic views are two-dimensional or flat views of objects. One of the reasons orthographic drawing is used instead of pictorial drawing is that it is easy to place dimensions on these drawings, therefore avoiding confusion about measurements (Figure 4-1).

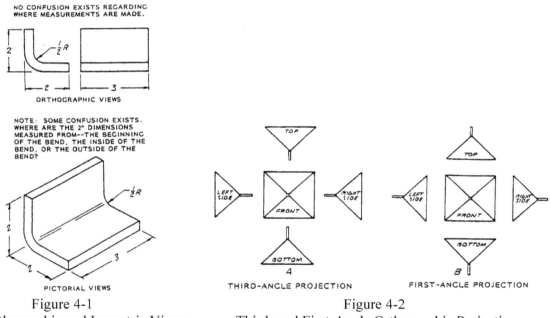

Figure 4-1
Orthographic and Isometric Views

Figure 4-2
Third- and First-Angle Orthographic Projection

There are two forms of orthographic projection that are commonly used: first-angle and third-angle (Figure 4-2). Third-angle projection is used in the United States and many other countries. First-angle projection is used in several European countries. This chapter presents third-angle orthographic projection in detail, but first describes how first-angle projection is different.

DIFFERENCES BETWEEN FIRST-ANGLE AND THIRD-ANGLE ORTHOGRAPHIC PROJECTION

In the third-angle projection shown in Figure 4-2, think of the pyramid shape as being attached in the center and swinging to all four sides to give right side, left side, top, and bottom views. First-angle projection is viewed as if the object were tipped to the sides to give the four views. Third-angle orthographic projection is used in the rest of this book, so no further reference will be made to first-angle projection.

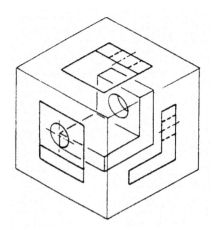

Figure 4-3
Transparent Box Model

Third-angle projection theory

One of the best ways to explain third-angle projection is the transparent box theory (Figure 4-3), in which an imaginary cube is placed around the object. The surfaces you would see if you looked into each side of the cube are registered on the cube. When the cube is unfolded, the views are arranged as shown in Figure 4-4. This arrangement of views is understood throughout the world. Your drawings must follow the same arrangement, with two exceptions, as shown in Figure 4-5.

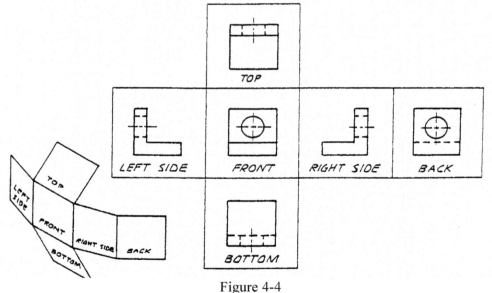

Figure 4-4
Standard View Arrangement

VIEWS

The transparent box theory shows that every object has six possible views: front, back, top, bottom, left side, and right side. Often an object can be fully described using three of these views, or sometimes fewer. Many objects such as screws and other fasteners need only one view to completely describe them. Other more complex objects require all six views and several auxiliary, section, and detail views for complete description. These other types of views will be presented in later chapters.

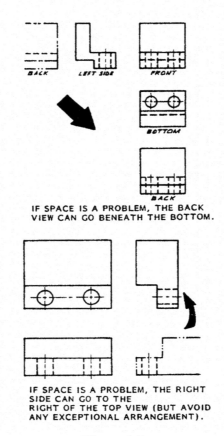

Figure 4-5
Exceptions to the Standard View Arrangement

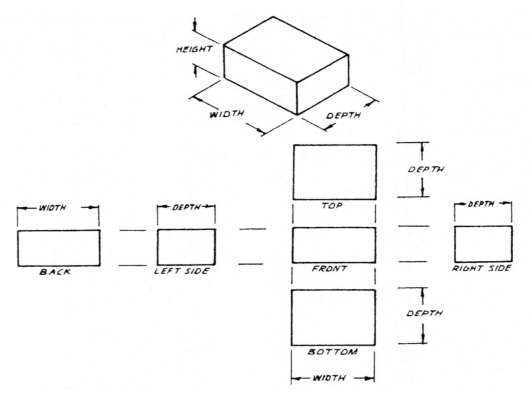

Figure 4-6
Each View Shows Only Two Dimensions

Height, width, and depth dimensions

Each view of the object contains only two of its three dimensions: The top and bottom views show width and depth; the right and left side views show height and depth; and the front and back views show width and height (Figure 4-6). The most commonly used combination of views is the top, front, and right side views, and the next most commonly used combination is top, front, and left side (Figure 4-7). Usually the front view is drawn first, and then either the top or side view is drawn. Height and width dimensions are easily projected into the adjacent view, but depth dimensions must be transferred using either a scale or a piece of paper or they must be projected through a 45 degree angle (Figure 4-8).

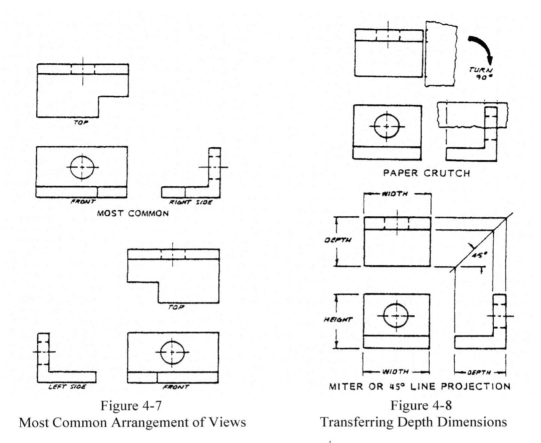

Figure 4-7	Figure 4-8
Most Common Arrangement of Views	Transferring Depth Dimensions

Identifying surfaces and features

To make two-dimensional drawings from three-dimensional drawings or an actual part you must learn to identify surfaces, edges, and other features. The following paragraphs and exercises will give you practice in doing that.

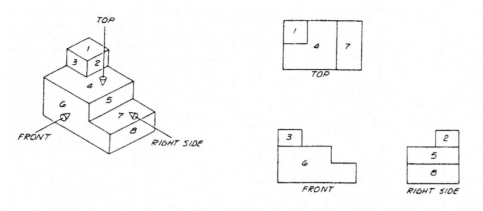

Figure 4-9
Normal Surfaces

Normal surfaces

The easiest surfaces to read are the flat, unslanted surfaces. These are called normal (meaning perpendicular) surfaces because they are perpendicular to your line of sight when you look at the object. Figure 4-9 shows an object that has all normal surfaces. Exercise 4-1 will test your skill in identifying normal surfaces from a three-dimensional drawing.

EXERCISE 4-1:
Identifying Normal Surfaces

Step 1. Remove the sheet labeled Exercise 4-1 from your book.
Step 2. Identify the numbered surfaces in the normal views in the spaces provided. Use the numbers from the pictorial view. Use your best lettering with guidelines top and bottom.
Step 3. Fill in the date, class, and your name with your best lettering.

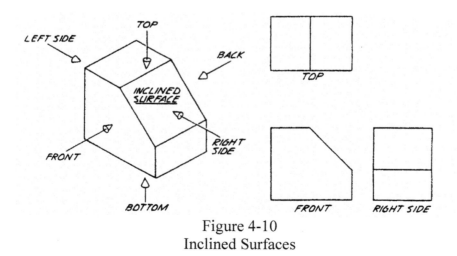

Figure 4-10
Inclined Surfaces

Inclined or slanted surfaces

An inclined or slanted surface is perpendicular to two of the normal surfaces, but at an angle other than 90 degrees to the other four normal surfaces. The slanted surface in Figure 4-10 is perpendicular to the front and back surfaces but inclined to the top, bottom, right side, and left side. The surface is said to be foreshortened when its true length is not shown. When you view this inclined surface, you see it slanted in only the front view. (You could see it slanted in the back view, but because it would appear exactly as it does in the front view, only the front is shown.)

Complete Exercise 4-2 now to see how well you can identify inclined and normal surfaces.

EXERCISE 4-2:
Identifying Inclined Surfaces

Step 1. Remove the sheet labeled Exercise 4-2 from your book.
Step 2. Identify the numbered surfaces in the normal views in the spaces provided. Use the numbers from the pictorial view. Use your best lettering with guidelines top and bottom.
Step 3. Fill in the date, class, and your name with your best lettering.

Oblique surfaces

Slanted surfaces that are inclined to all the normal surfaces are called oblique surfaces (Figure 4-11). Notice that the oblique surface appears in all three views and that only one line of the surface is true length in each view. Try Exercise 4-3 to identify oblique and normal surfaces.

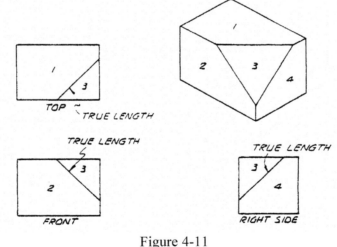

Figure 4-11
Oblique Surfaces

EXERCISE 4-3:
Identifying Oblique Surfaces

Step 1. Remove the sheet labeled Exercise 4-3 from your book.
Step 2. Identify the numbered surfaces in the normal views in the spaces provided. Use the numbers from the pictorial. Use your best lettering with guidelines top and bottom.
Step 3. Fill in the date, class, and your name with your best lettering.

Identifying edges

In reading two-dimensional drawings, it is often helpful to identify surfaces where they appear as an edge. As shown in Figure 4-12, when you look at a very thin sheet of metal from the front, you see it in the true shape of its front surface. When you view it from its right side, you see it as an edge. Then when you flip it over, you see the true shape of its back surface.

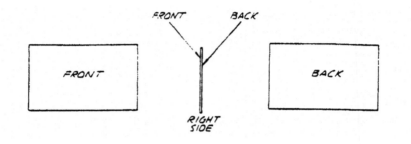

Figure 4-12
Edges on a Thin Sheet

If the metal is thicker, as in Figure 4-13, the edges are farther apart and the side view takes on a shape. In Figure 4-14 notice that edges in one view line up with edges in the view adjacent to it. Surfaces 2, 5, 7, and 10 in the top view, for example, line up with the same surfaces in the front view. Surfaces 1, 4, and 11 line up with the same surfaces in the right side view.

Study Figure 4-14 for a few minutes until you feel certain that you understand these views and can number edges correctly. After you feel confident about Figure 4-14, complete Exercise 4-4.

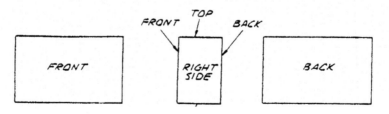

Figure 4-13
Edges on a Thicker Part

4 - 8

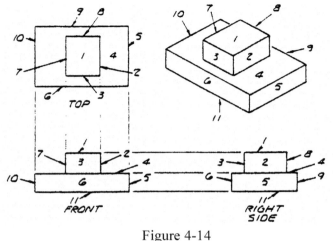

Figure 4-14
Identifying Edges

EXERCISE 4-4:
Identifying Edges

Step 1. Remove the sheet labeled Exercise 4-4 from your book.
Step 2. Identify the numbered surfaces as edges in the normal views in the spaces provided. Use the numbers from the pictorial. Use your best lettering with guidelines top and bottom.
Step 3. Fill in the date, class, and your name with your best lettering.

Cut cylinders

When cylinders are cut at right angles, their shapes in adjacent views do not change (Figure 4-15). When they are cut at an angle, their shapes appear as ellipses in one of the adjacent views (Figure 4-16).

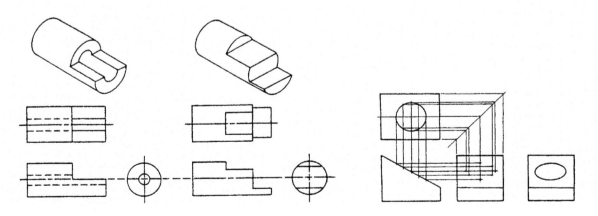

Figure 4-15
Cylinders Cut at Right Angles

Figure 4-16
Cylinders Cut at an Angle

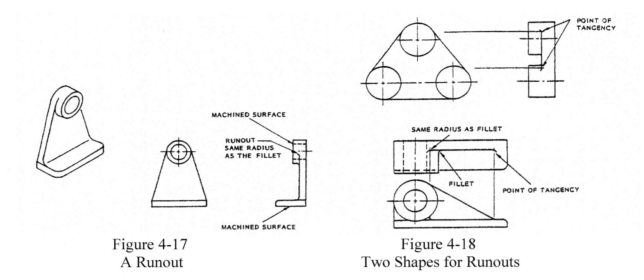

Figure 4-17
A Runout

Figure 4-18
Two Shapes for Runouts

Runouts

A **runout** is a surface that blends into another surface without forming an edge at the point where the runout ends. Figure 4-17 shows a runout on a casting. Castings and other molded parts often have runouts. Castings also often have rounded edges because of the way they are manufactured. The only sharp edges on most castings are surfaces that have been machined to allow a part to fit or function better. Some rounds of the cast parts are usually found connected to the runout. Figure 4-18 shows two shapes of runouts. Runouts are drawn just as you see them in this figure. The edge view line ends with the radius of the fillet drawn at the end. The point of tangency, where the flat surface meets the cylindrical surface, is where the runout ends.

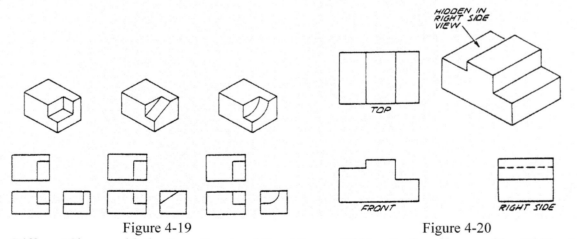

Figure 4-19
Different Shapes with the Same Front and Top Views

Figure 4-20
Hidden Surface Shown with a Hidden Line

Different shapes that look the same in one or more views

In reading two-dimensional views, it is easy to make a mistake about the shape of an object if you look at only two views. Figure 4-19 shows several objects that have the same appearance in two views. Only the right side view shows the true shape of each object.

Hidden features

To describe many objects fully, hidden surfaces must often be shown. These surfaces are shown with hidden lines (Figure 4-20).

Notice that the right side view would not be complete if the hidden surface were not shown with a hidden line.

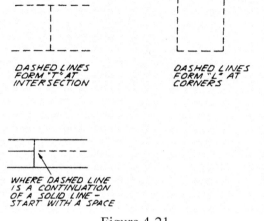

Figure 4-21
Rules for Drawing Hidden Lines

When hidden lines are drawn at a corner, they should form an L shape (Figure 4-21). When they intersect, they should form a T or a cross if one line crosses over the other. If they are a continuation of a solid line, there should be a break between the solid line and the first dash of a hidden line. The dashes should be about 1/8" long, with 1/16" between dashes. They can be longer on larger drawings.

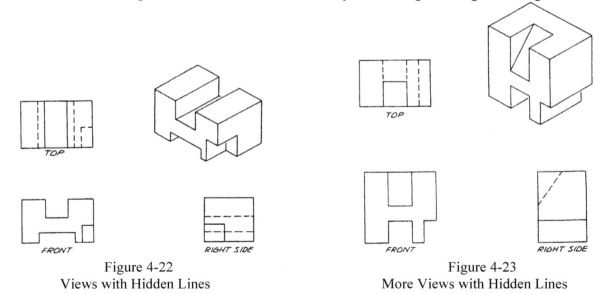

Figure 4-22
Views with Hidden Lines

Figure 4-23
More Views with Hidden Lines

Figures 4-22 and 4-23 show several hidden lines. In Figure 4-23 notice that the solid line in the top view takes precedence over the hidden line that shows the hidden slot. On complex objects, the number of hidden lines often can be very confusing, so it is generally understood that only one layer of hidden lines is shown (Figure 4-24).

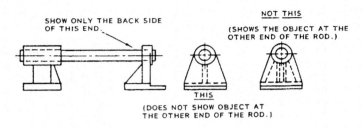

Figure 4-24
Showing Only One Layer of Hidden Features

Normal cylinders

Cylinders that are perpendicular to the normal surfaces of an object are called normal cylinders. These cylinders might be round holes or round rods. Figure 4-25 shows how normal cylinders look in two-dimensional views. Notice that the edges of the holes are shown with hidden lines in the view where they are hidden. The hidden lines in the front view that show the holes in front exactly cover the hidden lines that show the holes in the back.

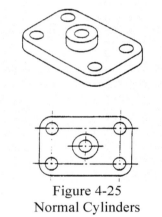

Figure 4-25
Normal Cylinders

When holes do not go all the way through the object, the bottom of the hole is shown with a hidden line as in Figure 4-26. Notice that the hole shown in the right-hand side of Figure 4-26 is slanted so that the circle at the bottom of the hole is smaller than the circle at the top of the hole.

Countersinks and counterbores

Figure 4-27 shows the countersink and counterbore features. The countersink feature is used to allow a flathead screw that has the same shape as the countersunk hole to fit below the surface of the part. A hole is drilled in the part first and then the countersink is added. The counterbore is composed of two holes, one larger than the other. The smaller hole is drilled first, and then the counterbore is added. Notice that the bottom of the larger hole, which does not go through the part, is shown with a hidden line. A counterbore is used to allow parts to fit deeper into the material. A variation of the counterbore, called a spotface, is a shallow counterbore that makes the surface smoother so that the head of a screw or bolt fits better.

Now use your hidden line skills to fill in the hidden lines on the views in Exercise 4-5.

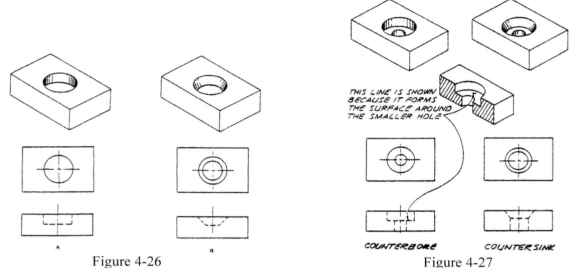

Figure 4-26
Holes that Do Not Go Through

Figure 4-27
Counterbore and Countersink

EXERCISE 4-5:
Sketching Hidden Lines

Step 1. Remove the sheet labeled Exercise 4-5 from your book.

Step 2. Add missing object lines and the missing hidden lines in the top and front views of sheet 1, and in the front and right side views of sheet 2. Make the dashes about 1/8" long with a 1/16" space between dashes. Make sure the hidden lines are aligned with features in the adjacent views and that your hidden lines follow the rules described in Figure 4-21. Use the pictorial drawing as a guide.

Step 3. Fill in the date, class, and your name with your best lettering.

SKETCHING ORTHOGRAPHIC VIEWS

Although you have already begun sketching in the previous chapters, we need to review some of the common practices in technical sketching and add some other information that will make your sketches professional quality.

Materials

The materials you will need have already been listed in a previous chapter. They are paper (the exercises in this book), pencils, triangle, eraser, and circle template. If you are making sketches on your own, you may prefer gridded paper for some objects, but you will find that plain paper is just as easy to use for some drawings. Be sure the eraser you use makes a clean erasure, because you will make some mistakes; and erasing is not only OK, it is encouraged.

Lines

You have already begun using lines in your sketches. If you are not certain about how they should appear, review Chapter 3 before you complete the remaining exercises in this chapter.

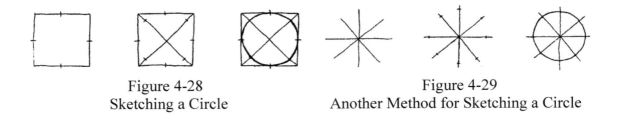

Figure 4-28
Sketching a Circle

Figure 4-29
Another Method for Sketching a Circle

Circles

Some of the circles you will sketch will be bigger than the largest circle on your circle template. These circles will not look as good as the ones you draw with the circle template, but they should be as accurate as you can make them. Figure 4-28 shows an easy method for drawing circles.

Step 1. Determine the diameter of the circle you want to sketch.
Step 2. Using light lines, draw a square the size of the diameter of the circle.
Step 3. Find the center of the circle by drawing diagonals across the corners of the square.
Step 4. Using the center as a guide, estimate the midpoint of each side and mark it.
Step 5. Along the diagonals, mark the radius of the circle from its center.
Step 6. Connect the construction points using a dark sketch line.

Figure 4-29 shows another method for drawing circles.

Step 1. Determine the diameter of the circle you want to sketch.
Step 2. Draw horizontal, vertical, and 45 degree construction lines through a center point.
Step 3. Mark the radius of the circle on the construction lines.
Step 4. Connect the construction points using a dark sketch line.

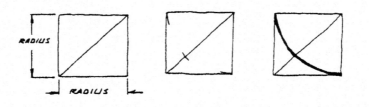

Figure 4-30
Sketching an Arc

Arcs

Arcs larger than your circle template are sketched in a manner similar to that used for circles. To draw an arc using the method shown in Figure 4-30, follow these steps:

Step 1. Sketch a square the size of the radius of the arc.
Step 2. Draw a construction line across a diagonal of the square.
Step 3. Mark the radius on the diagonal.
Step 4. Sketch the radius using a dark sketch line from one corner of the square through the mark on the diagonal to the other corner.

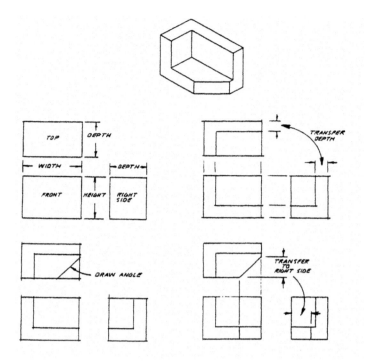

Figure 4-31
Aligning Features in Adjacent Views

Aligning views

As noted earlier, all features of an object in one view must be lined up with those same features in another view. Often one view will have a feature that must be completed before it can be projected into the adjacent view, as shown in Figure 4-31. The 45 degree miter-line method shown in Figure 4-32 can be used to project depth dimensions from the top view to the right side view.

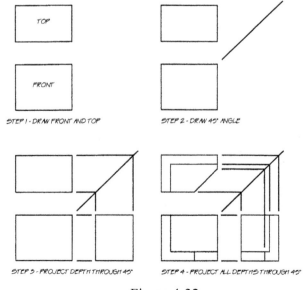

Figure 4-32
Miter-Line Method for Projecting Depth

4-15

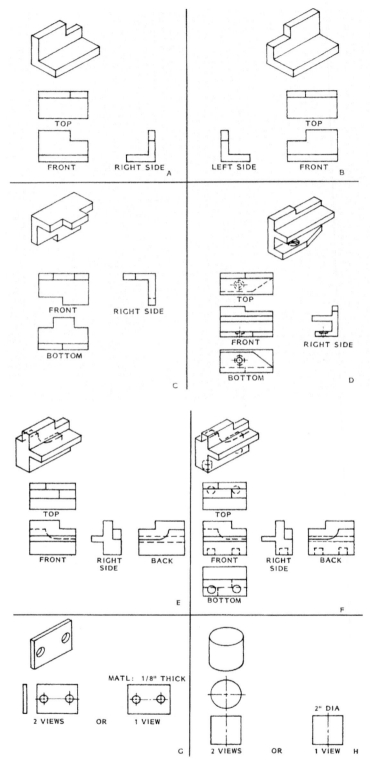

Figure 4-33
View Selection

4-16

View selection

Selecting the least number of views that best describe the object completely is very important. The views that show the least number of hidden lines and fully describe all contours of all surfaces should be selected. Figure 4-33 shows several objects and the correct view selection for them.

In Figure 4-33A, the top, front, and right side views show no hidden surfaces. Any other view selection would have shown hidden lines and would not have been as clear. The top view is necessary to show the shape of the surface, which could have had rounded corners, for example.

The description for 4-33A applies to the objects in 4-33B and C as well.

The objects in 4-33D, E, and F are more complex, so additional views are necessary to describe fully the features that appear only as hidden lines in all other views.

The object in 4-33G is an example of a flat object that can be described with only one view by placing a note on the drawing giving the thickness of the object.

The object in 4-33H is an example of a round object that can be described with either two views or one view by showing the diameter on that view. The notation DIA means that the only shape the object can have is round.

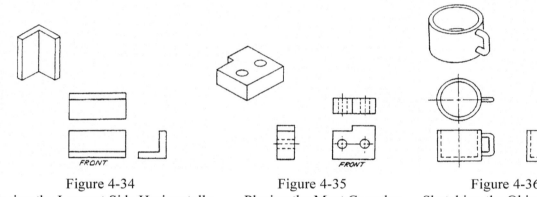

Figure 4-34	Figure 4-35	Figure 4-36
Placing the Longest Side Horizontally on the Front	Placing the Most Complex View on the Front	Sketching the Object in the Position Most Often Seen

Front view selection

The front view is usually the starting point for all orthographic drawings. There are three factors to consider when deciding which surfaces to use as the front view.

Place the longest side horizontally on the front (Figure 4-34).

Place the most complex feature on the front (Figure 4-35).

Sketch the object in the position in which it is used or seen most often (Figure 4-36).

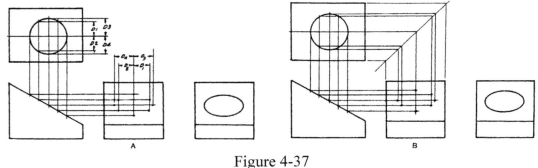

Figure 4-37
Sketching Ellipses

Drawing circles and curves on a slanted surface

Circular holes that have been cut at other than a 90 degree angle to their center appear as ellipses. An ellipse has the same major diameter as the circle but a smaller minor diameter. In other words, an ellipse is a circle that has been flattened. Figure 4-37 shows two methods for sketching an ellipse:

In Figure 4-37A, the circle has been divided into four parts so that points on the circle can be identified. These points are then projected onto the slanted surface in the front view and then into the right side view. Depth measurements are taken from the center of the circle on the top view and transferred to the right side view.

In Figure 4-37B, the miter-line method was used to transfer depth dimensions. Ellipses and other curved shapes can be sketched more accurately by dividing the circle or other shape into a greater number of parts.

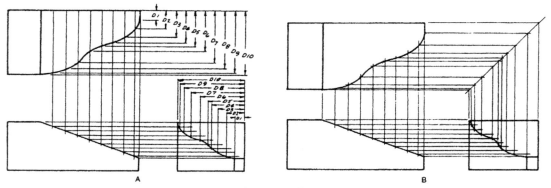

Figure 4-38
Sketching Curved Surfaces

Figure 4-38 shows a curved surface that has been drawn using the same methods as those shown in Figure 4-37. The only difference is that the depth dimensions in 4-38A were taken from the back surface.

Placement of views on the drawing

Placing of the views on the page is important to the appearance of the drawing. At first, you should center the views in the drawing. Later, notes, dimensions, revisions, and parts lists will require a different arrangement. You will have to know how to center the drawing before you can use the other arrangements.

4-18

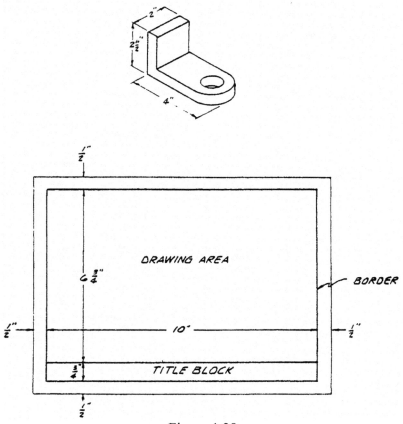

Figure 4-39
The Object and the Drawing Format

As an example of centering, assume that the drawing will contain the top, front, and right side views of the object shown in Figure 4-39.

Step 1. Calculate the area called the field of the drawing that will contain the complete drawing. The drawing will be placed on an 11" x 8 1/2" sheet. The border is 1/2" on all sides and the title block measures 3/4" deep. The drawing area is 10" x 6 3/4".

Step 2. Calculate where to start the left side of the front and top views (Figure 4-40). Add the width and depth dimensions (4" + 2" = 6"). Subtract this total from 10", the width of the drawing field (10" – 6" = 4"). Divide this number by 4 (4" / 4 = 1"). Place one quarter of the space (1") on the left, one quarter on the right (1"), and half the available space between the views (2"). The 1" dimension is not critical. You can make it a little more or less if you choose.

Step 3. Calculate where to start the bottom of the front and right side views. Add the height and depth dimensions (2 1/2" + 2" = 4 1/2"). Subtract this total from 6 3/4", the height of the drawing field (6 3/4" – 4 1/2" = 2 1/4"). Divide this number by 4 (2 1/4" / 4 = 9/16"). Place one quarter of the space above the top view, one quarter below the front view, and half of the available space between views. The 9/16" dimension is not critical. You could make the top and bottom spaces 1/2", 5/8", or 3/4" if you choose.

Please be aware that views must be moved farther apart when dimensions and notes are added. The preceding example is a guide only. Many other methods will work just as well.

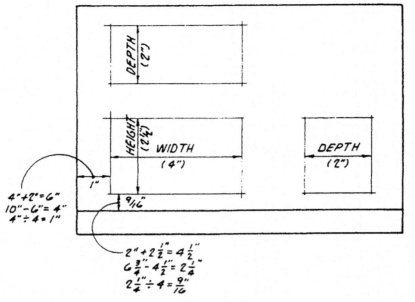

Figure 4-40
Centering Views in the Field of the Drawing

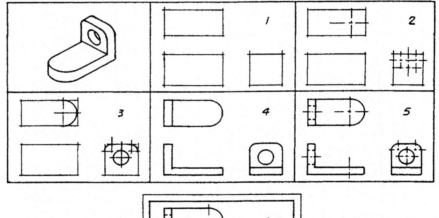

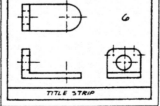

Figure 4-41
Order of Drawing

Order of sketching

The order of sketching is important to maintain accurate sizes and to improve speed (Figure 4-41).

Step 1. Block in the overall dimensions of all views, using very light construction lines.
Step 2. Locate and mark the center lines of all circles and arcs using light construction lines.
Step 3. Darken all circles and arcs.
Step 4. Darken all other object lines.
Step 5. Add hidden lines by projecting the surfaces from views where the features are visible.
Step 6. Darken the border and title block if the form is not preprinted, and letter the title block using guide lines and your best lettering.

Now use what you have learned about sketching to complete Exercises 4-1 through 4-10.

_____EXERCISES

EXERCISE 4-1   Complete Exercise 4-1 using steps 1 through 3 listed in this chapter. Fill in the date, class, and your name with your best lettering.

EXERCISE 4-2   Complete Exercise 4-2 using steps 1 through 3 listed in this chapter. Fill in the date, class, and your name with your best lettering.

EXERCISE 4-3   Complete Exercise 4-3 using steps 1 through 3 listed in this chapter. Fill in the date, class, and your name with your best lettering.

EXERCISE 4-4   Complete Exercise 4-4 using steps 1 through 3 listed in this chapter. Fill in the date, class, and your name with your best lettering.

EXERCISE 4-5   Complete Exercise 4-5 using steps 1 through 3 listed in this chapter. Fill in the date, class, and your name with your best lettering.

EXERCISE 4-6   Complete Exercise 4-6, **a robot hand,** using the following steps:
Step 1. Remove the sheet labeled Exercise 4-6 from your book.
Step 2. Complete object and hidden lines in the front view of Exercise 4-6.
Be sure to line up all features of the object with the adjacent views. Make sure that your lines are the correct weight and are of even width and darkness. Try to match the thickness and darkness of the existing lines.
Step 3. Fill in the date, class, and your name with your best lettering.

EXERCISE 4-7   Complete Exercise 4-7, **a hummer like model,** using the following steps:
Step 1. Remove the sheet labeled Exercise 4-7 from your book.
Step 2. Complete the object and hidden lines in the top and right side views of Exercise 4-7.
Be sure to line up all features of the object with the adjacent views. Make sure that your lines are the correct weight and are of even width and darkness.
Step 3. Be sure to line up all features of the object with the adjacent views.
Step 4. Fill in the date, class, and your name with your best lettering.

EXERCISE 4-8   Complete Exercise 4-8 using the following steps:

Step 1. Remove the sheet labeled Exercise 4-8 from your book. Use light lines to sketch the object lines of the top, front, and right side views. Use one unit on the three-dimensional drawing (Figure 4-42) to equal one unit on the two-dimensional sketch.
Be sure to line up all features of the object with the adjacent views.

Step 2. Use light construction lines to locate centers for the arcs in the front and right side views.

Step 3. Use light construction lines to draw the top half of the 3/4" diameter arc in the front view and the 1 /4" arc in the right side view. Draw all remaining lines and darken all lines as follows:

Step 4. Draw hidden lines in the top, front, and right side views.
Be sure to line up all features of the object with the adjacent views.
Make hidden lines the same width and darkness as the object lines.

Step 5. Fill in the date, class, and your name with your best lettering.

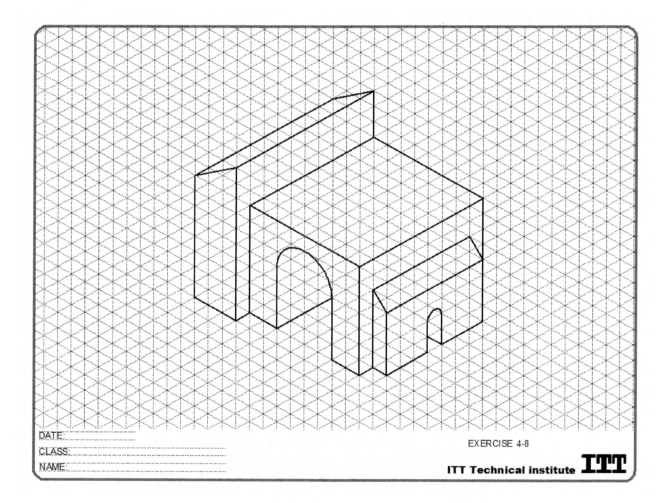

DATE
CLASS
NAME

EXERCISE 4-8

ITT Technical institute **ITT**

Figure 4-42
Dimensions for Exercise 4-8

4 - 22

EXERCISE 4-9   Complete Exercise 4-9, **a jeeplike model,** using the following steps:

Step 1. Remove the sheet labeled Exercise 4-9 from your book.

Step 2. Complete the object and hidden lines in the top and right side views of Exercise 4-9.

Be sure to line up all features of the object with the adjacent views. Make sure that your lines are the correct weight and are of even width and darkness.

Step 3. Be sure to line up all features of the object with the adjacent views.

Step 4. Fill in the date, class, and your name with your best lettering.

EXERCISE 4-10   Complete Exercise 4-10, **a robot head,** using the following steps:

Step 1. Remove the sheet labeled Exercise 4-10 from your book. Use light construction lines to complete the right side view and sketch the top view using your own ideas about what the robot head should look like. Be sure to line up all features of the object with the adjacent views.

Step 2. Darken all lines in all views.

Step 3. Fill in the date, class, and your name with your best lettering.

CHAPTER SUMMARY

This chapter contains information on reading and sketching orthographic views. You have read and sketched lines, circles, and arcs with solid lines, hidden lines, and center lines to make and interpret orthographic views. Now you will be able to continually improve your ability to use these items to make effective sketches.

REVIEW QUESTIONS

Circle the best answer.

1. The method of technical drawing used in the United States is

    a. First-Angle Orthographic Projection
    b. Second-Angle Orthographic Projection
    c. Third-Angle Orthographic Projection
    d. Fourth-Angle Orthographic Projection

2. The top view of an object should be drawn

    a. to the right of the front view
    b. directly above the front view
    c. to the left of the front view
    d. anywhere on the same sheet with a label

3. Lines of sight are at what angle to the sides of the projection box?

    a. 30 degrees
    b. 45 degrees
    c. 90 degrees (perpendicular)
    d. 100 degrees

4. When the box unfolds, where is the right side view in relation to the front view?

    a. to the right of the front view
    b. to the left of the front view
    c. above the front view
    d. below the front view

5. The three dimensions used in referring to the measurements of objects are

    a. height, width, and length
    b. height, width, and thickness
    c. height, width, and depth
    d. depth, thickness, and length

6. The total number of possible normal views in orthographic projection is

   a. 1
   b. 2
   c. 4
   d. 6

7. As few as _____ view(s) may be drawn if adequate information is given.

   a. 1
   b. 2
   c. 4
   d. 6

8. Hidden surfaces are shown with

   a. shaded areas
   b. light lines
   c. colored areas
   d. short dashed lines

9. The first view chosen for most drawings should show

   a. contour or shape
   b. length
   c. height
   d. width

10. The first view chosen for most drawings should be used as

    a. the right side view
    b. the top view
    c. the left side view
    d. the front view

11. A surface that is seen foreshortened in two views and appears as a line in the third view is called an inclined view.

    a. True   b. False

12. An object line (visible line) should be thin and light.

    a. True   b. False

13. Dimension lines, extension lines, and center lines should be thin and light.

    a. True   b. False

14.	All lines except construction lines and projection lines should be light.

	a.	True				b.	False

15.	When two views of an object give the same information, both of them should be sketched.

	a.	True				b.	False

Matching:
Write the number of the correct answer on the line.

	a. _____ Shows width and height			1.	Left Side View

	b. _____ Shows width and depth			2.	Bottom View

	c. _____ Shows height and depth			3.	Front View

	d. _____ Shows width and depth			4.	Top View

	e. _____ Shows height and depth			5.	Right Side View

General Questions:
Review the following questions.

	1.	Why does the United States use third-angle orthographic projection while Europe uses first-angle orthographic projection?

	2.	When would you want to sketch only the front view of an object?

	3.	When would you want to sketch all views of an object?

	4.	How can hidden lines be used to show counterbores and countersinks?

	5.	What can be done to make orthographic sketches the most effective way to communicate manufacturing and construction information?

5 Sketching Sectional Views

OBJECTIVES

After completing this chapter, you will be able to:

Correctly sketch to scale architectural section drawings from unsectioned two-dimensional or isometric drawings.

Correctly answer questions regarding sectional drawings.

USES OF SECTIONAL SKETCHES

It is often necessary to use a drawing technique known as sectioning. Sectional drawings are used to show the internal construction of parts (Figures 5-1 and 5-2). In many cases, sectional drawings are used not only to show someone how to make a part but also how several parts fit together (Figures 5-3 and 5-4). The use of sectional views requires many conventional practices and symbols, which are described in this chapter.

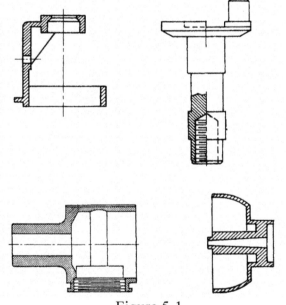

Figure 5-1
Sections Showing Internal Constructions

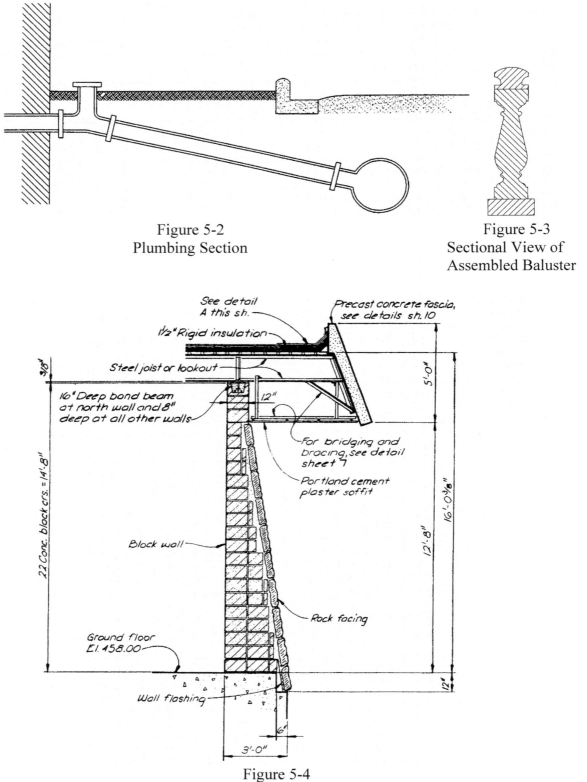

Figure 5-2
Plumbing Section

Figure 5-3
Sectional View of
Assembled Baluster

Figure 5-4
Sectional View Showing How a Wall Is Constructed

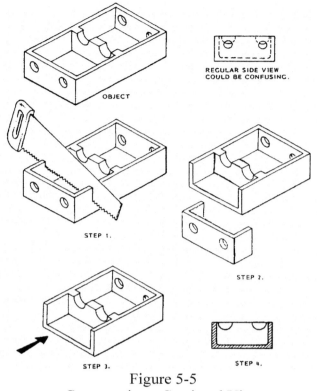

Figure 5-5
Constructing a Sectional View

CONSTRUCTING A SECTIONAL VIEW

The object shown in Figure 5-5 is a complex shape. Its features could be misunderstood if only external views were used. Therefore, to avoid any misunderstanding, a sectional view is constructed. Sectional views are easy to construct if you follow these steps:

Step 1. Decide which view will best show the hidden feature. In your mind, cut off the part that is hiding the feature. The cut, in this case, should be straight and should extend completely across the object.

Step 2. Throw away the part you cut off, and do not think of it again. It is easy to be confused about which part to draw. Throwing away the cut part eliminates that confusion.

Step 3. Look into the part that is left. Your line of sight should be perpendicular or straight into the remaining piece.

Step 4. Draw the shape of what you see. Draw section or hatch lines on the part that was cut, as if you were drawing saw marks on the part of the object that the saw touched when the cut was made. The parts untouched by the saw are sketched without section lines.

ELEMENTS OF SECTIONAL SKETCHES

Now that you have read the steps for constructing a sectional view, descriptions of the elements of sectional views are needed.

Let's start with cutting plane lines.

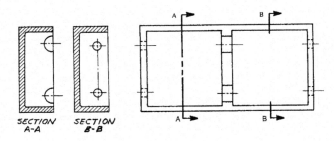

Figure 5-6
Cutting Plane Lines

Cutting plane lines

To show someone exactly where a cut was made, place an extra-heavy line with two dashes in it and arrows on the ends, showing the line of sight (Figure 5-6). This is a cutting plane line. It is about 3 times as thick as object lines. Another version of the cutting plane line is also shown in this figure. This cutting plane line, which does not extend across the object, is preferred by many companies because it does not hide other lines as often as the complete cutting plane line does. Many architectural drawings show construction features without the use of a cutting plane line.

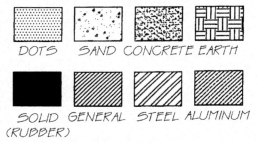

Figure 5-7
Patterns for Sectional Views

Hatch lines

Many materials that have been sectioned have a standard means of shading the cut material to identify the feature more easily. Figure 5-7 shows the shading patterns for several materials. Although these are commonly used, you will find many exceptions in drawings made by different architectural firms. Draw hatch lines about half as thick as object lines.

Using more than one sectional view

If more than one section is used on the same drawing, the sections are identified as details showing construction features throughout the structure.

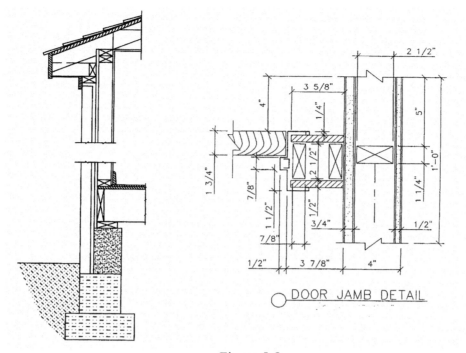

Figure 5-8
Wall Section and Door Jamb Detail

Standard architectural sectional details

Plan and elevation views show the complete structure, but the sectional drawings and other details show construction features throughout the building. The standard wall section and door jamb details (Figure 5-8) are found on many architectural plans.

Exceptions to conventional drawing practices

To avoid confusion, it is often necessary to treat some features of parts differently than with standard practices. The following are common exceptions to standard practices:

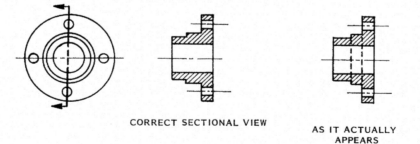

CORRECT SECTIONAL VIEW

AS IT ACTUALLY APPEARS

Figure 5-9
Hidden Lines Not Shown on a Sectional View

Eliminating Hidden Lines in Sectional Views

Sectional views are usually much clearer if hidden lines are not shown. The hidden lines are rarely necessary (Figure 5-9). You should eliminate hidden lines on sectional views unless it is absolutely necessary. In Figure 5-9, the hidden lines not only are unnecessary but would be confusing if they were drawn.

Not Sectioning Thin Features of a Part

To eliminate confusion, it is best not to section thin features, such as ribs and spokes (Figure 5-10). Although the cutting plane does cut through the ribs, the object looks like a shortened cone if it is drawn with hatch lines on the ribs.

Sketching hatch patterns on sectional views will make you appreciate the hatching feature of AutoCAD and AutoCAD LT, which is described in the following chapter. Now you will sketch some sectional views.

_____EXERCISES

EXERCISE 5-1 Complete Exercise 5-1 using the steps described:

Step 1. Remove the sheet labeled Exercise 5-1 from your book.

Step 2. Using the sketching and construction techniques you used in Chapter 4, complete the right side view as a sectional view. The depth dimensions are shown by the horizontal lines at the top and bottom of the vertical line. The smallest circles on the front view are holes that go all the way through the part.

Sprinkle drawing powder over your drawing before you begin to darken lines.

Be sure to line up all features of the object with the adjacent views.

Make sure that your lines are the correct weight and are of even width and darkness. Try to match the thickness and darkness of the existing lines.

Step 3. Draw 45 degree section lines in the right side view approximately 1/10" apart. Use the lines shown as an example. These lines should be thin and dark.

Step 4. Draw center lines in the right side view.

Step 5. Fill in the date, class, and your name with your best lettering.

EXERCISE 5-2 Complete Exercise 5-2 using the steps described:

Step 1. Remove the sheet labeled Exercise 5-2 from your book.

Step 2. Sketch the baluster of Figure 5-11 using the sketching and construction techniques you used in Chapter 5. Complete the view as a sectional view.
Draw it the same size as shown.
Sprinkle drawing powder over your drawing before you begin to darken lines.
Make sure that your lines are the correct weight and are of even width and darkness. Try to match the thickness and darkness of the existing lines.

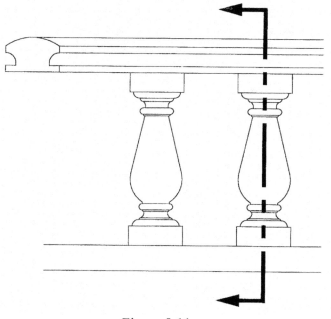

Figure 5-11
Cutting Plane for Exercise 5-2

Step 3. Draw 45 degree section lines approximately 1/10" apart. Make the top rail 45 degrees upward to the right. Make the support 45 degrees upward to the left. Use the lines shown in Exercise 5-1 as an example. These lines should be thin and dark.
Step 4. Fill in the date, class, and your name with your best lettering.

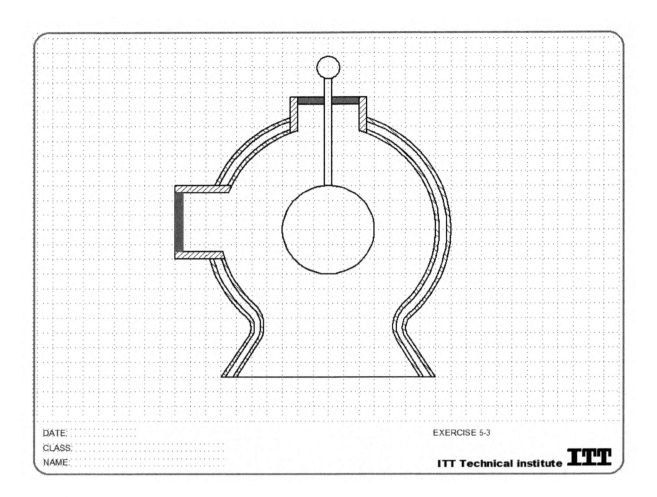

DATE:

CLASS:

NAME:

EXERCISE 5-3

ITT Technical institute ITT

Figure 5-12
Sizes for Exercise 5-3

EXERCISE 5-3 Complete Exercise 5-3 using the steps described:

    Step 1. Remove the sheet labeled Exercise 5-3 from your book.

    Step 2. Sketch the robot head as a sectional view (Figure 5-12) using the sketching and
                construction techniques you used in Chapter 5.
                Make sure that your lines are the correct weight and are of even width and
                darkness.
                Try to match the thickness and darkness of the existing lines.

    Step 3. Draw 45 degree section lines in the front view. Use the lines shown in Exercise 5-12 as
                an example. These lines should be thin and dark.

    Step 4. Fill in the date, class, and your name with your best lettering.

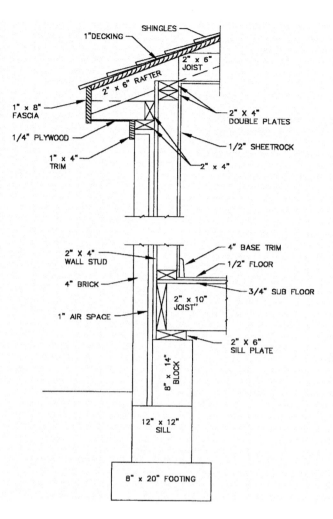

SHINGLES

1"DECKING

2" x 6"
JOIST

2" x 6" RAFTER

1" x 8"
FASCIA

2" X 4"
DOUBLE PLATES

1/4" PLYWOOD

1/2" SHEETROCK

1" x 4"
TRIM

2" x 4"

2" X 4"
WALL STUD

4" BASE TRIM

1/2" FLOOR

4" BRICK

3/4" SUB FLOOR

2" x 10"
JOIST"

1" AIR SPACE

2" X 6"
SILL PLATE

8" x 14"
BLOCK

12" x 12"
SILL

8" x 20" FOOTING

Figure 5-13
Sizes for Exercise 5-4

EXERCISE 5-4 Complete Exercise 5-4 using the steps described:

Step 1. Remove the sheet labeled Exercise 5-4 from your book.

Step 2. Sketch the lower half of the wall section (Figure 5-13) (from the break line down) using
sketching and construction techniques you used in Chapter 5.
Draw at a scale of 1" = 1'. Approximate any dimensions not shown.
Make sure that your lines are the correct weight and are of even width and
darkness.
Try to match the thickness and darkness of the existing lines.

Step 3. Fill in the date, class, and your name with your best lettering.

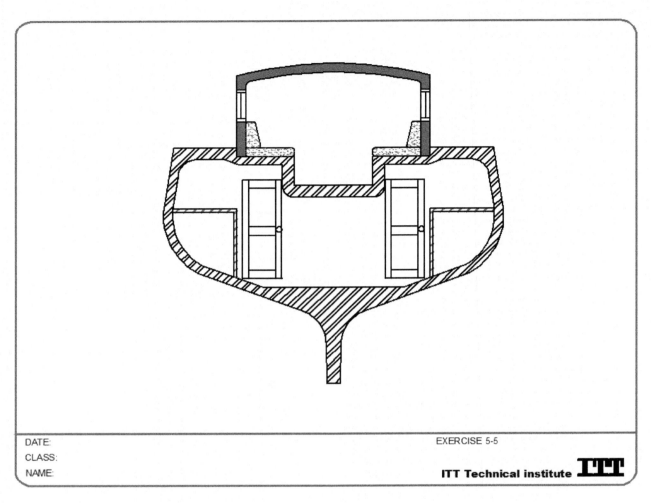

Figure 5-14
Exercise 5-5 Complete

EXERCISE 5-5 Complete Exercise 5-5 using the steps described:

Step 1. Remove the sheet labeled Exercise 5-5 from your book.

Step 2. Sketch the sailboat as a sectional view (Figure 5-14) using the sketching and construction
techniques you used in Chapter 5.
Make sure that your lines are the correct weight and are of even width and
darkness.
Try to match the thickness and darkness of the existing lines.

Step 3. Fill in the date, class, and your name with your best lettering.

CHAPTER SUMMARY

This chapter contains information on reading and sketching sectional views. You have read and sketched lines, circles, and arcs with solid lines, hidden lines, and center lines to make and interpret sectional views. Now you will be able to continually improve your ability to use these items to make effective sketches.

REVIEW QUESTIONS

Circle the best answer.
1. Why are sectional views needed to describe objects?
   a. to describe surface textures
   b. to show complex interior details
   c. to describe the overall shape of the structure
   d. to show different sides of a building

2. The object is cut by a _____ to describe the sectional view.
   a. cutting plane
   b. saw
   c. knife
   d. string

3. The solid material cut by the cutting plane is hatched with diagonal lines, usually drawn at
   a. 20 degrees
   b. 15 degrees
   c. 90 degrees
   d. 45 degrees

4. The line representing the edge view of the cutting plane is called
   a. the edge view line
   b. the section line
   c. the cut line
   d. the cutting plane line

5. Thin features such as ribs and spokes are often not cut on the sectional view because:
   a. It saves time.
   b. Ribs and spokes are not drawn at all.
   c. Sectioning of them gives a false impression of how the part is constructed.
   d. It takes up too much space on the drawing.

6. Hidden lines are not usually shown in sectional views.
   a. True   b. False

7.   Sectional views are not labeled when there are several sectional views on the same drawing.
     a.   True   b.   False

8.   The cutting plane line is sketched very thin in a sectional view.
     a.   True   b.   False

9.   Sectional views are often labeled A-A.
     a.   True   b.   False

10. The wall section is often shown on a set of plans.
     a.   True   b.   False

Matching:
Write the number of the correct answer on the line.

a. _____ Thin features not often cut   1. Cutting plane line
           on a sectional view

b. _____ Lines drawn at 45 degree   2. Ribs
           angles to show the cut surface

c. _____ Lines often not shown on a   3. Hidden lines
           sectional view

d. _____ Lines showing where the   4. Hatch lines
           imaginary cut is made

e. _____ A label for a sectional view   5. A-A

General Questions:
Review the following questions.

1.   Why are sectional views necessary?

2.   How much detail should there be in a wall section?

3.   When should sectional views be used?

4.   What types of sectional views are used most in the construction industries?

5.   What types of sectional views are used most in the manufacturing industries?

6   Perspective Sketching

_____OBJECTIVES

After completing this chapter, you will be able to:

Correctly sketch one-point perspective figures to scale on a one-point perspective grid.

Correctly sketch two-point perspective figures to scale on a two-point perspective grid.

Correctly answer questions regarding perspective drawing.

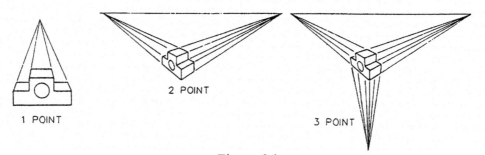

Figure 6-1
Perspective Sketching Methods

PERSPECTIVE SKETCHING FORMS

There are three perspective sketching methods: one-point, two-point, and three-point (Figure 6-1).

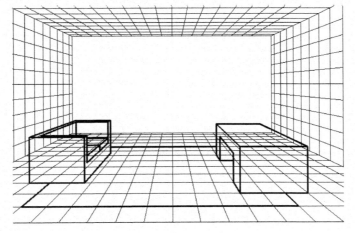

Figure 6-2
One-Point Perspective
Interior View

One-point perspective

This is a method in which the vertical and horizontal axes of the object being viewed are parallel to the picture plane, and the third axis appears at a right angle to the picture plane as shown in Figure 6-2.

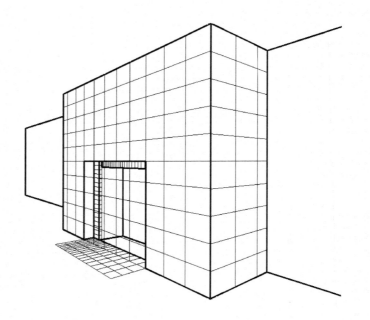

Figure 6-3
Two-Point Perspective
Interior View

Two-point perspective
This method has one axis of the object, usually the vertical axis, parallel to the picture plane, and the other two axes are inclined to the picture plane as shown in Figure 6-3.

Three-point perspective
This method has all three axes of the object inclined to the picture plane as shown in Figure 6-1. This method is not covered in detail in this book because it has limited usefulness.

BASIC ELEMENTS
The basics of perspective sketching are shown in Figure 6-4. They are:

1.   The object being viewed.
2.   The observer's eye, or the position of the observer's eye, called the station point (SP).
3.   The plane of projection, a drawing surface or a plane on which a picture of the object being viewed is projected. In perspective sketching this is called the picture plane (PP). The location of the picture plane plays an important part in perspective sketching.
4.   Imaginary lines of sight (to all points on the object), the lines of sight that pierce the plane of projection. They produce intersection points that, when connected together, make the perspective sketch.
5.   Center of vision (CV), a point on the horizon line opposite the observer's eye.
6.   Vanishing point (VP), a point at which receding parallel lines meet.
7.   Horizon line, an imaginary line on the eye level of the observer. The center of vision—the right and left vanishing points in two- and three-point perspective fall on this line.

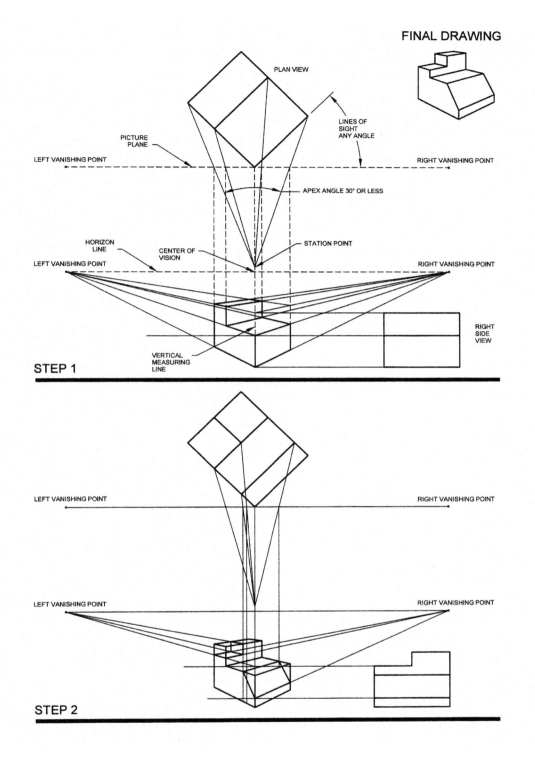

FINAL DRAWING

PLAN VIEW

LINES OF SIGHT ANY ANGLE

PICTURE PLANE

LEFT VANISHING POINT

RIGHT VANISHING POINT

APEX ANGLE 30° OR LESS

HORIZON LINE

CENTER OF VISION

STATION POINT

LEFT VANISHING POINT

RIGHT VANISHING POINT

RIGHT SIDE VIEW

VERTICAL MEASURING LINE

STEP 1

LEFT VANISHING POINT

RIGHT VANISHING POINT

LEFT VANISHING POINT

RIGHT VANISHING POINT

STEP 2

Figure 6-4
Elements of Two-Point Perspective

Sketching two boxes using one-point perspective

Step 1. Draw a **horizon line** about one-fourth of the way down the page. Mark a spot slightly to the right of the middle of the line to establish the **vanishing point.**

Step 2. Draw a rectangle below the horizon line in the approximate location shown in Figure 6-5 and draw light lines from the top two corners to the vanishing point.

Step 3. Draw a horizontal line between the two light lines to make the back of the box. Darken the lines of the box and erase the other parts of the light lines, and the first box is complete.

Step 4. Draw another rectangle in the approximate location shown in Figure 6-6 and draw light lines from the top two corners and the lower left corner of the box to the vanishing point.

Step 5. Draw a horizontal line and a vertical line to make the back of the box. Darken the lines of the box and erase the other parts of the light lines, and the second box is complete.

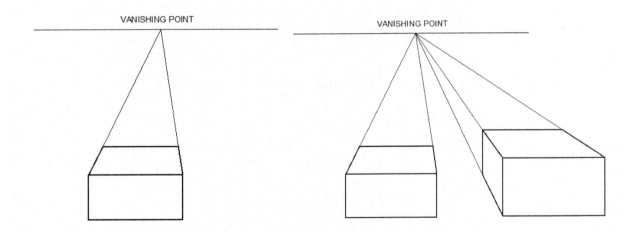

Figure 6-5
Drawing the First Box

Figure 6-6
Drawing the Second Box

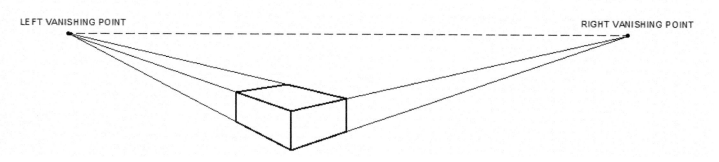

Figure 6-7
Sketching a Box Using Two-Point Perspective

Sketching a box using two-point perspective (Figure 6-7)

Step 1. Sketch a **horizon line** about one fourth of the way down the page. Mark two spots as far apart as possible to make the **two vanishing points**.

Step 2. Sketch a short vertical line for the front corner of the box, and then sketch a light line from the top and bottom of the line to each vanishing point.

Step 3. Sketch a vertical line to the left of the short vertical line, between the top and bottom light lines. From the top and bottom points of this line, sketch light lines back to the right vanishing point.

Step 4. Sketch a vertical line to the right of the front corner, and from the top and bottom points of this line, sketch construction lines back to the left vanishing point.

Step 5. Sketch a vertical line from the intersection of the top construction lines to the intersection of the bottom construction lines to make the back corners of the box.

Step 6. Darken the lines of the box and erase the other parts of the light lines, and the two-point perspective box is complete.

Try sketching a box using a horizon line at different heights. Place the box in different places in relation to the vanishing points. To make realistic appearing perspective objects requires vanishing points that are far apart. Try using a large piece of paper under your drawing and make your vanishing points as far apart as possible.

Sketching a cylinder using two-point perspective (Figure 6-8)

Step 1. Sketch a **horizon line** about one fourth of the way down the page. Mark two spots as far apart as possible to make the **two vanishing points**.

Step 2. Sketch a light short vertical line for the front corner of the box and then sketch a light line from the top and bottom of the line to each vanishing point.

Step 3. Sketch a light vertical line to the left of the short vertical line, between the top and bottom light lines. From the top and bottom points of this line, sketch light lines back to the right vanishing point.

Step 4.   Sketch a light vertical line to the right of the front corner, and from the top and bottom points of this line, sketch construction lines back to the left vanishing point.

Step 5. Sketch a light vertical line from the intersection of the top construction lines to the intersection of the bottom construction lines to make the back corners of the box.

Step 6. Sketch a line from each corner of the top surface of the box to the opposite corner to locate the center of the top surface. Do the same for the bottom surface of the box.

Step 7. Sketch an ellipse that touches the center of each side of the top surface of the box. Repeat for the bottom surface.

Step 8. Darken the top ellipse and the front of the bottom ellipse and sketch hidden lines for the back of the bottom ellipse.

Step 9. Sketch dark lines connecting the quadrants of the two ellipses, erase the construction lines, and the cylinder is finished.

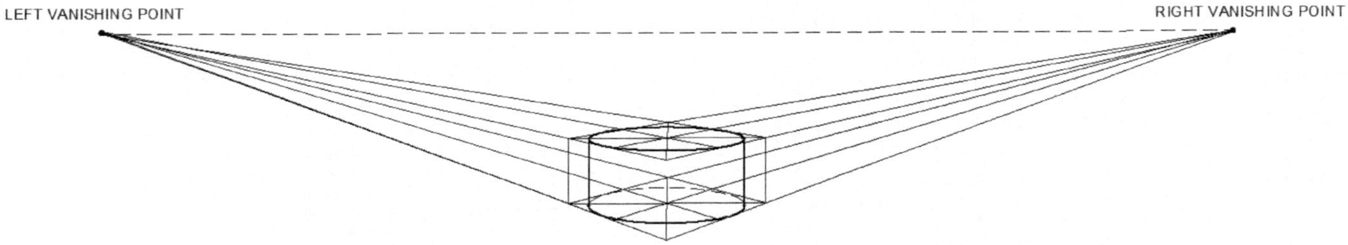

LEFT VANISHING POINT   RIGHT VANISHING POINT

Figure 6-8
Sketching a Cylinder Using Two-Point Perspective

Sketching equally spaced lines using two-point perspective (Figure 6-9)

Step 1. Sketch three lines to the left vanishing point as shown in Figure 6-9 and draw two lines on the right end of these three lines.

Step 2. Sketch a light dialog line from corner P1 to corner P2 through the intersection of the second line on the right end of the three lines.

Step 3. Sketch a line from corner P2 to the right vanishing point.

Step 4. Sketch a line from corner P3 to P4 and then extend it to P5.

Step 5. Repeat steps 2 through 4 for as many equally spaced lines as you need.

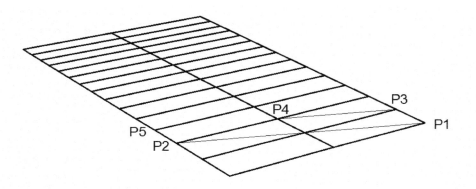

Figure 6-9
Sketching Equally Spaced Lines Using Two-Point Perspective

EXERCISES

EXERCISE 6-1 Complete Exercise 6-1 using the steps described:

    Step 1. Remove the sheet labeled Exercise 6-1 from your book.

    Step 2. Using the sketching and construction techniques presented in this chapter, complete the perspective sketch using the grid lines and the existing sketch lines as a guide. Make sure that your lines are the correct weight and are of even width and darkness. Try to match the thickness and darkness of the existing lines.

    Step 3. Compare your sketch with Figure 6-10 and make any necessary corrections.

    Step 4. Fill in the date, class, and your name with your best lettering.

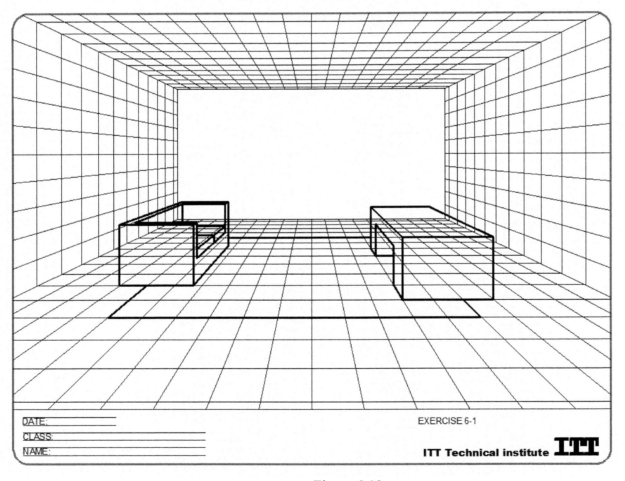

DATE:

CLASS:

NAME:

EXERCISE 6-1

ITT Technical institute **ITT**

Figure 6-10
Exercise 6-1

EXERCISE 6-2 Complete Exercise 6-2 using the steps described:

Step 1. Remove the sheet labeled Exercise 6-2 from your book.

Step 2. Using the sketching and construction techniques presented in this chapter, complete the perspective sketch using the grid lines and the existing sketch lines as a guide. Make sure that your lines are the correct weight and are of even width and darkness. Try to match the thickness and darkness of the existing lines.

Step 3. Compare your sketch with Figure 6-11 and make any necessary corrections.

Step 4. Fill in the date, class, and your name with your best lettering.

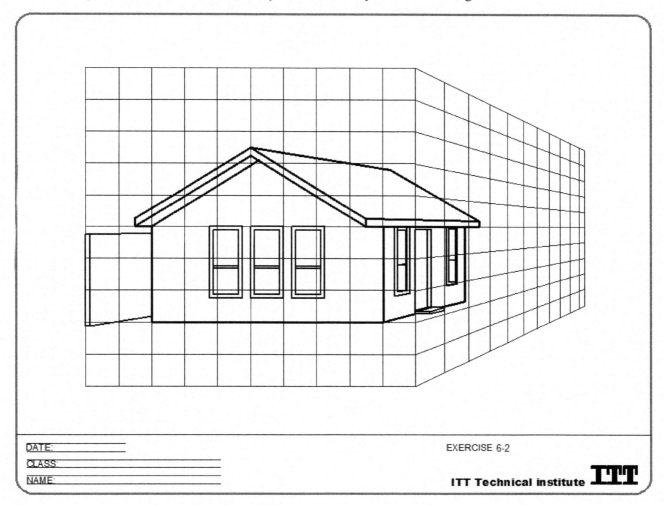

DATE:
CLASS:
NAME:

EXERCISE 6-2

ITT Technical institute **ITT**

Figure 6-11
Exercise 6-2

EXERCISE 6-3 Complete Exercise 6-3 using the steps described:

Step 1. Remove the sheet labeled Exercise 6-3 from your book.

Step 2. Using the sketching and construction techniques presented in this chapter, complete the perspective sketch using the grid lines and the existing sketch lines as a guide. Make sure that your lines are the correct weight and are of even width and darkness. Try to match the thickness and darkness of the existing lines.

Step 3. Compare your sketch with Figure 6-12 and make any necessary corrections.

Step 4. Fill in the date, class, and your name with your best lettering.

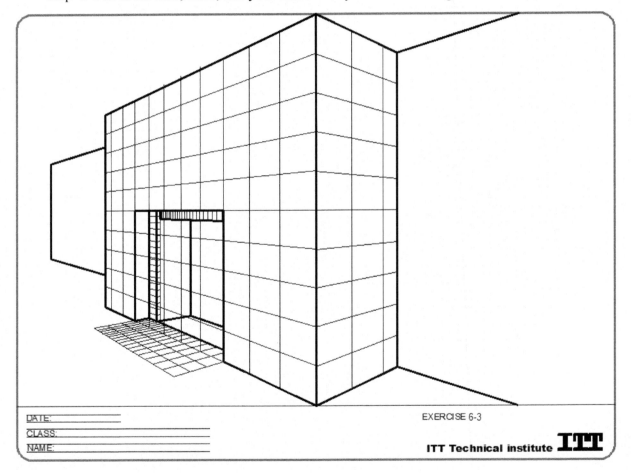

DATE:
CLASS:
NAME:

EXERCISE 6-3

ITT Technical institute ITT

Figure 6-12
Exercise 6-3

EXERCISE 6-4 Complete Exercise 6-4 using the steps described:

Step 1. Remove the sheet labeled Exercise 6-4 from your book.

Step 2. Using the sketching and construction techniques presented in this chapter, complete the perspective sketch using the grid lines and the existing sketch lines as a guide. Make sure that your lines are the correct weight and are of even width and darkness. Try to match the thickness and darkness of the existing lines.

Step 3. Compare your sketch with Figure 6-13 and make any necessary corrections.

Step 4. Fill in the date, class, and your name with your best lettering.

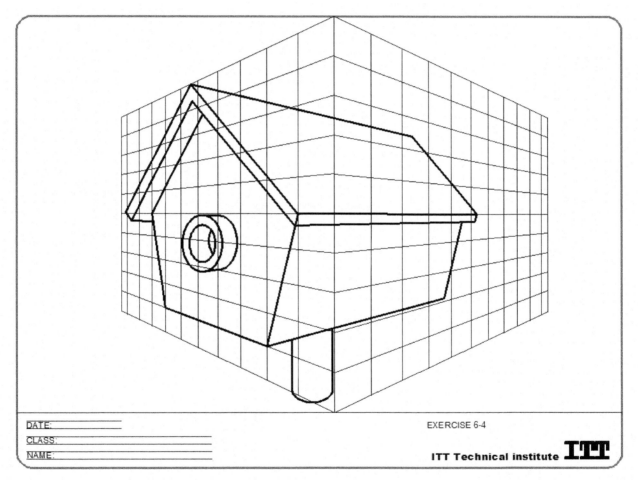

DATE:
CLASS:
NAME:

EXERCISE 6-4

ITT Technical institute **ITT**

Figure 6-13
Exercise 6-4

EXERCISE 6-5 Complete Exercise 6-5 using the steps described:

Step 1. Remove the sheet labeled Exercise 6-5 from your book and sketch the shape shown on the grid lines.

Step 2. Using the sketching and construction techniques presented in this chapter, complete the perspective sketch using the grid lines and extend light lines to the vanishing points as shown to aid in completing your sketch. You will need additional sheets of paper to extend lines to the vanishing points. Draw diagonal lines shown as hidden lines to locate the center of the rectangular opening, and draw it on the grid lines. Make sure that your lines are the correct weight and are of even width and darkness.

Step 3. Sketch the opening as shown on the grid lines and extend a light line to the right vanishing point to aid in drawing the depth of the opening.

Step 4. Sketch the arc above the opening on the left side.

Step 5. Fill in the date, class, and your name with your best lettering.

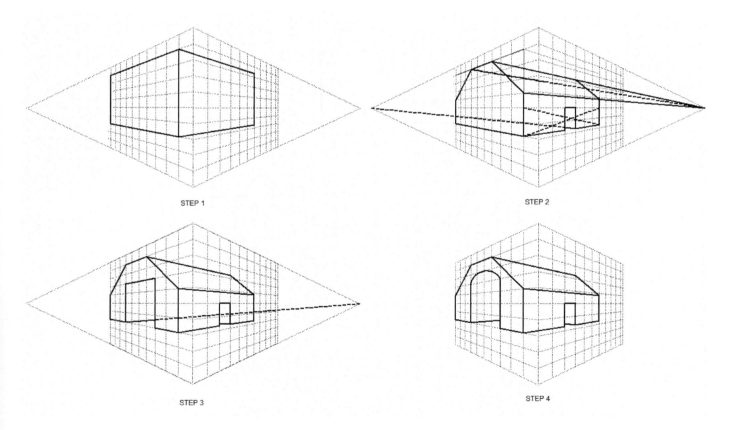

Figure 6-14
Exercise 6-5

This chapter gives you the information and techniques to make perspective sketches. These sketches consist of basic forms, more complex forms, buildings, and furniture. Now you have the skills and information needed to make perspective sketches that convey your ideas and those of others accurately.

_____**REVIEW QUESTIONS**

Multiple Choice

Circle the correct answer.

1. On which of the following is the station point located?
    a.   Vanishing lines
    b.   Horizon lines
    c.   Vertical measuring line
    d.   Ground line

2. On which of the following are the vanishing points located?
    a.   Vanishing lines
    b.   Horizon lines
    c.   Vertical measuring line
    d.   Ground line

3. When projecting a two-point perspective sketch, which of the following does the top view of the object touch?
    a.   Picture plane
    b.   Station point
    c.   Vanishing lines
    d.   Horizon line

4. Which of the following is the most difficult to sketch?
    a.   One-point perspective
    b.   Two-point perspective
    c.   Three-point perspective
    d.   None is more difficult than the others.

5. The apex angle (the cone of vision) should be
    a.   60 degrees or more
    b.   exactly 60 degrees
    c.   30 degrees or less
    d.   exactly 30 degrees

6. Perspective sketches and isometric sketches use the same vanishing points.
    a.   True   b.   False

7. Only two planes are visible in one-point perspective.
   a.   True   b.   False

8. Sketching accurate circles (ellipses) in two-point perspective requires you to draw a perspective box first.
   a.   True   b.   False

9. To accurately position equally spaced lines on a receding plane in two-point perspective you must draw diagonal lines through the centers of other lines.

   a.   True   b.   False

10. No complex figures can be sketched using one-point perspective.

    a.   True   b.   False

Matching

Write the number of the correct answer on the line.

a._____ The location of the observer's eye

b._____ The line that the top view is positioned on to sketch a two-point perspective

c._____ The points where vanishing lines intersect

d._____ The line where vanishing points are located

e._____ The line where heights are measured

1.   Picture plane

2.   Station point

3.   Vanishing points

4.   Horizon

5.   Vertical measuring line

General Questions

1. Why would you use one-point perspective instead of two-point perspective?

2. Why would you use two-point perspective instead of one-point perspective?

3. Where did perspective drawing originate?

4. What are the essential elements of perspective sketching?

5. Why is three-point perspective not used more in sketching.

7   People and Game Character Sketching

_____OBJECTIVES

After completing this chapter, you will be able to:

Correctly sketch people and game characters to scale on an orthographic grid.

Correctly sketch game characters to scale without an orthographic grid.

Correctly answer questions regarding people and game character sketching.

Figure 7-1
Types of People Sketching

INTRODUCTION TO PEOPLE SKETCHING
A sketch is a preliminary drawing. This means:
1.   It does not have to be perfect.
2.   It does not have to contain everything.
3.   You can erase part or all of the drawing if needed.
4.   Find something to measure with or something to compare to other objects and keep measuring as
            you sketch.
5.   Find a point you can measure distances from so that you can locate the sketch on the page.
6.   Sketch big shapes, not small details. Often only a few details are needed to sketch a shape
            such as three or four leaves on a tree or a few bricks in a wall.
7.   Try making lines in different ways and see which ones you like best.
8.   Check and correct your sketch carefully several times.

Sketching quickly

1. Sketching quickly requires practice and will improve over time.
2. You will learn to convey ideas with a few lines or marks.
3. Practice sketching quickly from any place you have the opportunity.
4. Choose people or objects as subjects and practice drawing them quickly.
5. Use a photograph, magazines, the Internet, or anything else to practice sketching quickly.
6. Give yourself 30 minutes to make:
   Four 5-minute sketches
   One 10-minute sketch

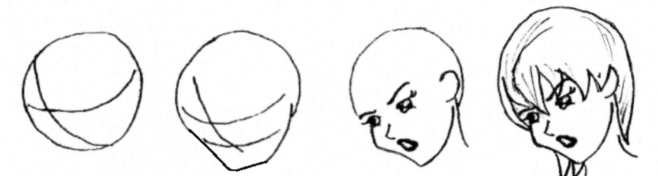

Figure 7-2
Sketching the Female Head

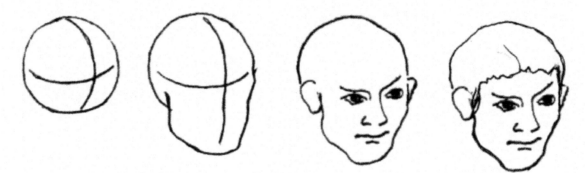

Figure 7-3
Sketching the Male Head

Sketching human heads

1. Start with a circle (Figures 7-2 and 7-3).
2. Sketch a line from the middle of the forehead.
3. Sketch a curved line down to the chin and complete the outline with a line on the other side.
4. Make the eyes, nose, chin, and ears.
5. Sketch large areas of hair with little detail, similar to the two figures.

You may also sketch even more simply by using an ellipse close to the shape of a head.

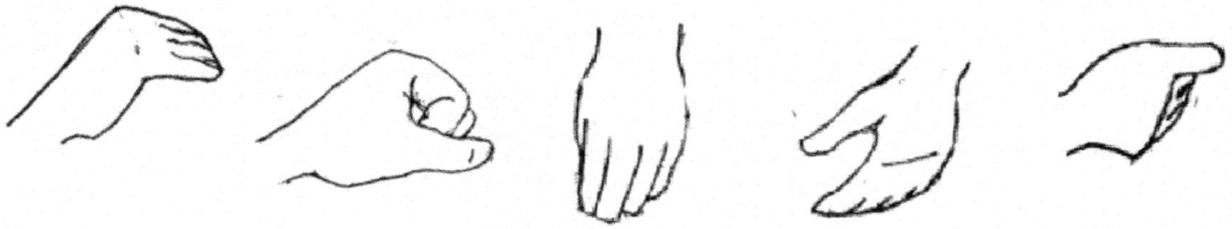

Figure 7-4
Sketching Hands

Sketching hands

Figure 7-4 shows hands in several positions. All of these can be sketched by following these steps:
1. Rough in the basic form and sketch light lines through the joints.
2. Form the fingers with simple lines.
3. Check the sketch and fix anything that looks weird.

Figure 7-5
Sketching Feet with Shoes on Them

Sketching feet with shoes on them

Figure 7-5 shows shoes in several positions. All of these can be sketched by following these steps:
1. Study shoes by looking through magazines, the Internet, your cell phone, or any other place where shoes can be observed.
2. Rough in the basic form and sketch light lines.
3. Darken the sketch when it looks right.
4. Check the sketch and fix it if necessary.

You may also want to spend some time learning how the human foot is constructed.
The more shoes you sketch, the better you will become at sketching them.

Figure 7-6
Sketches of People Standing

SKETCHING PEOPLE STANDING

Figure 7-6 shows several people in standing positions. All of these can be sketched by following these steps:

1.	Study the proportions listed below:

>	The average male is 7 and 1/2 heads tall.
>	Shoulders are 2 head lengths wide.
>	Hips are about 1 and 1/2 head lengths wide.

>	The average female is 7 heads tall.
>	Shoulders are 1 and 1/2 head lengths wide.
>	Hips are about 2 head lengths wide.

>	On both female and male, the hand is about as long as the length from the hairline to the bottom of the chin.

2.	Rough in the basic form and sketch light lines for the head, torso, hands, and feet.
3.	Darken the sketch when it looks right.
4.	Check the sketch and fix it if necessary.

Figure 7-7

SKETCHING PEOPLE SITTING

Figure 7-7 shows several people in sitting positions. All of these can be sketched by following these steps:

1.   Rough in the basic form and sketch light lines for the head, torso, hands, and feet.
2.   Darken the sketch when it looks right.
3.   Check the sketch and fix it if necessary.

Figure 7-8
Sketches of People in Action

SKETCHING PEOPLE IN ACTION

Figure 7-8 shows several people in action positions. All of these can be sketched by following these steps:

1.   Rough in the basic form and sketch light lines for the head, torso, hands, and feet.
2.   Darken the sketch when it looks right.
3.   Check the sketch and fix it if necessary.

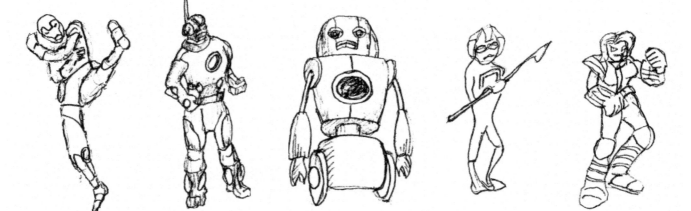

Figure 7-9
Types of Game Character Sketching

INTRODUCTION TO GAME CHARACTER SKETCHING

A sketch is a preliminary drawing. This means:

1.   It does not have to be perfect.
2.   It does not have to contain everything.
3.   You can erase part or all of the drawing if needed.
4.   Find something to measure with or something to compare to other objects and keep measuring as you sketch.
5.   Find a point you can measure distances from so that you can locate the sketch on the page.
6.   Sketch big shapes, not small details. Often only a few details are needed to sketch a shape such as three or four leaves on a tree or a few bricks in a wall.
7.   Try making lines in different ways and see which ones you like best.
8.   Check and correct your sketch carefully several times.

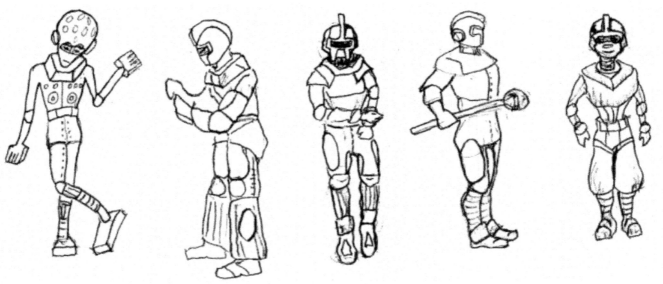

Figure 7-10
Sketches of Game Characters Standing

SKETCHING GAME CHARACTERS STANDING

Figure 7-10 shows several game characters in action positions. All of these can be sketched by following these steps:

1.   Rough in the basic form and sketch light lines for the head, torso, hands, and feet.
2.   Darken the sketch when it looks right.
3.   Check the sketch and fix it if necessary.

Figure 7-11
Sketches of Game Characters Sitting

SKETCHING GAME CHARACTERS SITTING

Figure 7-11 shows several game characters in sitting positions. All of these can be sketched by following these steps:
1. Rough in the basic form and sketch light lines for the head, torso, hands, and feet.
2. Darken the sketch when it looks right.
3. Check the sketch and fix it if necessary.

Figure 7-12
Sketches of Game Characters in Action

SKETCHING GAME CHARACTERS IN ACTION

Figure 7-12 shows several game characters in action positions. All of these can be sketched by following these steps:
1. Rough in the basic form and sketch light lines for the head, torso, hands, and feet.
2. Darken the sketch when it looks right.
3. Check the sketch and fix it if necessary.

EXERCISES

EXERCISE 7-1 Complete Exercise 7-1 using the steps described:

Step 1. Remove the sheet labeled Exercise 7-1 from your book.

Step 2. Using the sketching and construction techniques presented in this chapter, complete the sketch using the grid lines and the existing sketch lines as a guide.
Make sure that your lines are the correct weight and are of even width and darkness. Try to match the thickness and darkness of the existing lines.

Step 3. Compare your sketch with Figure 7-13 and make any necessary corrections.

Step 4. Fill in the date, class, and your name with your best lettering.

DATE:

CLASS:

NAME:

EXERCISE 7-1

ITT Technical institute

Figure 7-13
Exercise 7-1

EXERCISE 7-2 Complete Exercise 7-2 using the steps described:

Step 1. Remove the sheet labeled Exercise 7-2 from your book.

Step 2. Using the sketching and construction techniques presented in this chapter, complete the
sketch using the grid lines and the existing sketch lines as a guide.
Make sure that your lines are the correct weight and are of even width and
darkness. Try to match the thickness and darkness of the existing lines.

Step 3. Compare your sketch with Figure 7-14 and make any necessary corrections.

Step 4. Fill in the date, class, and your name with your best lettering.

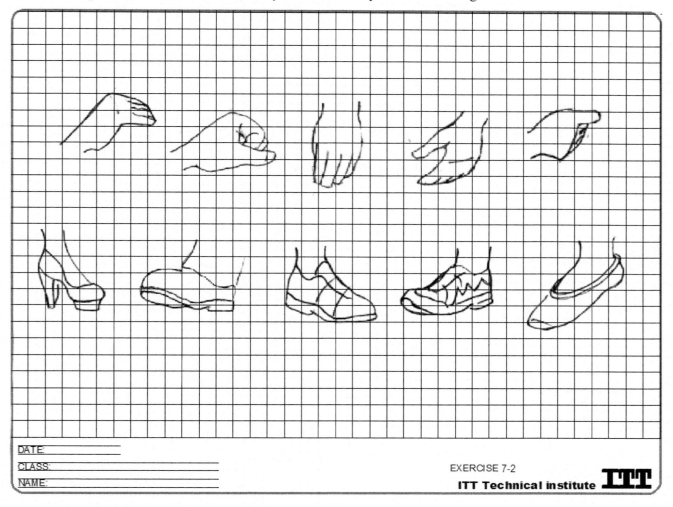

DATE:
CLASS:
NAME:

EXERCISE 7-2
ITT Technical institute ITT

Figure 7-14
Exercise 7-2

EXERCISE 7-3 Complete Exercise 7-3 using the steps described:

Step 1. Remove the sheet labeled Exercise 7-3 from your book.

Step 2. Using the sketching and construction techniques presented in this chapter, complete the
sketch using the grid lines and the existing sketch lines as a guide.
Make sure that your lines are the correct weight and are of even width and
darkness. Try to match the thickness and darkness of the existing lines.

Step 3. Compare your sketch with Figure 7-14 and make any necessary corrections.

Step 4. Fill in the date, class, and your name with your best lettering.

DATE:
CLASS:
NAME:

EXERCISE 7-3
ITT Technical institute

Figure 7-15
Exercise 7-3

EXERCISE 7-4 Complete Exercise 7-4 using the steps described:

Step 1. Remove the sheet labeled Exercise 7-4 from your book.

Step 2. Using the sketching and construction techniques presented in this chapter, complete the sketch using the grid lines and the existing sketch lines as a guide.
Make sure that your lines are the correct weight and are of even width and darkness. Try to match the thickness and darkness of the existing lines.

Step 3. Compare your sketch with Figure 7-16 and make any necessary corrections.

Step 4. Fill in the date, class, and your name with your best lettering.

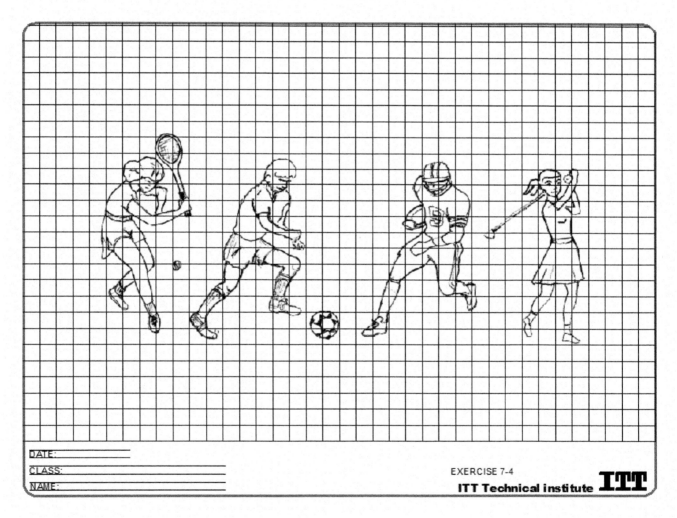

DATE:
CLASS:
NAME:

EXERCISE 7-4
ITT Technical institute ITT

Figure 7-16
Exercise 7-4

EXERCISE 7-5 Complete Exercise 7-5 using the steps described:

Step 1. Remove the sheet labeled Exercise 7-5 from your book.

Step 2. Using the sketching and construction techniques presented in this chapter, complete the sketch using the grid lines and the existing sketch lines as a guide.
Make sure that your lines are the correct weight and are of even width and darkness. Try to match the thickness and darkness of the existing lines.

Step 3. Compare your sketch with Figure 7-17 and make any necessary corrections.

Step 4. Fill in the date, class, and your name with your best lettering.

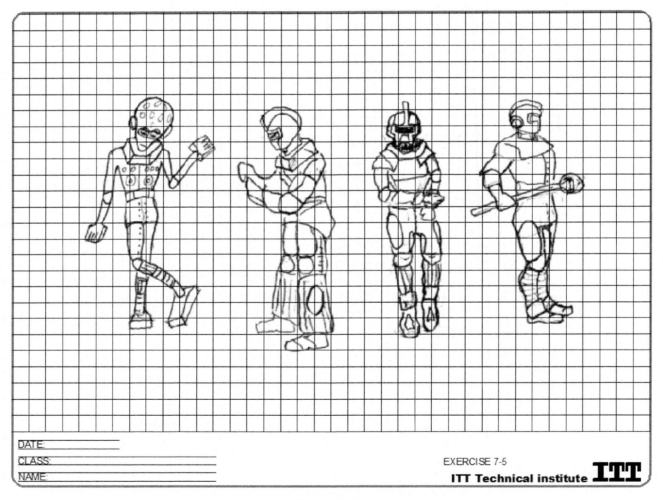

DATE:
CLASS:
NAME:

EXERCISE 7-5
ITT Technical institute **ITT**

Figure 7-17
Exercise 7-5

EXERCISE 7-6 Complete Exercise 7-6 using the steps described:

Step 1. Remove the sheet labeled Exercise 7-6 from your book.

Step 2. Using the sketching and construction techniques presented in this chapter, complete the sketch using the existing sketch lines as a guide.
Make sure that your lines are the correct weight and are of even width and darkness.

Step 3. Compare your sketch with Figure 7-18 and make any necessary corrections.

Step 4. Fill in the date, class, and your name with your best lettering.

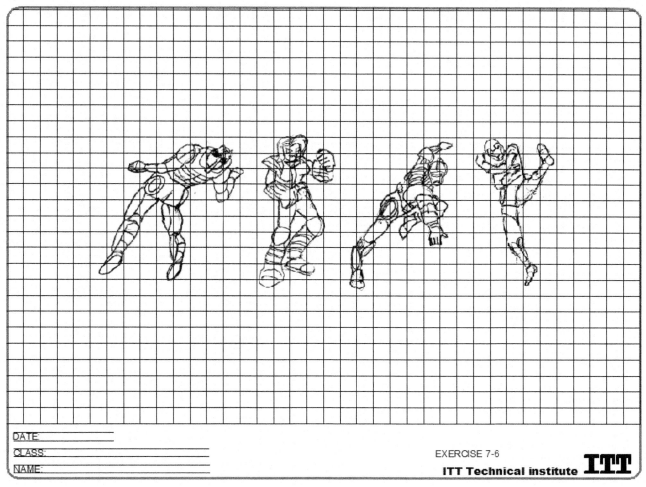

DATE:
CLASS:
NAME:

EXERCISE 7-6
ITT Technical institute ITT

Figure 7-18
Exercise 7-6

_____CHAPTER SUMMARY_

This chapter gives you the information and techniques to make perspective sketches of people and game characters. These sketches consist of basic forms and some more complex forms. Now you have the skills and information needed to make perspective sketches of people and game characters.

_____REVIEW QUESTIONS_

Multiple Choice

Circle the correct answer.

1. Which of the following is not true of a sketch?
    a. It does not have to be perfect.
    b. It does not have to contain everything
    c. Proportions in sketches are not important.
    d. You can erase all or part of it at any time.

2. Which of the following is true of a sketch?
    a. Check your sketch carefully.
    b. Sketch small details, always.
    c. The sketch must contain everything.
    d. The sketch must be perfect in every detail.

3. Which of the following is true of sketching quickly?
    a. Sketch only in your home.
    b. You do not have to practice sketching quickly.
    c. Sketch only from magazines.
    d. Sketching quickly improves over time.

4. Which of the following was one of the ways to sketch heads listed in this chapter?
    a. Start with a rectangle.
    b. Start with a circle.
    c. Start with an ellipse.
    d. Sketch a line from the middle of the chin to the nose.

5. Which of the following is not correct for the proportions of the average male?
    a. 7 and ½ heads tall
    b. Shoulders are 2 head lengths wide.
    c. 6 heads tall
    d. Hips are about 1 and ½ head lengths wide.

6. Sketches can only be made on a perspective grid.
    a. True   b. False

7. Game characters can be sketched sitting, standing, or in action.
    a. True   b. False

8. Game characters are always the same form.
    a.   True   b.   False

9. There is only one type of sketching that can be used to sketch game characters.
    a.   True   b.   False

10. Sketches must be checked several times.
    a.   True   b.   False

Matching

Write the number of the correct answer on the line.

a.____ Start with a circle.   1.   A sketch

b.____ Rough in the basic form first   2.   Sketching heads

c.____ A preliminary drawing   3.   Sketching hands

d.____ The width of the hips of the average female   4.   7 heads

e.____ The height of the average female   5.   2 head lengths

General Questions

1. Why would you use people sketches?

2. Why would you use game character sketches?

3. What type of sketching suits you best?

4. What are the essential elements of people and character sketching?

5. Where can you study people?

8   Sketching Pictorial Views Using Isometric (Axonometric) Sketching

_____OBJECTIVES

After completing this chapter, you will be able to:

Arrange correctly the three major forms of pictorial sketches in order of difficulty of sketching and shape distortion.

Correctly sketch isometric figures to scale from orthographic drawings on an isometric grid.

Correctly sketch isometric figures without an isometric grid.

Make isometric cutaway sketches that are in proportion and accurately show all parts of the assembly or structure.

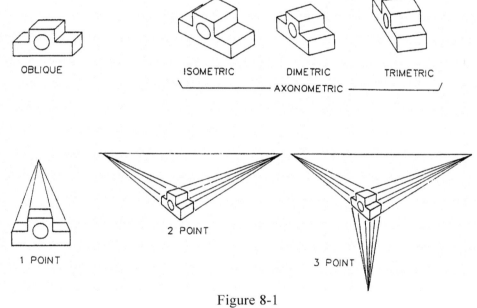

Figure 8-1
Pictorial Sketching Forms

PICTORIAL SKETCHING FORMS

There are three major pictorial sketching forms: oblique, axonometric, and perspective (Figure 8-1). Each of these methods has merits and drawbacks:

Oblique is usually the easiest to sketch, but is the most distorted.

Axonometric is more difficult to sketch, but is less distorted.
There are three forms of axonometric sketching: isometric, dimetric, and trimetric. By far the most commonly used is isometric. Isometric is the only axonometric form that will be covered in this book.

Perspective is the most difficult to sketch and is usually the least distorted. The perspective method is covered in Chapters 7, 8, and 12 of this book.

OBLIQUE SKETCHING

The distortions created by oblique sketching can be an advantage in sketching some objects but are unusable for others. A metal part that has the same cross-sectional shape along its length, for example, looks fine in oblique (Figure 8-2). An advantage of oblique sketching is that it shows the complete 2D shape of the front view, so there is no possibility of confusion.

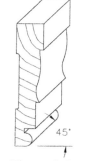

Figure 8-2
An Object with Uniform Contour

Oblique sketching simply involves sketching the front view of an object as an orthographic view and then adding depth to it at an angle, usually 45 degrees. To reduce the distorted appearance, the depth is often drawn half its true size. This technique is called cabinet oblique. When the depth dimension is full size, the sketching form is called cavalier oblique (Figure 8-3). In Exercise 8-1 you will sketch four shapes using the cabinet oblique sketching form.

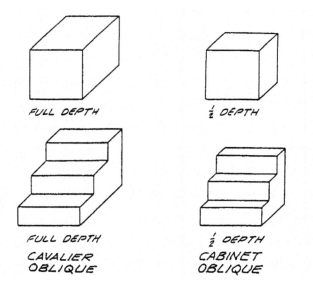

Figure 8-3
Cavalier and Cabinet Oblique

Figure 8-4 shows a technique for sketching ellipses in oblique. Avoid placing round shapes on the depth planes. Place them on the view where they appear as circles. If you have a shape that has round shapes on depth planes, the oblique method is probably not the one to use.

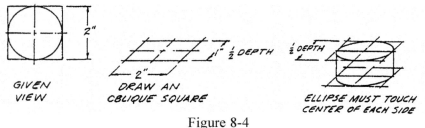

GIVEN VIEW

DRAW AN OBLIQUE SQUARE

ELLIPSE MUST TOUCH CENTER OF EACH SIDE

Figure 8-4
Sketching Ellipses in Oblique

ISOMETRIC SKETCHING

The isometric sketching form is used a great deal because it is easy to sketch and looks good for many objects. If you understand isometric well, the other two axonometric forms, dimetric and trimetric, are easy to learn.

Measurements in isometric are the same in all three dimensions—height, width, and depth. Figure 8-5 shows how to use this method for sketching a simple 4" x 2" x 2" box.

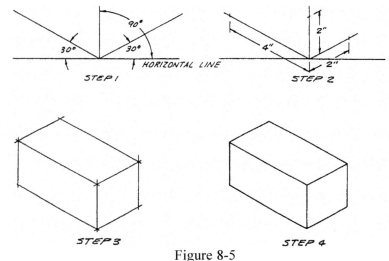

STEP 3

STEP 4

Figure 8-5
Measurements in Isometric

> Step 1. Lightly sketch the three isometric axes (or use isometric grid paper): 30 degrees right, 30 degrees left, and 90 degrees to a horizontal line.
> Step 2. Measure 4" along one of the 30 degree lines, 2" along the other 30 degree line, and 2" on the 90 degree line.
> Step 3. Extend height, width, and depth lines, making sure that all lines are parallel until they meet. Use your 30-60 degree triangle to sketch the 30 degree lines if you are not using isometric grid paper.
> Step 4. Darken all object lines to complete the sketch.

This simple example provides you with the basics of isometric sketching. There are some details of construction, which will be explained, but if you can sketch Figure 8-5, you have a good understanding of the basic principles. The following paragraphs give you the details of construction that you will need for complex shapes:

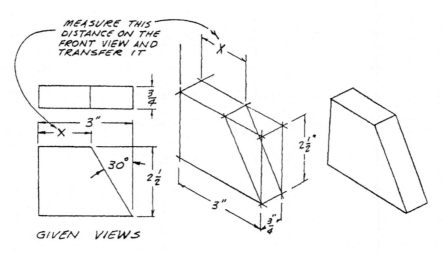

Figure 8-6
Sketching Angles in Isometric

Angles in isometric sketching

Without special tools, no measurements can be made on any lines that are not parallel to one of the isometric axes, and angles cannot be measured directly. Each end of the angle must be located and then joined as shown in Figure 8-6.

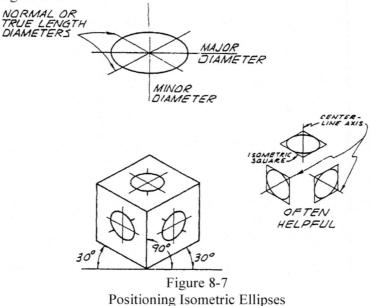

Figure 8-7
Positioning Isometric Ellipses

Circles in isometric sketching

Circles on the isometric planes appear as ellipses. The angle through which the circle is tilted is 35 degrees, 16 minutes. The positions for ellipses on each face of an isometric cube are shown in Figure 8-7. Notice that the minor diameter of the ellipse is always lined up on a center line that is parallel to one of

8 - 4

the isometric axes. Correct positioning of ellipses is very important to the appearance of a sketch and should be carefully studied. It is often helpful for beginners to sketch the center line axis and the isometric square inside which the ellipse will fit. The ellipse itself in the past was often drawn with an isometric ellipse template. To avoid the use of isometric ellipses, the exercises in this chapter will contain very few ellipses so you can sketch them without using a template.

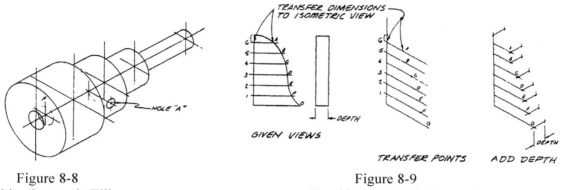

Figure 8-8
Sketching Isometric Ellipses
on a Curved Surface

Figure 8-9
Sketching Curves in Isometric

Cylindrical objects must be drawn so that the centers of their ellipses lie on a center line as shown in Figure 8-8. To simplify construction, holes on a curved surface, like hole A in Figure 8-8, are drawn as if they were lying on a flat surface.

Curves in isometric sketching

Isometric curves are drawn by locating a number of points (any number that is appropriate for the feature) on the curve in a flat (orthographic) view. Those points are then transferred to the isometric view, using the correct isometric measurements for each point. This process is illustrated in Figure 8-9.

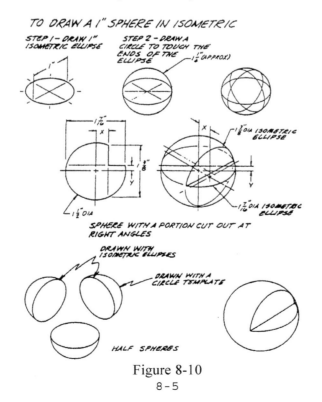

Figure 8-10

Spheres in isometric sketching

A sphere using any sketching method is drawn as a circle. If it is necessary to cut pieces out of it, isometric ellipses are helpful. Notice that the ellipses are drawn so that their minor diameters are lined up on one of the isometric axes (Figure 8-10). A sphere cannot be measured directly in isometric. You must take its measurement from the long diameter of an isometric ellipse. To sketch a 1" sphere in isometric, sketch a circle that touches the outside edges of the major diameter of a 1" diameter ellipse. It will measure about 1/4" more, or 1-1/4" in diameter.

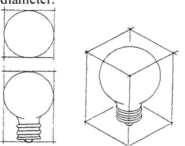

Figure 8-11
Sketching within a Box

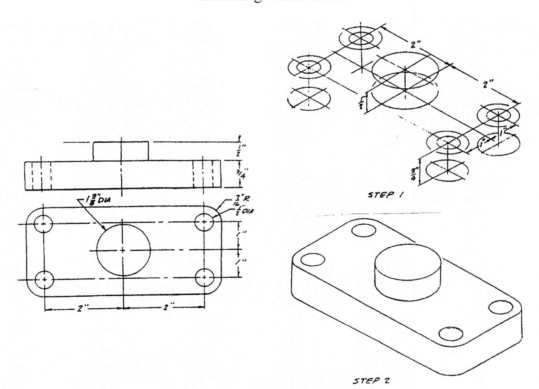

Figure 8-12
Locating Centers of Ellipses First

General guidelines for sketching in isometric

Some general guidelines for sketching in isometric are as follows:

> For complex shapes it is often helpful to sketch a box around the object and measure from the corners of the box to locate features (Figure 8-11).

Locate the centers of all holes and curves and sketch those first (Figure 8-12).

Be sure to locate points and features in all three dimensions: height, width, and depth

You cannot measure angles in isometric. Locate the ends of the angular line, using height, width, and depth dimensions, as was shown in Figure 8-6.

Be sure to position ellipses correctly, as was shown in Figure 8-7.

For cylindrical objects, work from a center line and locate ellipse centers on that line, as was shown in Figure 8-8.

For curves and irregular shapes, establish some points on the orthographic views and transfer them to the isometric view, as was shown in Figure 8-9.

Simplify the intersections of cylinders and holes, as was shown in Figure 8-8.

CUTAWAY SKETCHES

Cutaway sketches are among the most impressive technical sketches. They are used in many different types of publications such as advertising pieces, specification sheets, and repair manuals. Examples of cutaway sketches are shown in Figures 8-13 through 8-15.

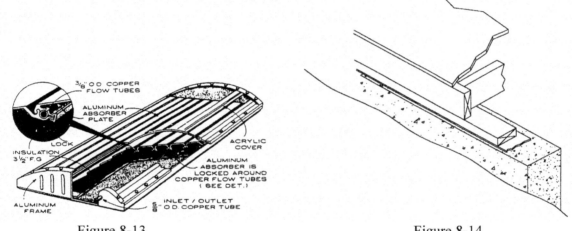

Figure 8-13
Cutaway Example

Figure 8-14
Cutaway Example

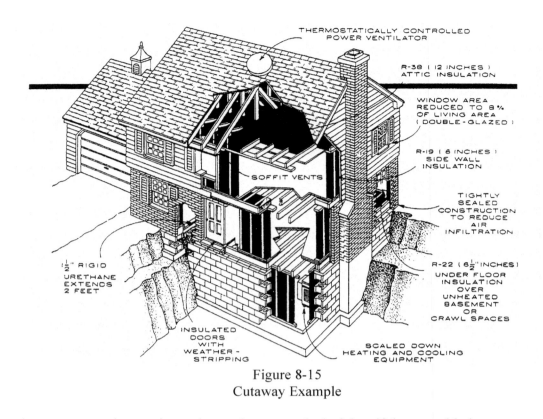

THERMOSTATICALLY CONTROLLED
POWER VENTILATOR

R-38 (12 INCHES)
ATTIC INSULATION

WINDOW AREA
REDUCED TO 8%
OF LIVING AREA
(DOUBLE-GLAZED)

R-19 (6 INCHES)
SIDE WALL
INSULATION

SOFFIT VENTS

TIGHTLY
SEALED
CONSTRUCTION
TO REDUCE
AIR
INFILTRATION

$1\frac{1}{2}$" RIGID
URETHANE
EXTENDS
2 FEET

R-22 ($6\frac{1}{2}$"INCHES)
UNDER FLOOR
INSULATION
OVER
UNHEATED
BASEMENT
OR
CRAWL SPACES

INSULATED
DOORS
WITH
WEATHER-
STRIPPING

SCALED DOWN
HEATING AND COOLING
EQUIPMENT

Figure 8-15
Cutaway Example

Although cutaways are impressive and can take a great deal of time if the assembly has many parts, they are not difficult to sketch. The main things to remember when sketching cutaways are to complete one part at a time and to make sure the parts are in the correct position. The sketch shown in Figure 8-15 is an excellent example of a complex cutaway. If you study a few individual parts for a moment, you will quickly see that there is nothing that you have not sketched or could not sketch if you knew the shape and size of the part. There are a few rules and details, however, that will help you with sketching cutaways.

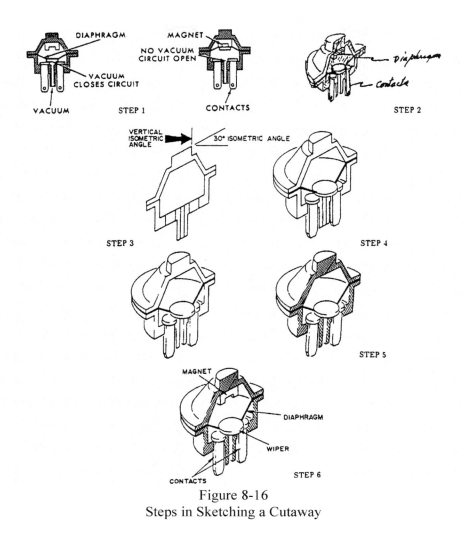

Figure 8-16
Steps in Sketching a Cutaway

The following steps, illustrated in Figure 8-16, cover those rules and details.

General guidelines for cutaway sketches
      Step 1. Determine the surfaces to be cut.
      Step 2. Make a rough freehand sketch.
      Step 3. Sketch the cut surfaces.
      Step 4. Sketch the full shapes.
      Step 5. Put shading on the cut surfaces.
      Step 6. Add callouts.

We shall examine each step in detail.

<u>Determine the surfaces to be cut.</u>
Find out exactly what the sketch is trying to show. When you know the parts to be shown and what position they should be in, you can determine which surfaces should be cut and how deep the cut should be. If the sketch in Figure 8-16 were to be shown as a cutaway, for example, and your instructions were to show how the vacuum switch works, a cut completely across the upper and lower housing through the magnet and the diaphragm would be used. To show less would hide some of the internal parts that reveal

how the switch functions.

Make a rough freehand sketch
Making a rough freehand sketch allows you to decide which isometric position to use and to make the correct decision about which surfaces to cut. In Figure 8-16, the sketch confirms that a full cut across the part is needed to show both contacts. It also indicates that the vertical isometric axis is a good position for the sketch because it shows how the part functions.

Sketch the cut surfaces
It is usually best to sketch the cut surfaces first. Sometimes this cannot be done before some of the uncut parts must be drawn. You will discover that as you proceed through the sketch. In Figure 8-16, notice that the cut surfaces were drawn just as they appear on the orthographic views, except that isometric angles have now taken the place of horizontal and vertical lines.

Sketch the full shapes
Sketch the full shapes and complete the uncut parts of the cut surfaces. You must be sure that the parts are shown in their correct positions, which you can determine by measuring. If they are not in the correct positions and still do not show clearly what is intended, do not hesitate to distort dimensions or to make additional cuts, so long as parts do not get too far out of proportion.

Put shading on the cut surfaces
In Figure 8-16, shading lines were used on the cut surfaces. Notice that the shading lines are at steep angles of approximately 60 degrees in opposite directions. It is important to make these lines different from isometric angles, because they can easily be confused with object lines.

Add callouts
Notice that the lettering in the callout is lined up horizontally. The blunt end of the leader points to the center of the line of lettering, and the arrow end breaks the part about 1/16". Keep leaders short and with a fan arrangement or with the same angle. Lines of lettering can be centered or arranged flush right or left, whichever is convenient or specified by your customer. Be sure to follow a consistent pattern and that all callouts are clear and easily read.

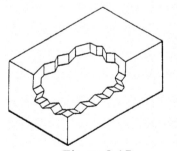

Figure 8-17
Use Obtuse Angles for Cut Surfaces

Further details
If you must cut a flat plane in a cutaway sketch, use obtuse angles for the cut as shown in Figure 8-17. This allows you to show uniform thickness easily by using the opposite isometric angle and does not distract from the sketch as extremely jagged cuts do.

Fasteners, shafts, and spheres are shown much more clearly if they are not cut on the sketch. Generally, nothing should be cut in a cutaway that is not necessary to show what is intended.

If you like this kind of sketching, study cutaways in books and magazines to decide what looks good and what does not. Not all the sketches you see printed in books and magazines are good ones.

EXERCISES

EXERCISE 8-1   Use the following instructions to sketch the final step shown in Figures 8-18, 8-19, 8-20, and 8-21, on the sheet labeled Exercise 8-1 using the cabinet oblique sketching form. Make sure your lines are dense and the same width as object lines. Your sketch will show only the final step in each of these figures.

Remove the sheet labeled Exercise 8-1 from your book.

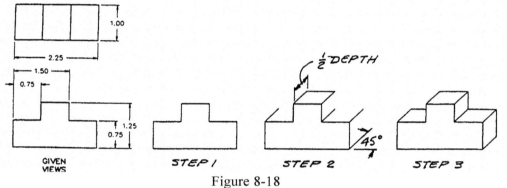

Figure 8-18
Exercise 8-1A

Figure 8-18   Step 1. Sketch the front view of the object using the dimensions shown in the given views. The lower left corner of the front view is in the upper left of the exercise sheet.

Step 2. Extend light construction lines from the front view at a 45 degree angle to show the depth. Make sure the dimension is one half the true depth (in this case, 1/2").

Step 3. Complete the illustration by connecting the points to form the back surface and darken all object lines.

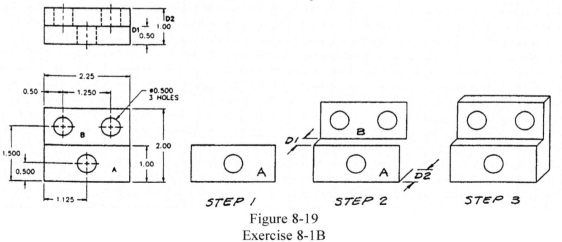

Figure 8-19
Exercise 8-1B

Figure 8-19   Step 1. Sketch front surface A using the dimensions shown in the given views.
                         The lower left corner of this sketch is in the upper right of the sheet.
                Step 2. Lightly sketch lines D1 and D2 at a 45 degree angle. Make D1
                         and D2 half their true length. Sketch front surface B using the
                         dimensions shown in the given views.
                Step 3. Darken the other depth lines and darken all object lines to complete the
                         illustration.

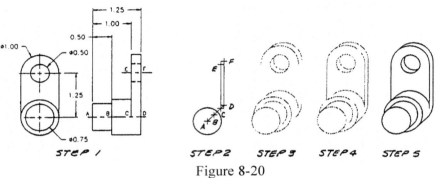

Figure 8-20

Exercise 8-1C

Figure 8-20   Step 1. Look at the given views to decide which circles are on the same center lines.
                Step 2. Locate the centers for all circles. Sketch a light 45 degree construction
                         line from the center of the circle on the exercise sheet. The center of this
                         circle is point A.
                         Measure half the distance from A to B and mark point B on the
                         construction line. Do the same for points C and D.
                         From points C and D sketch light construction lines straight up. Take
                         the distance from C to E on the given views and mark point E on the
                         vertical construction line.
                         From point E sketch a light 45 degree construction line to intersect with
                         the vertical line from point D. This locates point F.
                Step 3. Lightly sketch the parts of the circles that will show. You can tell which
                         ones will show by beginning with the circle at point A and working backward.
                Step 4. Locate the tangent points by sketching light 45 degree and vertical
                         construction lines. On this sketch, the tangent points are where
                         straight lines meet the circles. You need to find the tangent points so
                         that your lines have a nice, smooth flow and none of the circles
                         are flattened.
                Step 5. Darken all lines that show to complete the sketch.

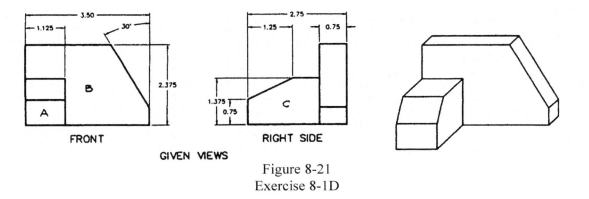

FRONT

RIGHT SIDE

GIVEN VIEWS

Figure 8-21
Exercise 8-1D

Figure 8-21.   On your own: Complete the oblique view on the right side of the figure at half scale. Surface A of this sketch is located in the lower right of the exercise sheet. The angle on surface B can be measured directly 1/2" up from its lower right corner. The angle on surface C cannot be measured. You must locate the ends of the line and connect those points to form the angle. Darken all lines after you have completed the construction.
Letter your name, the date, and the class with your best lettering.

EXERCISE 8-2   Use the following instructions to sketch the final step shown in Figures 8-22 and 8-23 on the sheet labeled Exercise 8-2 using the isometric sketching form. Make sure your lines are dense and the same width as object lines. Your sketch will show only the final step in each of these figures.
Remove the sheet labeled Exercise 8-2 from your book.

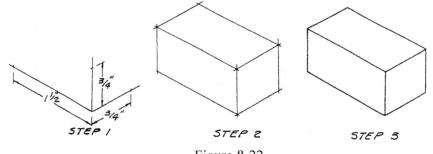

STEP 1   STEP 2   STEP 3

Figure 8-22
Exercise 8-2A

Figure 8-22   Step 1. Mark 3/4" from the lower left corner on the 30 degree axis to the right, 3/4" on the vertical axis, and 1-1/2" on the 30 degree axis to the left. The lower left corner of this sketch is on the left side of the exercise sheet.
     Step 2. Using light construction lines, extend height, width, and depth lines until they meet, and sketch parallel lines as needed.
     Step 3. Darken the object lines.

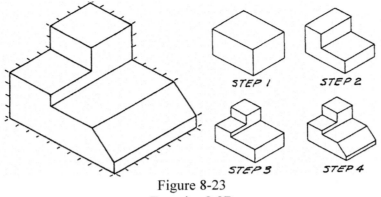

Figure 8-23
Exercise 8-2B

Figure 8-23.   Step 1. Using light construction lines, sketch an isometric box measuring 2" on the isometric axis to the right, 2-1/2" on the isometric axis to the left, and 1-1/2" on the vertical axis. Each mark on the 3D view represents 1/4". The lower right corner of the box is on the right side of the exercise sheet.

Step 2. Use light construction lines to sketch the general shape of the front view as shown.

Step 3. Use light construction lines to sketch the notch in the upper surface in the right side view as shown.

Step 4. Locate the ends of the angular shape and complete the shape as shown. Darken all object lines to complete the illustration.

Letter your name, the date, and the class with your best lettering.

EXERCISE 8-3   Use the following instructions to sketch the final step shown in Figure 8-24 and an isometric sketch of Figure 8-25 on the sheet labeled Exercise 8-3 using the isometric sketching form. Make sure your lines are dense and the same width as object lines. Your sketch will show only the final step in Figure 8-24.

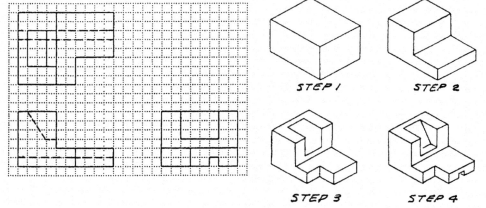

Figure 8-24
Exercise 8-3A

Figure 8-24   Step 1. Using light construction lines, sketch an isometric box measuring 2" on the isometric axis to the right, 2-1/2" on the isometric axis to the left, and 1-1/2" on the vertical axis. Each mark on the orthographic views represents 1/4".

Step 2. Use light construction lines to sketch the general shape of the front view as shown.

Step 3. Use light construction lines to sketch the top and right side of the notch in the upper surface. Sketch the notch in the base as shown.

Step 4. Complete the shape of the notch in the upper surface and sketch the .25 slot in the bottom of the right side of the base as shown. Darken all lines to complete the sketch.

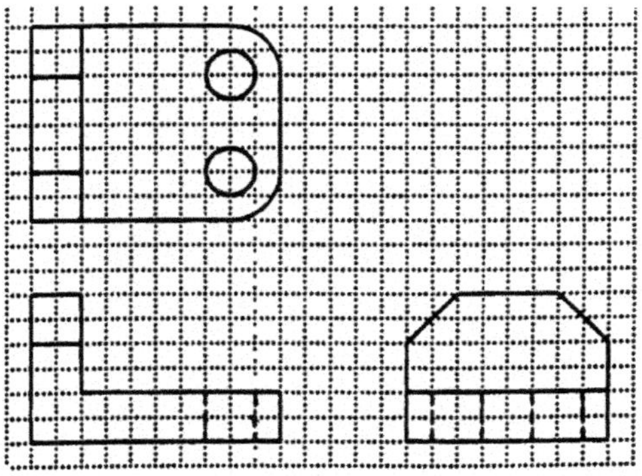

Figure 8-25
Exercise 8-3B

Figure 8-25   On your own: Make an isometric sketch from the top, front, and right side orthographic views shown in Figure 8-25. You will have to make isometric squares to help you sketch the ellipses forming the holes and the fillets at the corners of the base as shown in Figure 8-7. Use the same method you used for the other sketches in Exercise 8-2.

Letter your name, the date, and the class with your best lettering.

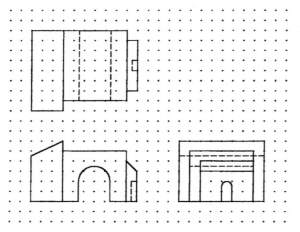

Figure 8-26
Exercise 8-4, Grids = 1/4"

EXERCISE 8-4 Make an isometric sketch from the top, front, and right side orthographic views shown in Figure 8-26 on the sheet labeled Exercise 8-4 in your book.
Each mark on the orthographic views represents 1/4".
Letter your name, the date, and the class with your best lettering.

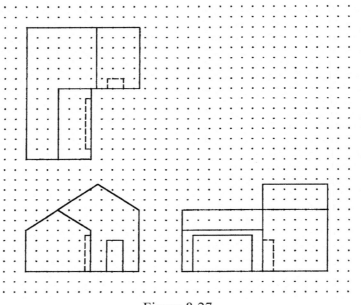

Figure 8-27
Exercise 8-5

EXERCISE 8-5 Make an isometric sketch from the top, front, and right side orthographic views shown in Figure 8-27 on the sheet labeled Exercise 8-5 in your book.
Each mark on the orthographic views represents 1/4". Center the sketch in the sheet by using light construction lines until you are sure the sketch is centered.
Letter your name, the date, and the class with your best lettering.

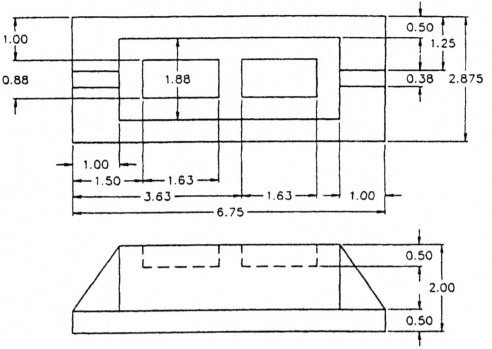

Figure 8-28
Exercise 8-6

EXERCISE 8-6   Make an ISOMETRIC sketch of Figure 8-28 on the sheet labeled Exercise 8-6 in your book. Sketch the figure 3/4 scale using the dimensions shown. **DO NOT SHOW ANY DIMENSIONS.**

Letter your name, the date, and the class with your best lettering.

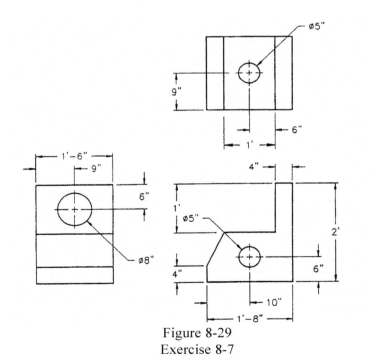

Figure 8-29
Exercise 8-7

EXERCISE 8-7   Make an ISOMETRIC sketch of Figure 8-29 on the sheet labeled Exercise 8-7 in your book.

Sketch the figure at a scale of 1"=1' using the dimensions shown. Center the sketch in the sheet by using light construction lines until you are sure the sketch is centered. You will have to make isometric squares to help you sketch the ellipses forming the holes as shown in Figure 8-7.

DO NOT SHOW ANY DIMENSIONS.

Letter your name, the date, and the class with your best lettering.

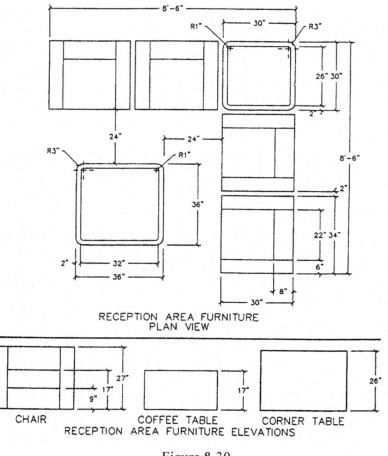

RECEPTION AREA FURNITURE
PLAN VIEW

CHAIR   COFFEE TABLE   CORNER TABLE
RECEPTION AREA FURNITURE ELEVATIONS

Figure 8-30
Exercise 8-8

EXERCISE 8-8   Make an ISOMETRIC sketch of Figure 8-30 on the sheet labeled Exercise 8-8 in your book.

Sketch the figure at a scale of 3/8"=1' using the dimensions shown.

DO NOT SHOW ANY DIMENSIONS.

Letter your name, the date, and the class with your best lettering.

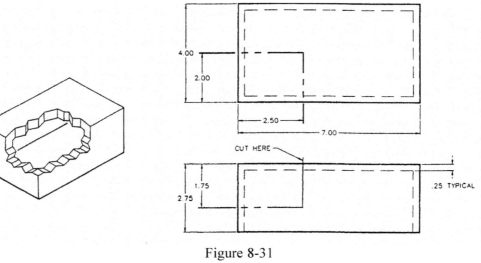

Figure 8-31
Exercise 8-9

EXERCISE 8-9   Make an ISOMETRIC cutaway sketch of Figure 8-31 on the sheet labeled
Exercise 8-9 in your book.
Sketch the figure full scale using the dimensions shown. Center the sketch in the
sheet by using light construction lines until you are sure the sketch is centered.
Make the cut with obtuse angle break lines. Notice that the thickness of all three
cut walls is the same.
DO NOT SHOW ANY DIMENSIONS.
Letter your name, the date, and the class with your best lettering.

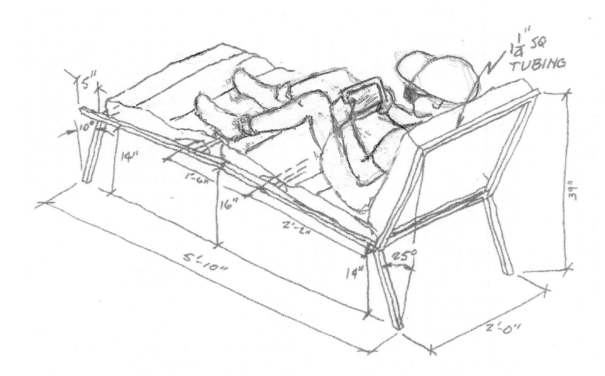

Figure 8-32
Exercise 8-10

EXERCISE 8-10   Make an ISOMETRIC sketch of Figure 8-32 on the sheet labeled Exercise 8-10 in your book.
Sketch the figure at a scale of 1"=1'-0" using the dimensions shown.
Estimate any dimensions not shown.
Center the sketch in the sheet by using light construction lines until you are sure the sketch is centered.
DO NOT SHOW ANY DIMENSIONS.
Letter your name, the date, and the class with your best lettering.

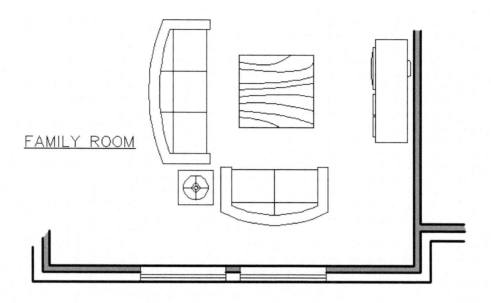

FAMILY ROOM

Figure 8-33 Sheet 1 of 2
Exercise 8-11

EXERCISE 8-11   Make an ISOMETRIC sketch of Figure 8-33, sheets 1 and 2, on the sheet labeled Exercise 8-11 in your book.
Measure the figure using a scale of 1/4"=1'-0" and draw it at the same scale. You can use both sheets for your measurements.
Add three people similar to the ones shown in Figure 8-33, sheet 2.
Your final sketch should look similar to Figure 8-33, sheet 2.
Letter your name, the date, and the class with your best lettering.

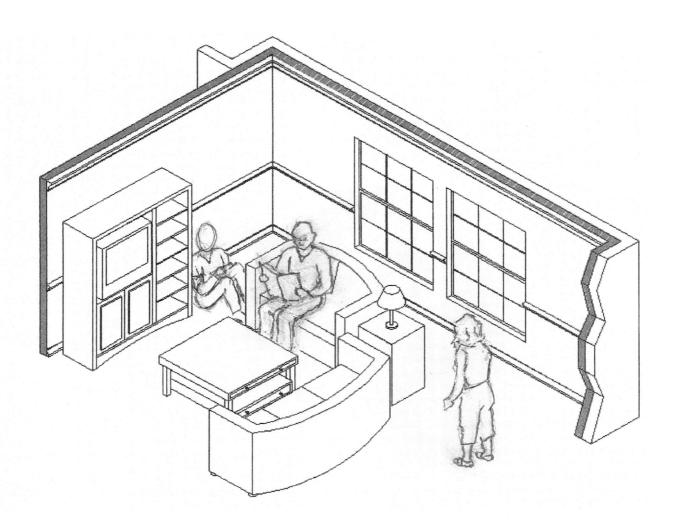

Figure 8-33 Sheet 2 of 2
Exercise 8-11

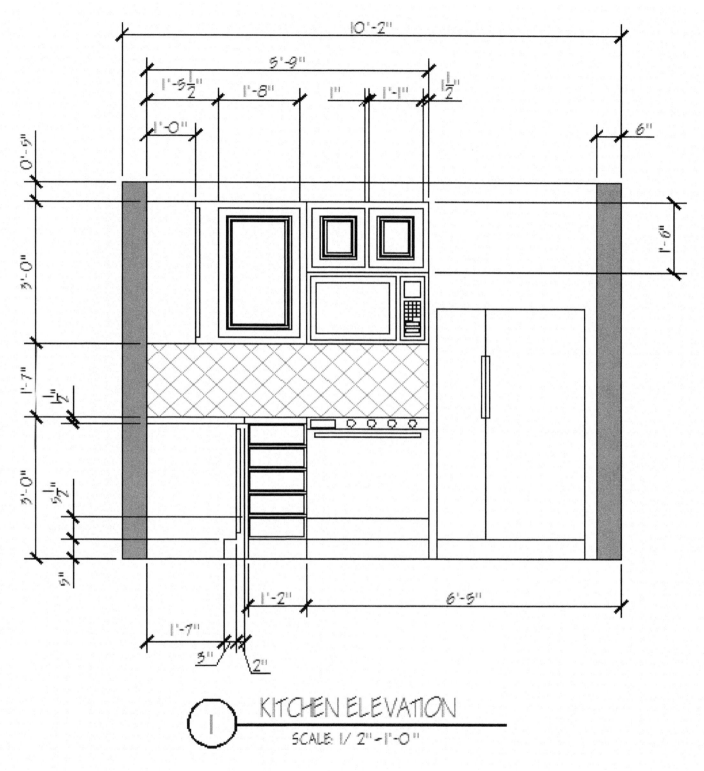

KITCHEN ELEVATION
SCALE: 1/ 2" = 1'-0"

Figure 8-34
Exercise 8-12

8-23

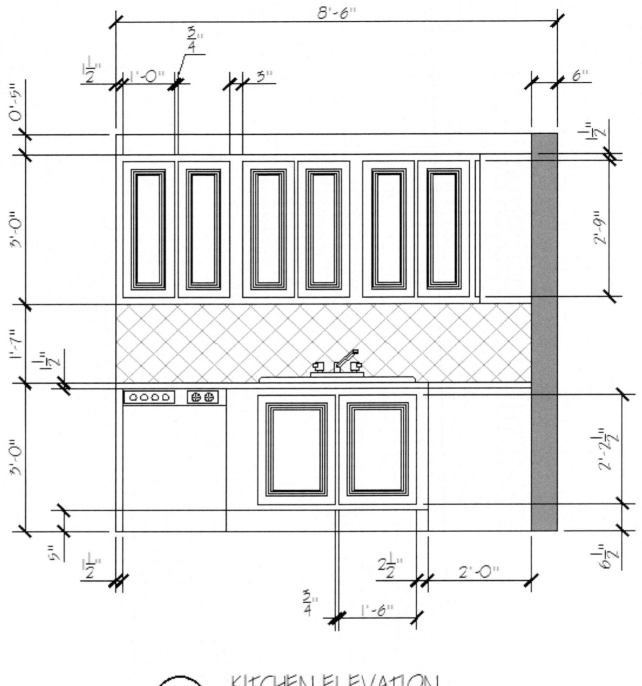

KITCHEN ELEVATION

SCALE: 1/2" = 1'-0"

Figure 8-35
Exercise 8-12

Figure 8-36
Exercise 8-12
(Scale 1"=1'-0")

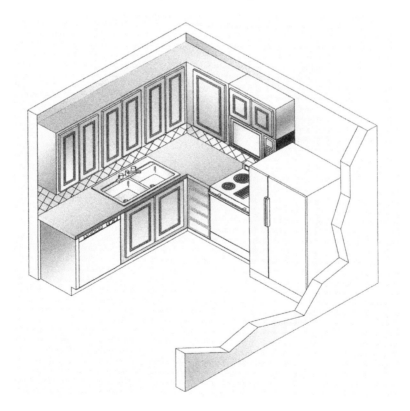

Figure 8-37
Exercise 8-12
(Scale 1/4"=1'-0")

EXERCISE 8-12   Make an ISOMETRIC sketch of Figure 8-37 on the sheet labeled Exercise 8-12 in your book using a scale of 3/8"=1'-0".

Use the dimensions from Figures 8-34 and 8-35 and, if necessary, measure some of the features in the isometric drawings (Figures 8-36 and 37) using the scales indicated.

Add a person of your choice to the area, making sure it is proportional to the rest of the sketch.

Shade your sketch with pencil, charcoal, or a medium of your choice so that it appears approximately as shown in Figure 8-37.

Letter your name, the date, and the class with your best lettering.

This chapter gives you the information and techniques to make isometric sketches. These sketches consist of basic forms, more complex forms, buildings, furniture, and people. Now you have the skills and information needed to make isometric sketches that convey your ideas and those of others accurately.

_____REVIEW QUESTIONS

Multiple Choice

Circle the correct answer.

1.   Which of the following is usually the least distorted type of pictorial but the most difficult to sketch?

      a.   Oblique

      b.   Isometric

      c.   Dimetric

      d.   Two-point perspective

2.   Which of the following is not one of the isometric axes?

      a.   30

      b.   60

      c.   90

      d.   210

3.   An isometric gives equal presentations of

      a.   front, top, and right side views

      b.   front and left side views

      c.   top and right side views

      d.   left and right side views

4.   On isometric sketches _____ are used.

      a.   isometric measurements

      b.   pictorial measurements

      c.   oblique measurements

      d.   true length measurements

5.   The three isometric axes are

      a.   30 degrees left, 60 degrees right, and vertical

      b.   30 degrees left, 45 degrees right, and vertical

      c.   30 degrees left, 30 degrees right, and vertical

      d.   60 degrees left ,30 degrees right, and vertical

6.   Isometric lines are lines that are parallel to

      a.   a level line

      b.   the front view

      c.   the right side view

      d.   isometric axes

7. Spheres in isometric sketching appear as
   a. circles
   b. ellipses
   c. straight lines
   d. irregular curves

8. Cylindrical objects in isometric sketching are best drawn by locating centers on
   a. a box around the surface
   b. an outside surface
   c. a center line or center lines
   d. the edges of preceding ellipses

9. An isometric cutaway sketch is best described as
   a. an isometric sectional view
   b. a perspective
   c. an exploded view
   d. an orthographic sectional view

10. Which of the following should be done first in making an isometric cutaway sketch?
    a. Make a freehand sketch
    b. Shade the cut surfaces
    c. Sketch the cut surfaces in isometric
    d. Sketch the uncut surfaces in isometric

11. Angles are measured in isometric sketching by adding the angle of the isometric axis to the angle to be drawn.
    a. True
    b. False

12. Cylinder walls are usually cut on a cutaway.
    a. True
    b. False

13. To sketch a line at an angle that is not on an isometric axis locate both ends of the line first, then sketch the line.
    a. True
    b. False

14. Break lines on cutaway sketches should be drawn with lines parallel to an isometric axis.
    a. True
    b. False

15. Trimetric is a form of axonometric sketching.
    a. True
    b. False

Matching

Write the number of the correct answer on the line.

a.____ A 2D sketching method using 30 and 90 degree
angled lines that gives the appearance of three
dimensions   1.   Shaft

b.____ The least distorted of pictorial sketching forms   2.   Circle

c.____ The shape of a sphere in isometric sketching   3.   Isometric

d.____ The starting point for sketching cylindrical objects   4.   Perspective

e.____ A part that is not cut in a cutaway sketch   5.   Center line

General Questions

1. What is isometric sketching and how is it used?

2. Why are isometric ellipses used to sketch holes and cylinders?

3. Why must angles in isometric be sketched by locating the ends of the angle instead of sketching a line
at a specific angle?

4. What are cutaway sketches and why are they used?

5. Why are freehand sketches done first in making an isometric cutaway sketch?

9 Sketching Floor Plans

OBJECTIVES

After completing this chapter, you will be able to:

Correctly sketch floor plans to scale from a given set of specifications.

Correctly answer questions regarding floor plan sketches.

INTRODUCTION

Floor plans are created by using the ideas of many people. Clients, architects, city inspectors, builders, salespeople, and others may have input into many final floor plans. The purpose of this chapter is to develop the skills necessary to correctly draw a sketch of a proposed floor plan and scale and dimension it. The design of the plan has already been developed. You are to draw the sketch as designed from specifications furnished to you.

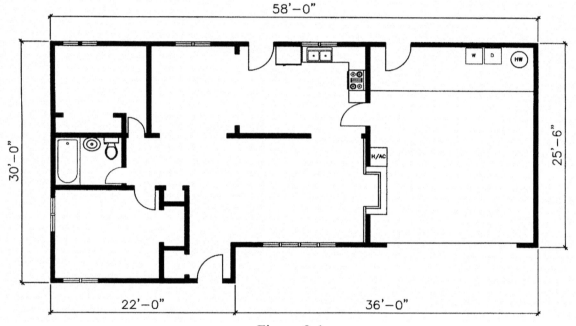

Figure 9-1
Exercise 9-1 Complete

STEPS IN SKETCHING THE PROPOSED FLOOR PLAN (Figure 9-1)

Figure 9-1 shows how your final sketch will appear.

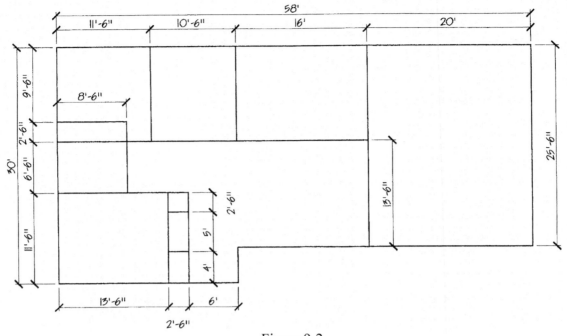

Figure 9-2
Sketch Outline Lightly

_____**EXERCISES**

EXERCISE 9-1
   Step 1. Remove the sheet labeled Exercise 9-1 from the back of your book.
   Step 2. Draw the outline of the plan very lightly on the paper (Figure 9-2). The outline will be from the outside of outside walls to the center of inside walls.
   Step 3. With light lines, add thickness to all walls (Figure 9-3). Because the scale is very small, 1/8"=1', make all walls approximately 1/16" (5" to 6").
   Step 4. Locate all windows, doors, and the fireplace (Figure 9-4) with light construction lines.

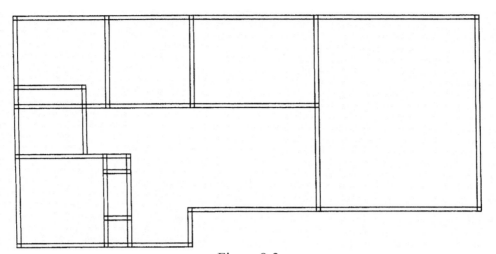

Figure 9-3
Add Thickness to All Walls Using Light Construction Lines

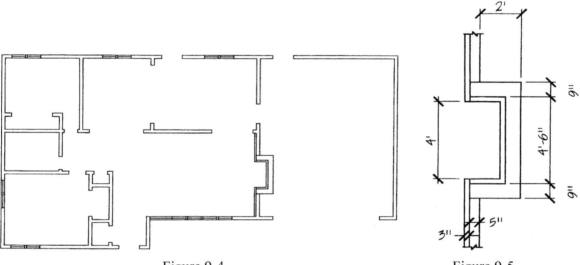

Figure 9-4
Locate Windows, Doors, and the Fireplace

Figure 9-5
Fireplace Dimensions (Not to Scale)

Step 5. With light construction lines, sketch sinks, counter tops, cabinets, bathroom fixtures,
water heater, washer, dryer, heating, and A/C equipment (Figure 9-5). Use the sizes
shown in Figure 9-6. These symbols are 1/8"=1', so draw them the size shown in this
figure.

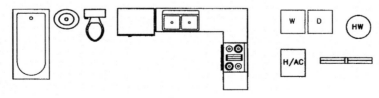

Figure 9-6
Symbols for Kitchen, Bath, Utilities, and Windows at 1/8"=1'-0" Scale

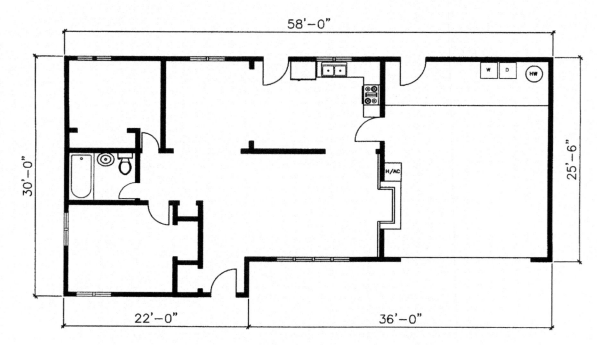

Figure 9-7
Exercise 9-1 Complete

Step 6. Darken all lines (Figure 9-7).

Step 7. Compare your sketch with Figure 9-7 and make any necessary corrections.

Step 8. Fill in the date, class, and your name with your best lettering.

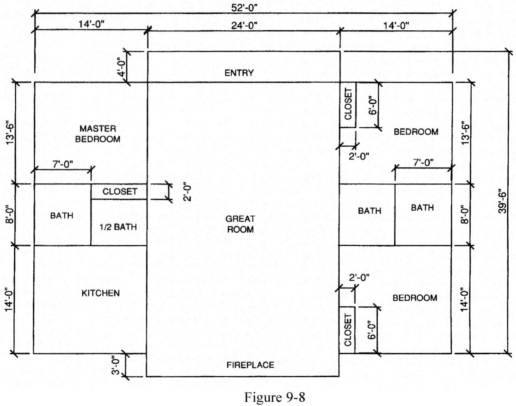

Figure 9-8
Dimensions for Exercise 9-2

EXERCISE 9-2
Step 1. Complete Exercise 9-2 using the specifications described in Figure 9-8 and the sheet labeled

Exercise 9-2. Use the sketching technique described in Exercise 9-1. Locate the windows, doors, fireplace, kitchen, and all other items shown in Exercise 9-1. Use the sizes shown in Figure 9-6.

9-5

Step 2. Using the sketching and construction techniques presented in this chapter, complete the sketch using the grid lines and the existing sketch lines as a guide.
Make sure that your lines are the correct weight and are of even width and darkness.
Try to match the thickness and darkness of the existing lines.

Step 3. Check your sketch and make any necessary corrections.

Step 4. Fill in the date, class, and your name with your best lettering.

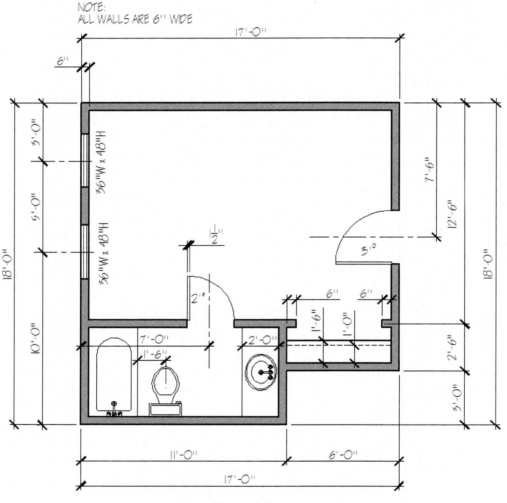

Figure 9-9
Dimensions for Exercise 9-3

EXERCISE 9-3
Step 1. Complete Exercise 9-3 using the specifications shown in Figure 9-9 and the sheet labeled Exercise 9-3. Use the sketching technique described in Exercise 9-1.

Step 2. Using the sketching and construction techniques presented in this chapter, complete the sketch

using the grid lines and the existing sketch lines as a guide.
Make sure that your lines are the correct weight and are of even width and darkness.
Try to match the thickness and darkness of the existing lines.

Step 3. Check your sketch and make any necessary corrections.

Step 4. Fill in the date, class, and your name with your best lettering.

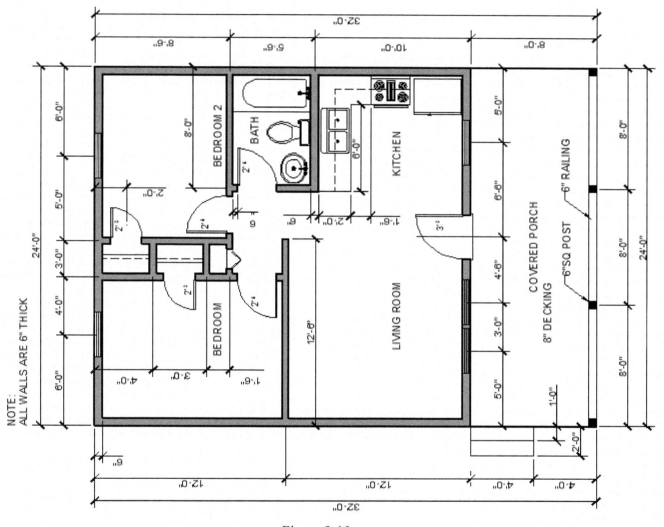

Figure 9-10
Dimensions for Exercise 9-4

EXERCISE 9-4

Step 1. Complete Exercise 9-4 using the specifications shown in Figure 9-10 and the sheet labeled
Exercise 9-4. Use the sketching
technique described in Exercise 9-1.

Step 2. Using the sketching and construction techniques presented in this chapter, complete the sketch

using the grid lines and the existing sketch lines as a guide.
Make sure that your lines are the correct weight and are of even width and darkness.
Try to match the thickness and darkness of the existing lines.

Step 3. Check your sketch and make any necessary corrections.

Step 4. Fill in the date, class, and your name with your best lettering.

_____CHAPTER SUMMARY

This chapter gives you the information and techniques to make floor plans. These sketches consist of basic forms and some more complex forms. Now you have the skills and information needed to make floor plans.

_____REVIEW QUESTIONS

Multiple Choice

Circle the correct answer.

1.   The walls shown in these sketches are approximately:
       a.   2" thick
       b.   5" thick
       c.   8" thick
       d.   10" thick

2.   The scale for Exercise 9-1 is:
       a.   1/16"=1'
       b.   1/8"=1'
       c.   ¼"=1'
       d.   ½"=1'

3.   Which scale is on the same edge as the 1/8 scale?
       a.   1/16
       b.   ¼
       c.   ½
       d.   3/8

4.   On a scale of 1/8"=1', a 3' door will actually measure:
       a.   3"
       b.   3/8"
       c.   ¾"
       d.   1-1/2"

5.   On a scale of 1/8"=1', a 16' room will actually measure:
        a.   3"
        b.   16"
        c.   2"
        d.   4"

6.   On a scale of 1/8"=1', a 20' room will actually measure 6".
        a.   True   b.   False

7.   The floor plan can best be described as an orthographic top view.
        a.   True   b.   False

8.   The inputs from all of the people who have an interest in what the final floor plan looks like
        require that the designer ensure that no one changes the preliminary plan.
        a.   True   b.   False

9.   The lines in the preliminary sketch (Figure 9-1) show the inside of the outside walls.
        a.   True   b.   False

10.   The lines in the preliminary sketch show the centers of the inside walls.
        a.   True   b.   False

Matching

Write the number of the correct answer on the line.

a.____ Drawn with arcs and straight lines.   1.   A window

b.____ Drawn with inside and outside lines   2.   A sink

c.____ Drawn with straight lines only   3.   A water heater

d.____ In Exercise 9-1, drawn with a circle only   4.   A wall

e.____ In Exercise 9-1, drawn with ellipses and a circle 5.   A door

General Questions

1. Why would you use sketches of floor plans?

2. When would you need sketches of floor plans?

3. What information must you have to make sketches of floor plans?

4. What are the essential elements of floor plan sketches?

5. Where can you sketch floor plans?

10 Sketching Dimensions

OBJECTIVES

After completing this chapter, you will be able to:

Correctly sketch dimension lines, extension lines, center lines, architectural ticks, arrowheads, and leaders.

Correctly dimension rectangles, angles, circles, and arcs.

Correctly dimension doors, windows, and interior and exterior walls.

Use the unidirectional and aligned systems for dimensioning.

Correctly select and place dimensions.

Use current symbols for diameter and radius.

Correctly answer questions regarding sketching dimensions.

INTRODUCTION

Most architectural drawings are used for assembling an architectural detail or constructing a building. The person who builds or assembles the product must know not only the shape of the object but also its exact size, where its features are located, and what materials and finishes are to be used.

Although you may know basic construction techniques and can issue correct instructions to contractors through dimensions and notes, most of the problems of basic dimensioning are covered by a few simple rules. You will have little difficulty if you follow these rules carefully and apply them knowing that someone must actually build the object from your drawing or sketch.

STANDARD DIMENSIONING PRACTICES

Each part of the dimensioning process has specific rules governing it. These parts include:

Lines, symbols, and abbreviations
Size and location dimensions
Drawing to scale
Placement of dimensions
Aligned and unidirectional systems of dimensioning
Dimensioning features
Notes
Tabular dimensioning

Lines, symbols, and abbreviations

The four types of lines used in dimensioning are the extension line, dimension line, center line, and the leader. All of the four lines are drawn thin and dark.

The symbols for diameter and radius are also described in this chapter.

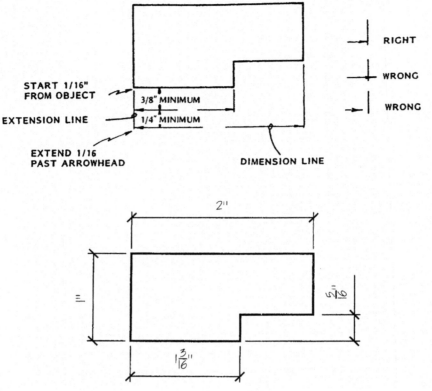

Figure 10-1
Extension and Dimension Lines and their Spacing

Extension line

The extension line (Figure 10-1) extends from the object, with a gap of about 1/16" next to the object, and goes to about 1/16" beyond the arrowhead. Leave a gap where extension lines cross other extension lines or dimension lines.

Dimension line

The dimension line (Figure 10-1) has an arrowhead or some other symbol (such as a slash, called a tick mark) at each end to show where the measurement is made. The arrowhead just touches the extension line. The arrowhead is approximately three times as long as it is wide. The wings of the arrowhead are straight and very close to the shaft. A gap is often left near the middle for the dimension text. In architectural drawings, the dimension line is often unbroken and the text is placed above a horizontal dimension or to the left of a vertical one. The arrowhead may also be a different shape such as the one shown in Figure 10-3. The dimension line may also extend beyond the extension line a short distance if the architect chooses to do so. On small drawings such as the ones in this chapter, dimension lines are spaced 1/2" from the object and 3/8" apart. The minimum of 3/8" and 1/4" shown in Figure 10-1 is used where space is very limited. On larger drawings, the spacing can be greater, but the first dimension is always placed further from the object lines of the drawing than the spacing between dimensions.

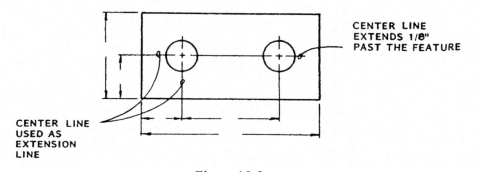

Figure 10-2
Center Lines

Center line

Center lines (Figure 10-2) are used to show the centers of symmetrical features and are used in place of extension lines for locating holes and other round features. Make center lines end about 1/16" to 1/8" outside the hole or feature.

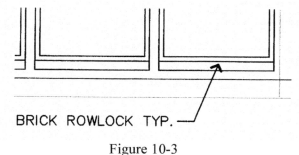

Figure 10-3
Leaders

Leader

A leader (Figure 10-3) is a thin solid line that leads from a note or dimension and ends with an arrowhead touching the part.

Leaders are often straight, inclined lines (never vertical or horizontal) that are usually drawn at 45, 60, or 30 degree angles, but may be drawn at any convenient angle. A short horizontal shoulder may be extended out from mid-height of the lettering of the note accompanying the leader. Leaders may extend from either the center of the beginning line or the ending line of the note, **NOT** from the inside lines. Leaders may also be curved to add character to the drawing if the architect chooses.

Symbols and abbreviations

The standard symbols and abbreviations used in this chapter are:

Diameter - Ø

Radius - R

Places - PL (as in the "dimension occurs in 4 places")

Typical - TYP (as in "this thickness is the same or typical throughout the part")

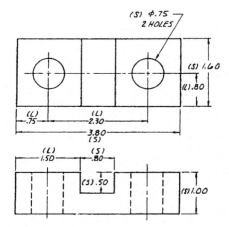

Figure 10-4
Size and Location Dimensions

Size and location dimensions

There are two types of dimensions: those that show the size of a feature and those that show the location of the feature (Figure 10-4).

Drawing to a scale

Drawings and sketches are often made to a scale. This scale is shown on the drawing, usually in the title block. If a minor change is to be made in one of the dimensions, a wavy line may be placed under the dimension to show that the dimension is not to scale. Regardless of the scale used, dimensions are always those of the feature to be built, not the size of that feature on the drawing.

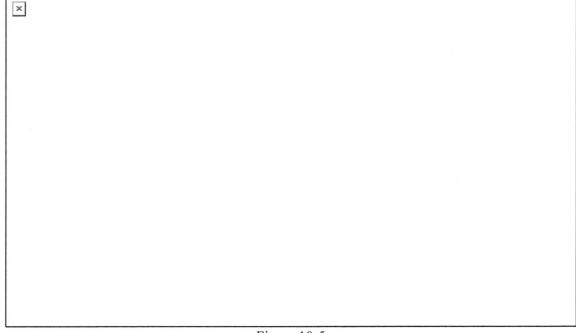

Figure 10-5
Correct and Incorrect Placement of Dimensions

Placement of dimensions

Examples of correct and incorrect placement of dimension lines are shown in Figure 10-5. The shortest dimensions are closest to the object outline.

Dimension lines should not cross extension lines, which results from placing the shorter dimensions outside. (This is sometimes unavoidable, however.) Be aware that it is acceptable for extension lines to cross each other.

A dimension line should never coincide with or form a continuation of any line of the drawing.

Avoid crossing dimension lines with other dimension lines whenever possible.

In general, avoid dimensioning to hidden lines (Figure 10-6). Place dimensions where the feature is seen as a solid line. (A section drawing may be necessary.)

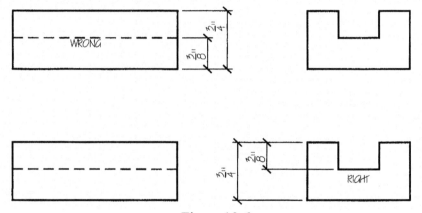

Figure 10-6
Avoid Dimensioning to Hidden Lines

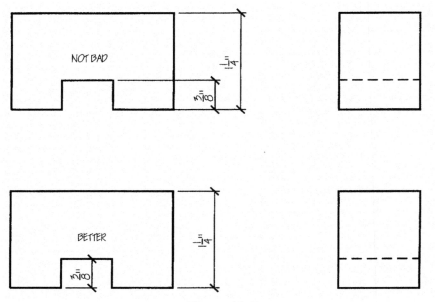

Figure 10-7
Place Dimensions Close to the Feature

If possible, dimensions should be placed in close relationship to the feature shown (Figure 10-7). Place as many of the dimensions as possible between the views and on the view that shows the shape of the feature best (Figure 10-8).

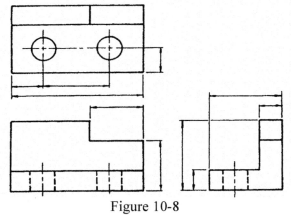

Figure 10-8
Place Dimensions between Views Where Possible

If the drawing contains fractional dimensions that run into each other, stagger the dimensions one above the other so that both are easily read.

Unidirectional and aligned systems of dimensioning

Both the aligned and the unidirectional systems of dimensioning have been widely used. Each system has advantages and disadvantages.

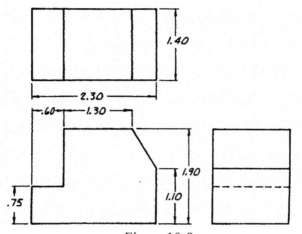

Figure 10-9
Unidirectional System of Dimensioning

Unidirectional system

In the unidirectional system (Figure 10-9), the dimensions are placed to read from the bottom of the drawing, and fraction bars (if any) are parallel with the bottom of the drawing.

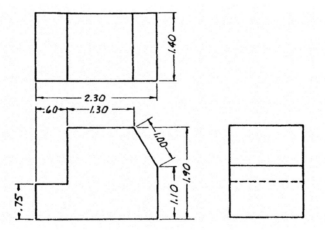

Figure 10-10
Aligned System of Dimensioning

Aligned system

In the aligned system of dimensioning (Figure 10-10), the dimensions are placed parallel to the lines of the drawing, and they are read from the bottom or right side of the drawing.

Dimensions and notes with leaders are aligned with the bottom of the drawing (placed in a horizontal position) in both systems.

Dimensioning features

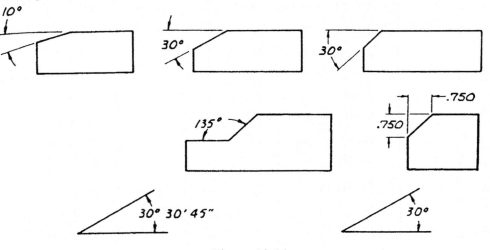

Figure 10-11
Dimensioning Angles

Angles

Angles are dimensioned in degrees (Figure 10-11). All the methods of dimensioning angles shown in the figure are acceptable. You will find occasion to use all of them if you dimension many angles.

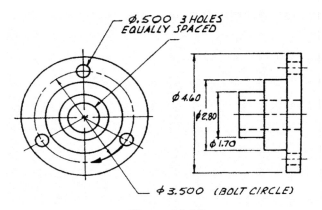

Figure 10-12
Dimensioning Holes and Cylinders

Circles

There are two common types of circular features: holes and cylinders (Figure 10-12). Holes are dimensioned on the view in which the hole is seen as a circle. Cylinders are dimensioned on the view where the cylinder is seen as a rectangle.

A circular center line (called a bolt circle) is used to locate holes from the center of a cylindrical piece.

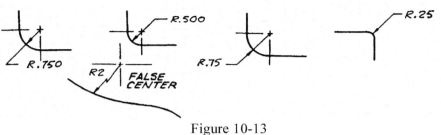

Figure 10-13
Dimensioning Radii

Radius

A radius is dimensioned in the view in which its true shape is seen (Figure 10-13). The abbreviation R is used for radius. If a large radius cannot be located because of lack of space, a false center can be located.

Notes

Two types of notes are shown on drawings: general and specific. General notes pertain to the whole drawing, and specific notes apply to one feature on the drawing. These notes are usually located on the drawing in a specific place that is preprinted with the drawing format. If these is no specific place for notes, they can be placed anywhere on the field of the drawing where they will not be crowded and can be read easily.

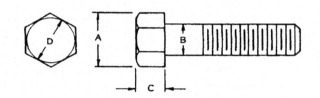

SIZE	A	B	C	D
1/2	0.866	0.515	11/32	3/4
3/4	1.299	0.768	1/2	1-1/8
1	1.732	1.022	43/64	1-1/2
1 1/4	2.165	1.277	27/32	1-7/8

Figure 10-14
Tabular Dimensioning

Tabular dimensioning

Some drawings can be used for several sizes of an object that have the same appearance. Figure 10-14 is an example of tabular dimensioning.

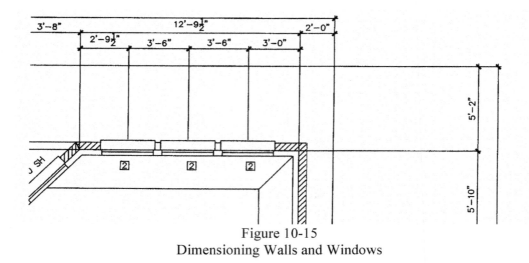

Figure 10-15
Dimensioning Walls and Windows

DIMENSIONING TO WINDOWS, DOORS, EXTERIOR AND INTERIOR WALLS

The sizes of windows and doors are not shown on the floor plan. Instead, the windows are identified with a letter inside a polygon, and the doors are identified with a number inside a circle. The specifications for both windows and doors are shown on a window and door schedule (a table) elsewhere in the set of plans. Windows and doors are located, however, by showing the measurement from a wall to the center of the window or door. Measurements are often shown from the outside of an exterior wall to the center of an inside wall; from the outside to outside of exterior walls and from the center of an inside wall to the center of another inside wall. There are exceptions to these guidelines, however, which you will see in the dimensioning examples. These variations are a result of construction methods and the architect's individual preference. Figures 10-16 through 10-20 show the placement of these dimensions.

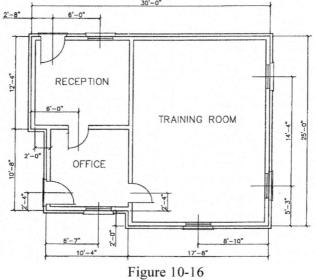

Figure 10-16
Dimensioning Example

10-10

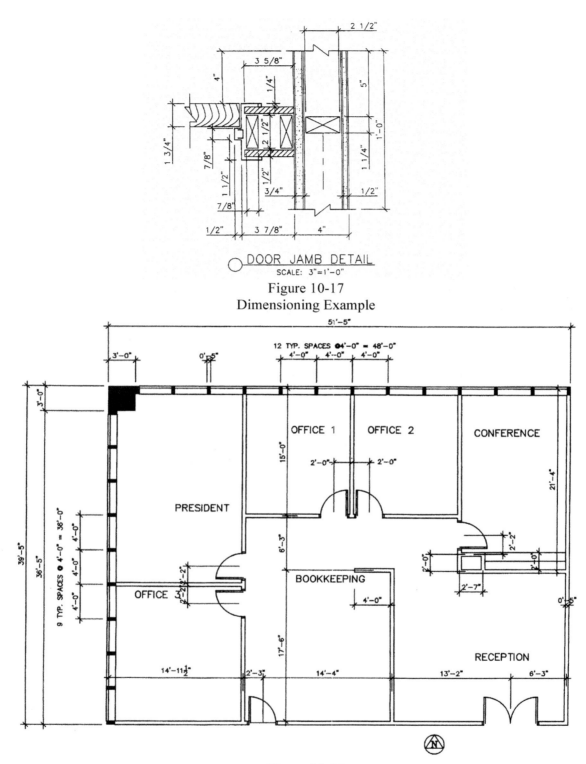

DOOR JAMB DETAIL
SCALE: 3"=1'-0"

Figure 10-17
Dimensioning Example

Figure 10-18
Dimensioning Example

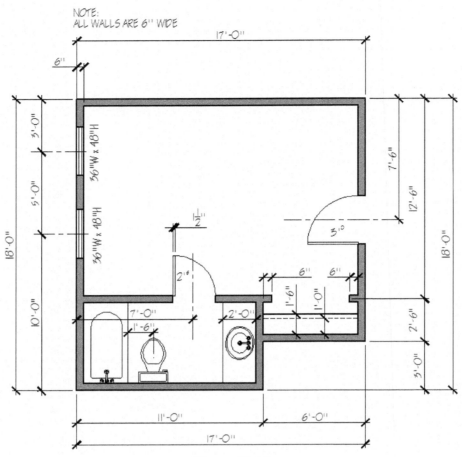

Figure 10-19
Dimensioning Example

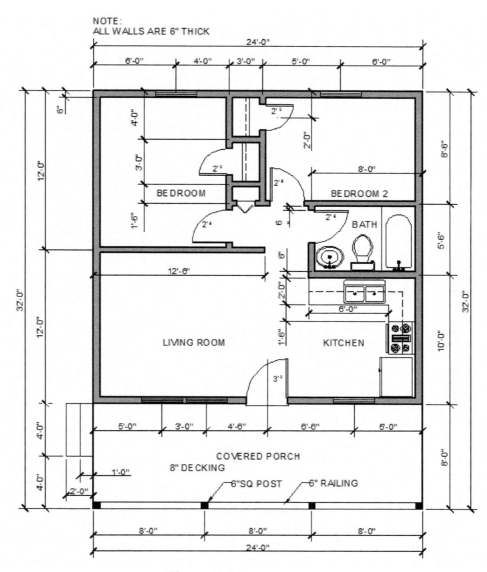

Figure 10-20
Dimensioning Example

EXERCISE 10-1   Sketch the dimensions on the sheet labeled Exercise 10-1. Refer to Figures 10-5 through 10-10 if necessary to determine what dimensions are necessary and where they should be placed.

Step 1. Use three place decimal dimensions.

Step 2. Leave 1/2" (2 grid marks) between the drawing and the first dimension.

Step 3. Leave 3/8" (1-1/2 grid marks) between dimension lines.

Step 4. Use good line weights and be consistent with letter size, arrowheads, and extension line offset from the part and extension line extension past the arrow head.

Step 5. Fill in the date, class, and your name with your best lettering.

EXERCISE 10-2   Sketch the dimensions on the sheet labeled Exercise 10-2. Refer to Figures 10-5 through 10-10 if necessary to determine what dimensions are necessary and where they should be placed.

Step 1. Use three place decimal dimensions.

Step 2. Leave 1/2" (2 grid marks) between the drawing and the first dimension.

Step 3. Leave 3/8" (1-1/2 grid marks) between dimension lines.

Step 4. Use good line weights and be consistent with letter size, arrowheads, and extension line offset from the part and extension line extension past the arrow head.

Step 5. Fill in the date, class, and your name with your best lettering.

EXERCISE 10-3   Use the sheet marked Exercise 10-3. Place dimensions showing the following

Step 1. The measurement from the outside of outside walls to the center of inside walls.

Step 2. The measurement from the center of inside walls to the center of inside walls.

Step 3. Measurements to the centers of all windows and doors.

Step 4. Refer to Figure 10-19 for ideas about how to dimension this floor plan.

Step 5. Match the existing method of dimensioning using the same spacing, line weight, and letter height as shown on the exercise sheet.

Step 6. Leave a greater space between the drawing and the first line of dimensions than between the first and second line of dimensions.

Step 7. Use good line weights and be consistent with letter size, ticks, and extension line offset from the part and extension line extension past the tick mark.

Step 8. Fill in the date, class, and your name with your best lettering.

EXERCISE 10-4   Use the sheet marked Exercise 10-4. Place dimensions showing the following:

Step 1. The measurement from the outside of outside walls to the center of inside walls.

Step 2. The measurement from the center of inside walls to the center of inside walls.

Step 3. Measurements to the centers of all windows and doors.

Step 4. Refer to Figure 10-19 for ideas about how to dimension this floor plan.

Step 5. Match the existing method of dimensioning using the same spacing, line weight, and letter height as shown on the exercise sheet.

Step 6. Leave a greater space between the drawing and the first line of dimensions than between the first and second line of dimensions.

Step 7. Use good line weights and be consistent with letter size, ticks, and extension line offset from the part and extension line extension past the tick mark.

Step 8. Fill in the date, class, and your name with your best lettering.

_____CHAPTER SUMMARY

This chapter gives you the information and techniques to place dimensions on sketches. These sketches consist of machine parts and architectural floor plans. Now you have the skills and information needed to place dimensions on sketches accurately and correctly.

_____REVIEW QUESTIONS

Circle the best answer.

1. How much space should be left between the dimension line arrowhead and the extension line to which it points?
    a.   1/2"
    b.   3/8"
    c.   1/16"
    d.   None

2. How much space should be left between the object and the first dimension line on the small drawings in the exercises in this chapter?
    a.   1/4"
    b.   3/8"
    c.   1/2"
    d.   3/4"

3. Is it permissible for dimension lines to cross extension lines or other dimension lines?
    a.   Yes, in all cases
    b.   Never
    c.   Avoid, if possible.
    d.   No, leave off the crossing dimension.

4. If more than one dimension containing a fraction is given on one side of a view, what should be done to make the fractions more legible?
    a.   Make the fractions twice the normal size.
    b.   Stagger the numbers containing the fractions.
    c.   Line up the numbers containing the fractions.
    d.   Make the fractions half the normal size.

5. Cylindrical objects are dimensioned in the rectangular view with
    a.   extension lines and dimension lines
    b.   a leader and a note
    c.   dimension lines only
    d.   a leader and a center line

6. The dimension line can extend beyond the extension line if the architect chooses to select that method of dimensioning.
    a.   True   b.   False

7.	A 180 degree angle would be best for drawing a leader.
	a.	True	b.	False

8.	Small holes are dimensioned in the circular view with extension lines and dimension lines.
	a.	True	b.	False

9.	Floor plans do not show the sizes of windows and doors.
	a.	True
	b.	False

10.	Dimensions should be made from the outside of the outside wall to the center of the window.
	a.	True
	b.	False

Matching

Write the number of the correct answer on the line.

a.____	A line leading from the floor plan to the dimension
	line	1.	3/8"

b.____	The space between dimension lines on small drawings	2.	Center lines

c.____	Used to locate holes	3.	1/2"

d.____	A good angle for a leader	4.	Extension line

e.____	The space between the object and the first
	dimension line on small drawings	5.	45 degree

General Questions

1.	What are dimensions used for on sketches?

2.	Why are dimensions important on drawings?

3.	When should you use dimensions on sketches?

4.	Where should dimensions be placed on sketches?

5.	Why would you use aligned dimensioning instead of unidirectional dimensioning?

11 Sketching Elevations

OBJECTIVES

After completing this chapter, you will be able to:

Correctly sketch exterior elevations to scale from floor plans and other specifications.

Correctly sketch interior elevations to scale.

Correctly answer questions regarding sketching elevations.

INTRODUCTION

and city officials how the building will
look from the front, rear, right, and left sides when it is completed. These are two-dimensional drawings that do not show depth as you would find in perspective drawings. Elevations show exterior details such as:

the style and sizes of windows and doors
the type of siding or brick
gutters
roof style and pitch
porches and decks
chimneys
molded concrete features
finished floor level
finished ceiling level
wood trim

STEPS IN SKETCHING THE FRONT ELEVATION

All elevations must show all features in the same location and the same size as they appear on the floor plan. Therefore, the first step in drawing the elevation is to locate the floor plan and any other specifications that show sizes and shapes of windows, doors, roofs, and any other features that are needed to complete the exterior details of the building.

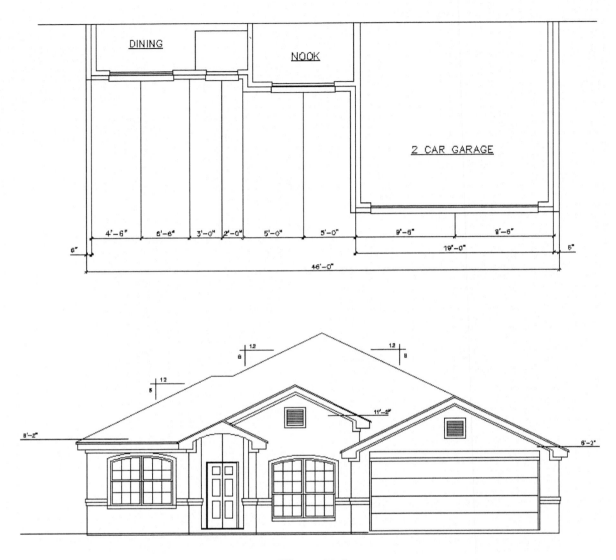

Figure 11-1
Partial Floor Plan and Front Elevation

_____**EXERCISES**

EXERCISE 11-1

Step 1. Remove the sheet labeled Exercise 11-1 from the back of your book.

Step 2. Collect the information needed to complete the drawing.

The upper part of Figure 11-1 is the partial floor plan that shows the location of all windows, doors, and other features on the front elevation. The lower part of Figure 11-1 is a scaled drawing showing the front elevation of a house similar to the one you will be drawing. All windows, doors, and roofs are the same as on your drawing.

Step 3. Sketch the outside limits of the elevation as shown in Figure 11-2. Also, show center lines to locate windows and doors.

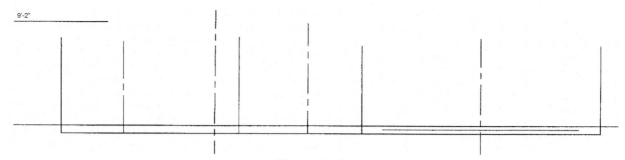

9'-2"

Figure 11-2
Sketch Outside Dimensions

Step 4.   Sketch the roof as shown in Figure 11-3. Notice the numbers shown above the
diagonal lines of the roof (Figure 11-1). These represent run and rise dimensions. Run
is the horizontal dimension (in this case, 12) and rise is the vertical dimension (6). This
means that for each 12 feet in the horizontal direction, the roof will rise 6 feet. Be sure your
run/rise is 12/6.

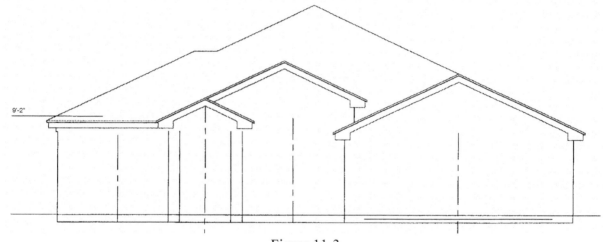

9'-2"

Figure 11-3
Sketch the Roof

Step 5.   Locate windows and doors, sketch them in place as shown in Figure 11-4, and
add details under the eaves of the roof. Dimensions from the floor plan must be used
to place the windows and doors in their correct locations.
Make sure that your lines are the correct weight and are of even width and darkness.
Try to match the thickness and darkness of the existing lines.
Step 6.   Sketch other details and add notes as shown in Figure 11-4.

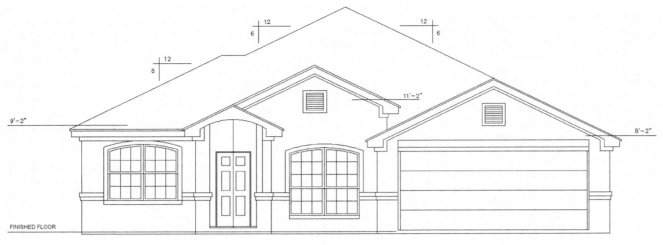

Figure 11-4
Sketch Other Details and Add Notes

Step 7. Compare your sketch with Figure 11-5 and make any necessary corrections.

Step 8. Fill in the date, class, and your name with your best lettering.

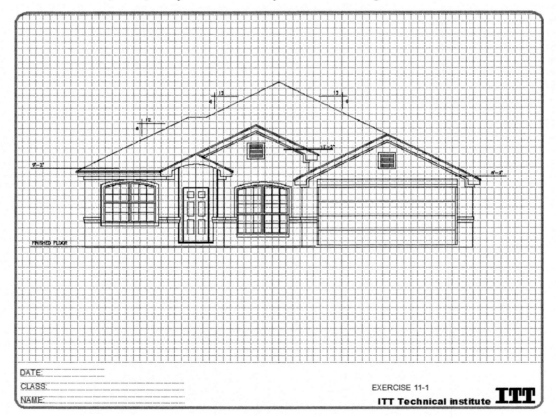

Figure 11-5
Exercise 11-1 Complete

EXERCISE 11-2

Step 1. Complete Exercise 11-2 using the specifications shown in Figure 11-7 and the sheet labeled
Exercise 11-2.

Step 2. Using the sketching and construction techniques presented in this chapter, complete the sketch
using the grid lines and the existing sketch lines as a guide.

Make sure that your lines are the correct weight and are of even width and darkness.

Try to match the thickness and darkness of the existing lines.

Step 3. Compare your sketch to Figure 11-7 and make any necessary corrections.

Step 4. Fill in the date, class and your name with your best lettering.

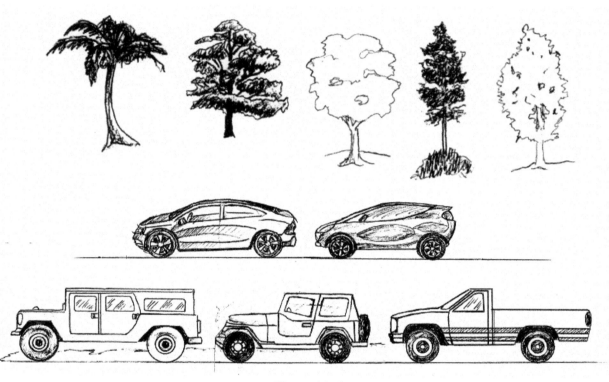

Figure 11-6
Sketches of Cars and Trees for Exercise 11-2

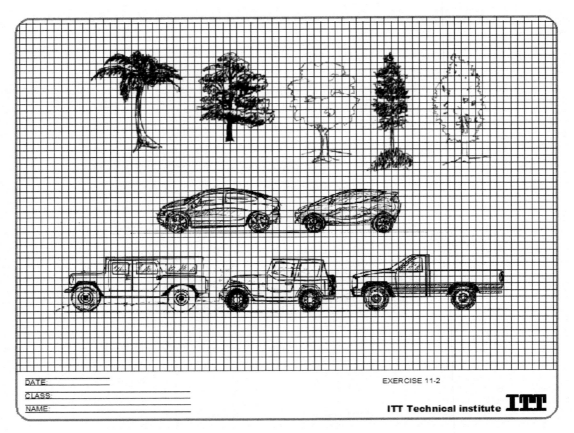

Figure 11-7
Exercise 11-2 Complete

Figure 11-8
Specifications for Exercise 11-3

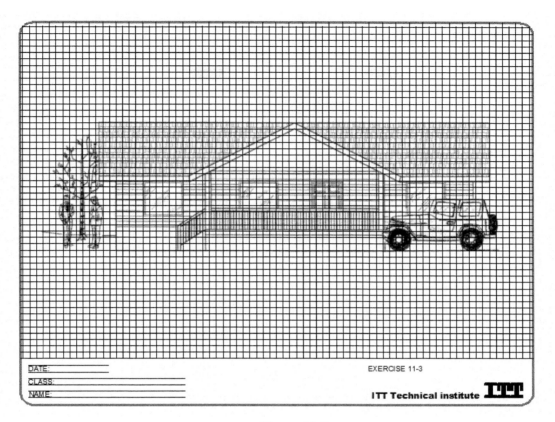

Figure 11-9

Exercise 11-3 Complete

EXERCISE 11-3

Step 1. Complete Exercise 11-3 using the specifications described in Figure 11-9 and the sheet labeled Exercise 11-3. Use the sketching technique described in Exercise 11-1. Locate the windows, doors, and all the other

items shown in Figure 11-8. Use the sizes shown in Figure 11-9.

Step 2. Using the sketching and construction techniques presented in this chapter, complete the sketch using the grid lines and the existing sketch lines as a guide.

Make sure that your lines are the correct weight and are of even width and darkness.

Try to match the thickness and darkness of the existing lines.

Step 3. Check your sketch and make any necessary corrections.

Step 4. Fill in the date, class, and your name with your best lettering.

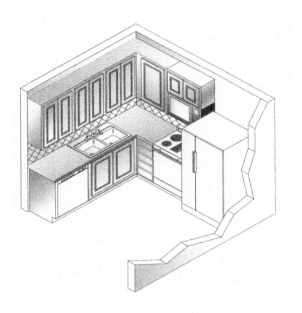

Figure 11-10
Isometric View of Exercise 11-4

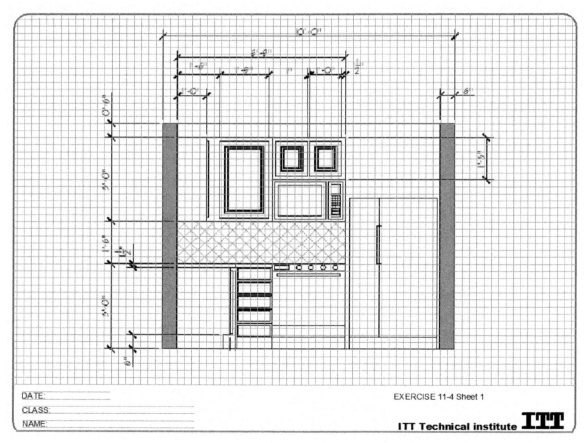

Figure 11-11

Exercise 11-4, Sheet 1, Complete

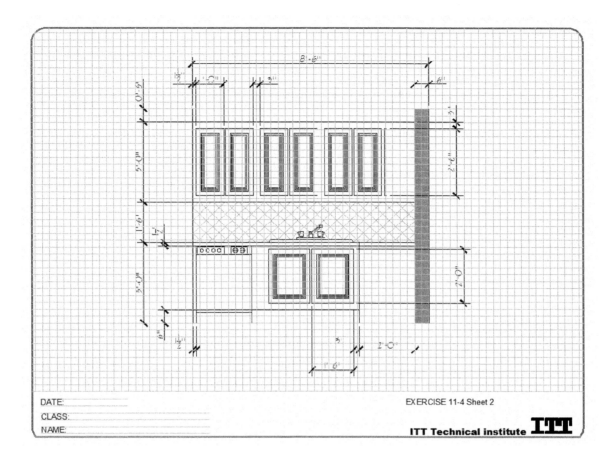

Figure 11-12
Exercise 11-4, Sheet 2, Complete

EXERCISE 11-4

Step 1. Complete Exercise 11-4 using the sizes shown in Figures 11-11 and 11-12. This is a two-page exercise, so you will need both of the exercise sheets for Exercise 11-4 from the back of your book.

Step 2. Using the sketching and construction techniques presented in this chapter, complete the sketch as two interior elevations using the grid lines and the existing sketch lines as a guide.
Make sure that your lines are the correct weight and are of even width and darkness.
Try to match the thickness and darkness of the existing lines.

Step 3. Check your sketches and make any necessary corrections.

Step 4. Fill in the date, class, and your name with your best lettering.

This chapter gives you the information and techniques to make sketches of elevations. These sketches consist of interior elevations with people and furniture, and exterior elevations with people, cars, and trees. Now you have the skills and information needed to make sketches of elevations accurately and correctly.

_____**REVIEW QUESTIONS**

Circle the best answer.

1. Which of the following that is on the floor plan will not appear on the front elevation?
   a. Chimney
   b. Front door
   c. Roof style
   d. Kitchen cabinet

2. Which of the following appears on the elevation of the house shown in Figure 11-1?
   a. Front door
   b. Back door
   c. Garage door
   d. Chimney

3. Run and rise refers to which of the following?
   a. Roof
   b. Finished floor height
   c. Finished ceiling height
   d. Siding

4. Which of the following will provide an incline of 45 degrees?
   a. Run 6 rise 12
   b. Run 12 rise 6
   c. Run 6 rise 6
   d. Run 6 rise 9

5. The distance from the left corner of the front of the house in Figure 11-1 (inside surface of the brick) to the center of the front door is:
   a. 4'-10"
   b. 12'-7"
   c. 9'-9"
   d. 15'-0"

6. The living room width measures 15'-0".
   a. True b. False

7. It is not necessary to make sure that the location of windows and doors on the elevation are the same as on the floor plan.
   a. True b. False

8. The garage measures approximately 24'-0".
   a. True b. False

9. There are two windows in the nook.
   a. True b. False

10. Exterior elevations do not show interior details.
    a. True b. False

Matching

Write the number of the correct answer on the line.

a.____ Shows the fireplace

b.____ Used to identify the angle of the roof

c.____ Used to give information for an exterior elevation

d.____ Shows the front door

e.____ Used to show the size of the garage

1. Floor plan

2. Exterior elevations

3. Interior elevations

4. Dimensions

5. Run and rise

General Questions

1. What items are often shown on interior elevations?

2. Why do you need exterior elevations?

3. Why do you need interior elevations?

4. When would you need to use a floor plan to make an exterior elevation?

5. Where could you sketch elevations and how detailed should they be?

12 Sketching Perspective Scenes

OBJECTIVES

After completing this chapter, you will be able to:

> Correctly sketch exterior perspective scenes.
> Correctly sketch interior perspective scenes.
> Correctly add shading to a perspective scene
> Correctly answer questions regarding sketching perspectives.

INTRODUCTION

The three perspective sketching methods, one-point, two-point, and three-point, were introduced in Chapter 6. In this chapter you will sketch interior perspective scenes with shading. You also will sketch exterior perspective scenes with shading.

We will begin with a review of one-point and two-point perspective methods (Figures 12-1 and 12-2). A discussion of how to add shading to the scenes you create will follow that. You will then proceed to create the perspective scenes with shading.

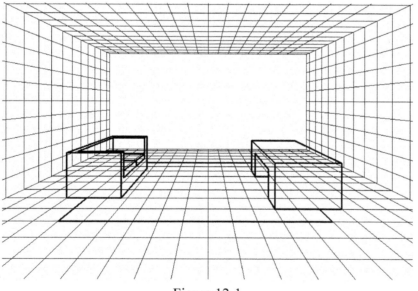

Figure 12-1
One-Point Perspective Example

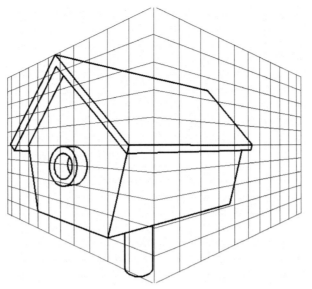

Figure 12-2
Two-Point Perspective Example

ONE-POINT PERSPECTIVE

This a method in which the vertical and horizontal axes of the object being viewed are parallel to the picture plane and the third axis appears at a right angle to the picture plane as shown in Figures 12-3 and 12-4.

Sketching an exterior scene using one-point perspective (Figures 12-3 and 12-4)

Step 1. Sketch a **horizon line** about one fourth of the way down the page. Mark a spot slightly to the left of the middle of the line to establish the **vanishing point**.

Step 2. Sketch the scene as shown in Figure 12-3. You will have to draw a rectangular box to locate the centers of the ellipses that form the cylinder shown on the right.

Step 3. Add the figure from Chapter 7 and the tree from Chapter 11. Clean up the cylinder and add lines to indicate that it is round.

Step 4. Clean up any features that need it and complete the sketch as shown in Figure 12-4.

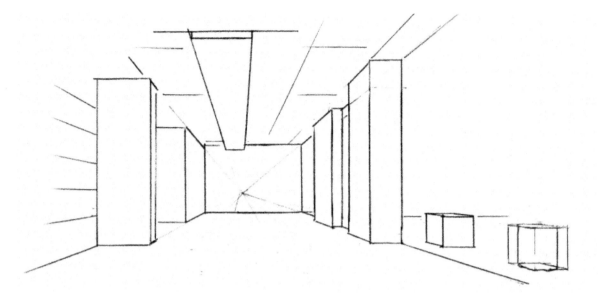

Figure 12-3
One-Point Perspective Interior View
Part 1

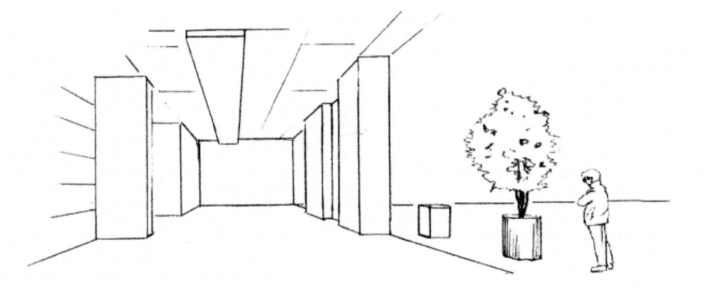

Figure 12-4
One-Point Perspective Interior View
Part 2

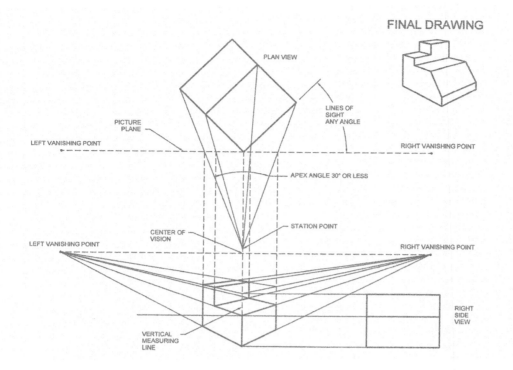

Figure 12-5
Elements of Two-Point Perspective

BASIC ELEMENTS

The basics of perspective sketching are shown in Figure 12-5. They are:

1. The object being viewed.

2. The observer's eye, the position of the observer's eye, called the station point (SP).

3. The plane of projection, a drawing surface or a plane on which a picture of the object being viewed is projected. In perspective sketching this is called the picture plane (PP). The location of the picture plane plays an important part in perspective sketching.

4. Imaginary lines of sight (to all points on the object), the lines of sight that pierce the plane of projection. They produce intersection points that when connected together make the perspective sketch.

5. Center of vision (CV), a point on the horizon line opposite the observer's eye.

6. Vanishing point (VP), a point at which receding parallel lines meet.

7. Horizon line, an imaginary line on the eye level of the observer. The center of vision— the right and left vanishing points in two and three-point perspective fall on this line.

TWO-POINT PERSPECTIVE
Sketching an exterior scene using two-point perspective (Figures 12-6 and 12-7)

Step 1. Sketch a **horizon line** about one fourth of the way down the page. Sketch lines to establish the **vanishing points** similar to Figure 12-5. Your lines of sight will be above and below the horizon line so that you will be able to make the sketch shown in Figure 12-7.

Step 2. Sketch light lines from the top and bottom corners to the vanishing point.

Step 3. Sketch the two buildings and the other features as shown in Figure 12-6. Sketch lines from the corners of the lower window in the building on the left to locate the center of the window. Use a similar method to locate the upper windows and the lower window in the building on the right.

Step 4. Add go marks in the windows to represent glass or use another method that you like better.

Step 5. Add figures from Chapter 7 and trees from Chapter 11 and complete the sketch as shown in

Figure 12-7.

Figure 12-6
Sketching a Two-Point Perspective Exterior Scene, Part 1

Figure 12-7
Sketching a Two-Point Perspective Exterior Scene, Part 2

Sketching an exterior scene using one-point perspective (Figures 12-8 and 12-9)

Step 1. Sketch a **horizon line** about one fourth of the way down the page. Mark a spot slightly to the left of the middle of the line to establish the **vanishing point**.

Step 2. Sketch the three buildings and the other features as shown in Figure 12-8. Sketch lines beneath the balloons to form boxes as shown in Figure 12-8. These boxes will be used to sketch and locate the ellipses that form the bottom part of the balloon that carries people.

Step 3. Add go marks in the windows to represent glass or use another method that you like better.

Step 4. When you sketch the windows of the receding surface of the building on the right, use the method of sketching the first two vertical lines, sketching a line through the center of the second line from the lower corner of the first line, and sketching the third line and continue locating lines in the same manner.

Step 5. Add go marks in the windows to represent glass or use another method that you like better and complete the sketch as shown in Figure 12-9.

Figure 12-8
Sketching a One-Point Perspective Exterior Scene
Part 1

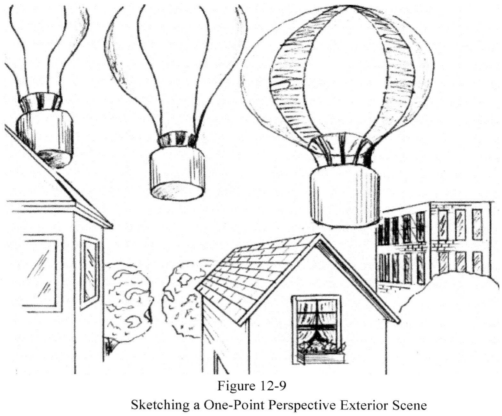

Figure 12-9
Sketching a One-Point Perspective Exterior Scene
Part 2

SHADING

Shading will not be necessary in many of the sketches you will make, but it will be important to some of your clients. Therefore, you need to have a mastery of at least a simple method of applying shading to objects. The basics of perspective shading are shown in Figures 12-10 through 12-18. They are:

Figure 12-10
Flat Areas on a Rectangular Box

1.   Flat areas as shown in Figure 12-10. Notice that dark areas are placed next to light areas. Although there are many sources of light and ways to apply shading, do not be too concerned about where the light is coming from. Just try to keep dark areas next to light areas and vary the areas to produce a pleasing appearance.

Figure 12-11
Holes in a Square Box

2.   Holes as shown in Figure 12-11. Notice that there is a larger area of dark on one side of the hole than the other. This gives the hole a more natural and pleasing appearance.

Figure 12-12
Cylindrical Areas on a Hex-Head Fastener

3.   Cylindrical area as shown in Figure 12-12. The same method of using a larger area of dark on one side of the cylinder as in the hole of Figure 12-11 is employed here. Notice how the flat ellipse is shaded on the top of the hex head. This method is acceptable, but you may find that the flat top of Figure 12-10 will be a better choice for some applications.

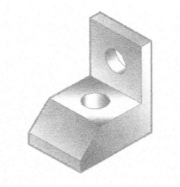

Figure 12-13
Flat Areas and Holes in an Object with Several Areas

4.   Figure 12-13 shows the top two shading techniques applied to an object with several areas. Notice how areas of dark are placed next to light areas.

Figure 12-14
Shaded Spheres

5.   Spherical areas are shown in Figure 12-14. Several sizes of spheres are shown with varying patterns. Notice that a dark area is placed on one area of the sphere in every case.

6.   Figures 12-15 through 12-18 show examples of scenes that have been shaded. Refer to all these figures for information on the methods you can use to shade your sketches. You also may want to assemble a collection of pictures that have been shaded using reflected light and other sources that produce pleasing and effective sketches.

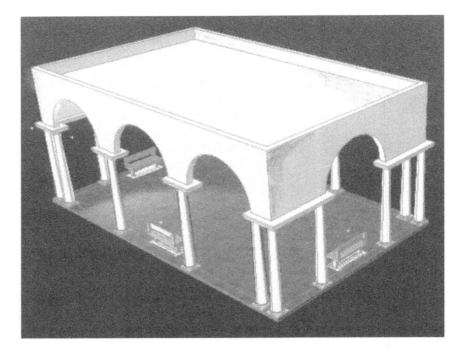

Figure 12-15
Shading Example

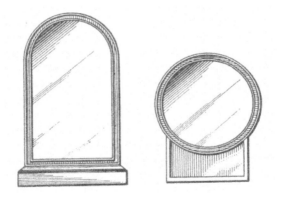

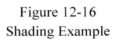

Figure 12-16
Shading Example

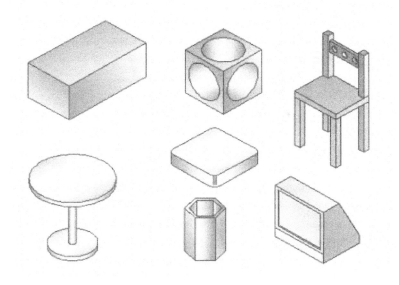

Figure 12-17
Shading Example

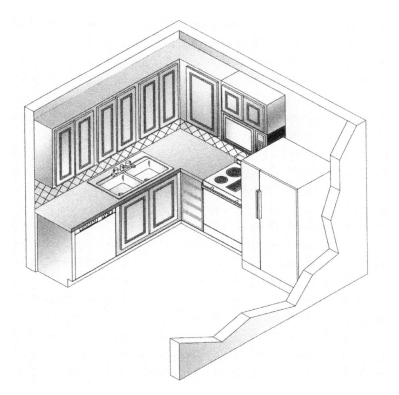

Figure 12-18
Shading Example

Figure 12-19
Exercise 12-1 Complete

EXERCISE 12-1

Step 1. Complete Exercise 12-1 using the specifications shown in Figure 12-19 and the sheet labeled Exercise 12-1.

Step 2. Using the sketching and construction techniques presented in this chapter, complete the sketch using the existing sketch lines as a guide.

Make sure that your lines are the correct weight and are of even width and darkness.

Try to match the thickness and darkness of the existing lines.

Step 3. Compare your sketch to Figure 12-19 and make any necessary corrections.

Step 4. Fill in the date, class, and your name with your best lettering.

Figure 12-20
Exercise 12-2 Complete

EXERCISE 12-2

Step 1. Complete Exercise 12-2 using the specifications shown in Figure 12-20 and the sheet labeled Exercise 12-2.

Step 2. Using the sketching and construction techniques presented in this chapter, complete the sketch using the existing sketch lines as a guide.

Make sure that your lines are the correct weight and are of even width and darkness.

Try to match the thickness and darkness of the existing lines.

Step 3. Add shading as shown in Figures 12-10 through 12-18.

Step 4. Compare your sketch to Figure 12-20 and make any necessary corrections.

Step 5. Fill in the date, class, and your name with your best lettering.

Figure 12-21
Exercise 12-3 Complete

EXERCISE 12-3

Step 1. Complete Exercise 12-3 using the specifications shown in Figure 12-21 and the sheet labeled Exercise 12-3.

Step 2. Using the sketching and construction techniques presented in this chapter, complete the sketch using the existing sketch lines as a guide.

Make sure that your lines are the correct weight and are of even width and darkness.

Try to match the thickness and darkness of the existing lines.

Step 3. Add shading as shown in Figures 12-10 through 12-18.

Step 4. Compare your sketch to Figure 12-21 and make any necessary corrections.

Step 5. Fill in the date, class, and your name with your best lettering.

Figure 12-22
Exercise 12-4 Complete

EXERCISE 12-4

Step 1. Complete Exercise 12-4 using the specifications shown in Figure 12-22 and the sheet labeled Exercise 12-4.

Step 2. Using the sketching and construction techniques presented in this chapter, complete the sketch using the existing sketch lines as a guide.

Make sure that your lines are the correct weight and are of even width and darkness.

Try to match the thickness and darkness of the existing lines.

Step 3. Add shading as shown in Figures 12-10 through 12-18.

Step 4. Compare your sketch to Figure 12-22 and make any necessary corrections.

Step 5. Fill in the date, class, and your name with your best lettering.

Figure 12-23
Photo for Exercise 12-5

EXERCISE 12-5

Step 1. Make a sketch for Exercise 12-5 using the photograph in Figure 12-23. Your book has two sheets for this exercise, one with the photograph and the other without it. Trace the photograph onto the blank sheet as a sketch.

Step 2. Using the sketching and construction techniques presented in this chapter, complete the sketch using the existing sketch lines as a guide.
Make sure that your lines are the correct weight and are of even width and darkness.
Try to match the thickness and darkness of the existing lines.

Step 3. Add shading as shown in Figures 12-10 through 12-18.

Step 4. Compare your sketch to Figure 12-23 and make any necessary corrections.

Step 5. Fill in the date, class, and your name with your best lettering.

Figure 12-24
Photo for Exercise 12-6

EXERCISE 12-6

Step 1. Make a sketch for Exercise 12-6 using the photograph in Figure 12-24. Your book has two sheets for this exercise, one with the photograph and the other without it. Trace the photograph onto the blank sheet as a sketch.

Step 2. Using the sketching and construction techniques presented in this chapter, complete the sketch using the existing sketch lines as a guide.

Make sure that your lines are the correct weight and are of even width and darkness.

Try to match the thickness and darkness of the existing lines.

Step 3. Add shading as shown in Figures 12-10 through 12-18.

Step 4. Compare your sketch to Figure 12-24 and make any necessary corrections.

Step 5. Fill in the date, class, and your name with your best lettering.

Figure 12-25
Photo for Exercise 12-7

EXERCISE 12-7

Step 1. Make a sketch for Exercise 12-7 using the photograph in Figure 12-25. Your book has two sheets for this exercise, one with the photograph and the other without it. Trace the photograph onto the blank sheet as a sketch.

Step 2. Using the sketching and construction techniques presented in this chapter, complete the sketch using the existing sketch lines as a guide.

Make sure that your lines are the correct weight and are of even width and darkness.

Try to match the thickness and darkness of the existing lines.

Step 3. Add shading as shown in Figures 12-10 through 12-18.

Step 4. Compare your sketch to Figure 12-25 and make any necessary corrections.

Step 5. Fill in the date, class, and your name with your best lettering.

DATE: _____

CLASS: _____

NAME: _____

ITT Technical institute **ITT**

Figure 12-26
Photo for Exercise 12-8

EXERCISE 12-8

Step 1. Make a sketch for Exercise 12-8 using the photograph in Figure 12-26. Your book has two sheets for this exercise, one with the photograph and the other without it. Trace the photograph onto the blank sheet as a sketch.

Step 2. Using the sketching and construction techniques presented in this chapter, complete the sketch using the existing sketch lines as a guide.

Make sure that your lines are the correct weight and are of even width and darkness.

Try to match the thickness and darkness of the existing lines.

Step 3. Add shading as shown in Figures 12-10 through 12-18.

Step 4. Compare your sketch to Figure 12-26 and make any necessary corrections.

Step 5. Fill in the date, class, and your name with your best lettering.

This chapter gives you the information and techniques to make sketches of scenes with and without shading. These sketches consist of interior scenes with people and furniture, and exterior scenes with people, cars, and trees. Now you have the skills and information needed to make sketches of scenes accurately and correctly.

_____REVIEW QUESTIONS

Circle the best answer.

1. Which of the following is NOT one of the basic elements of perspective sketching?
   a. Object being viewed
   b. Center of vision
   c. Vanishing points
   d. Go marks

2. Which of the following is used to give shading a pleasing appearance?
   a. Light areas next to light areas
   b. Dark areas next to dark areas
   c. Light areas next to dark areas
   d. No shading at all

3. On which of the following are the vanishing points located?
   a. Vanishing line
   b. Ground line
   c. Vertical measuring line
   d. Horizon line

4. Which of the following is the most difficult to draw?
   a. One-point perspective
   b. Two-point perspective
   c. Three-point perspective
   d. None is more difficult than the others.

5. Which of the following is used to represent glass?
   a. Solid shading with no variation
   b. Go marks
   c. Nothing
   d. Several lines of the same length

6. Cylinders never require shading.
   a. True   b. False

7. Spheres are shaded with go marks.
   a. True   b. False

8. Two-point perspectives have two vanishing points.
   a. True   b. False

9. Locating equally spaced lines in a receding plane is done by sketching a line through the center of an existing line.
    a.   True   b.   False

10. Holes are shaded with one continuous area of the same density.
    a.   True   b.   False

Matching

Write the number of the correct answer on the line.

a.____ A point on the horizon line opposite the observer's eye 1.   Go marks

b.____ Used to represent glass   2.   Shading of flat planes

c.____ A point at which receding lines meet   3.   Shading of holes

d.____ Place dark areas next to light ones   4.   Vanishing point

e.____ A larger dark area on one side than the other
       side   5.   Center of vision

General Questions

1. What time of day is best for making sketches of perspective scenes?

2. Why do you need shading on sketches of perspective scenes?

3. Is shading effective and is it worth the time to do it?

4. When can you make sketches for perspective scenes?

5. Where could you sketch elevations and how detailed should they be?

Appendix

SECTION 2 EXERCISES

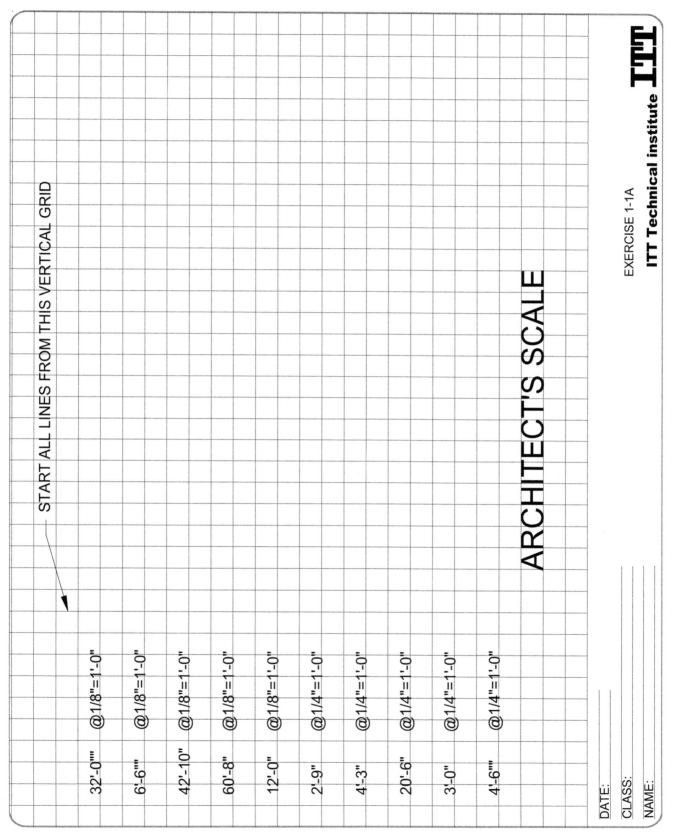

START ALL LINES FROM THIS VERTICAL GRID

ARCHITECT'S SCALE

32'-0""   @1/8"=1'-0"

6'-6""   @1/8"=1'-0"

42'-10"   @1/8"=1'-0"

60'-8"   @1/8"=1'-0"

12'-0"   @1/8"=1'-0"

2'-9"   @1/4"=1'-0"

4'-3"   @1/4"=1'-0"

20'-6"   @1/4"=1'-0"

3'-0"   @1/4"=1'-0"

4'-6""   @1/4"=1'-0"

DATE:

CLASS:

NAME:

EXERCISE 1-1A
ITT Technical institute

A–3

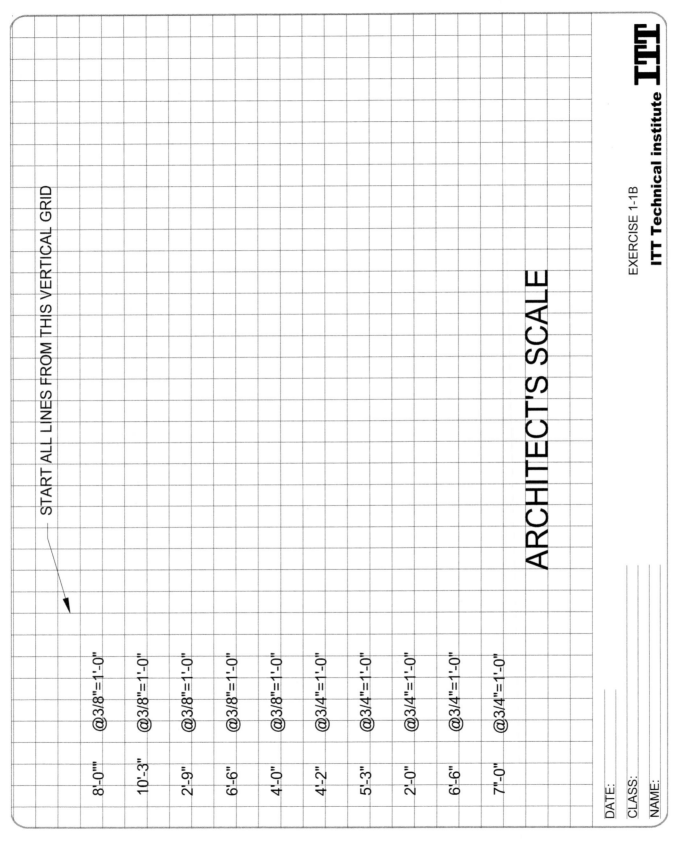

START ALL LINES FROM THIS VERTICAL GRID

8'-0"" @3/8"=1'-0"

10'-3" @3/8"=1'-0"

2'-9" @3/8"=1'-0"

6'-6" @3/8"=1'-0"

4'-0" @3/8"=1'-0"

4'-2" @3/4"=1'-0"

5'-3" @3/4"=1'-0"

2'-0" @3/4"=1'-0"

6'-6" @3/4"=1'-0"

7"-0" @3/4"=1'-0"

ARCHITECT'S SCALE

EXERCISE 1-1B

ITT Technical institute

ITT

DATE:

CLASS:

NAME:

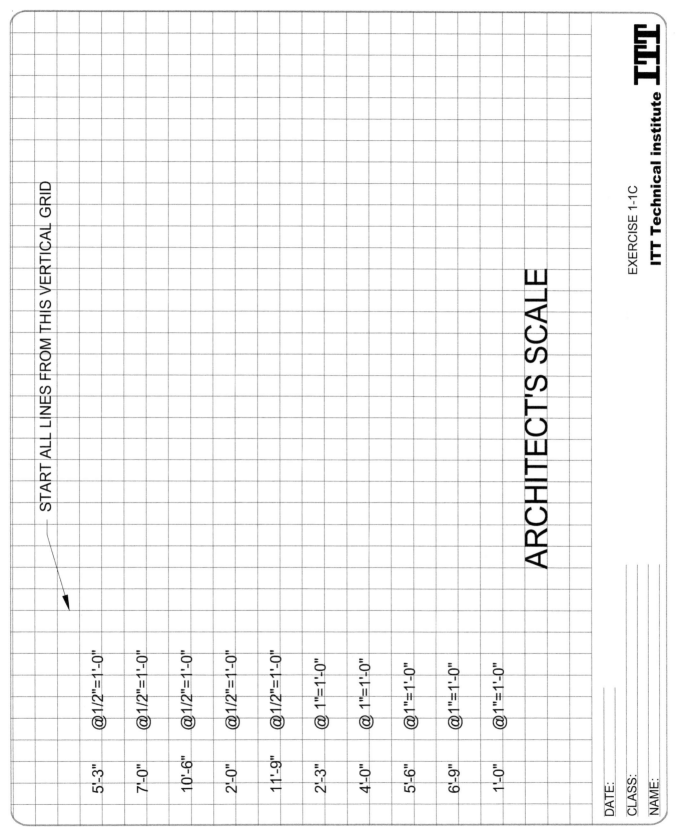

START ALL LINES FROM THIS VERTICAL GRID

ARCHITECT'S SCALE

5'-3"   @1/2"=1'-0"

7'-0"   @1/2"=1'-0"

10'-6"   @1/2"=1'-0"

2'-0"   @1/2"=1'-0"

11'-9"   @1/2"=1'-0"

2'-3"   @ 1"=1'-0"

4'-0"   @ 1"=1'-0"

5'-6"   @1"=1'-0"

6'-9"   @1"=1'-0"

1'-0"   @1"=1'-0"

EXERCISE 1-1C

ITT Technical institute

ITT

DATE:

CLASS:

NAME:

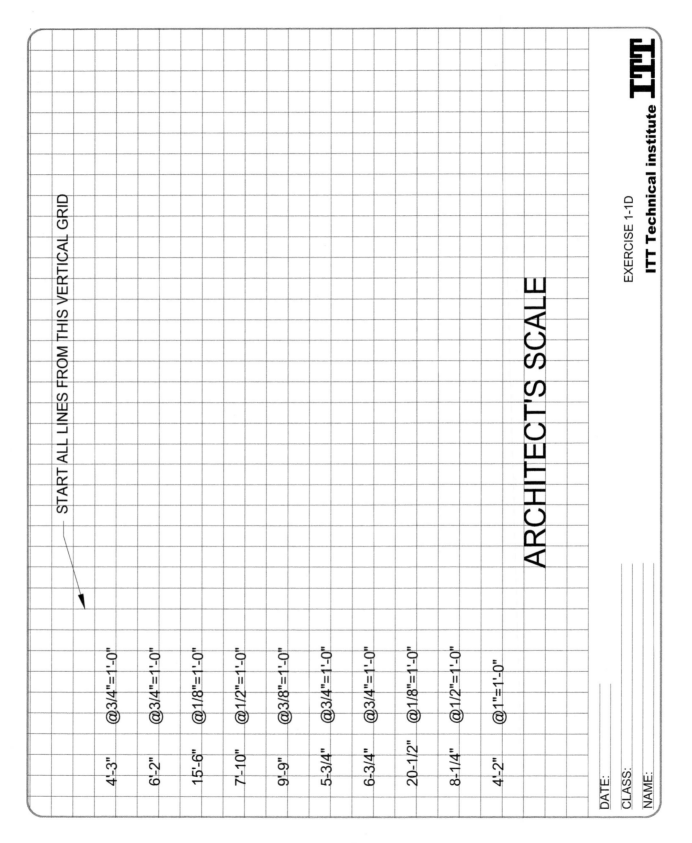

START ALL LINES FROM THIS VERTICAL GRID

ARCHITECT'S SCALE

4-3"   @3/4"=1'-0"

6'-2"   @3/4"=1'-0"

15'-6"   @1/8"=1'-0"

7'-10"   @1/2"=1'-0"

9'-9"   @3/8"=1'-0"

5-3/4"   @3/4"=1'-0"

6-3/4"   @3/4"=1'-0"

20-1/2"   @1/8"=1'-0"

8-1/4"   @1/2"=1'-0"

4'-2"   @1"=1'-0"

EXERCISE 1-1D

ITT Technical institute

ITT

DATE:

CLASS:

NAME:

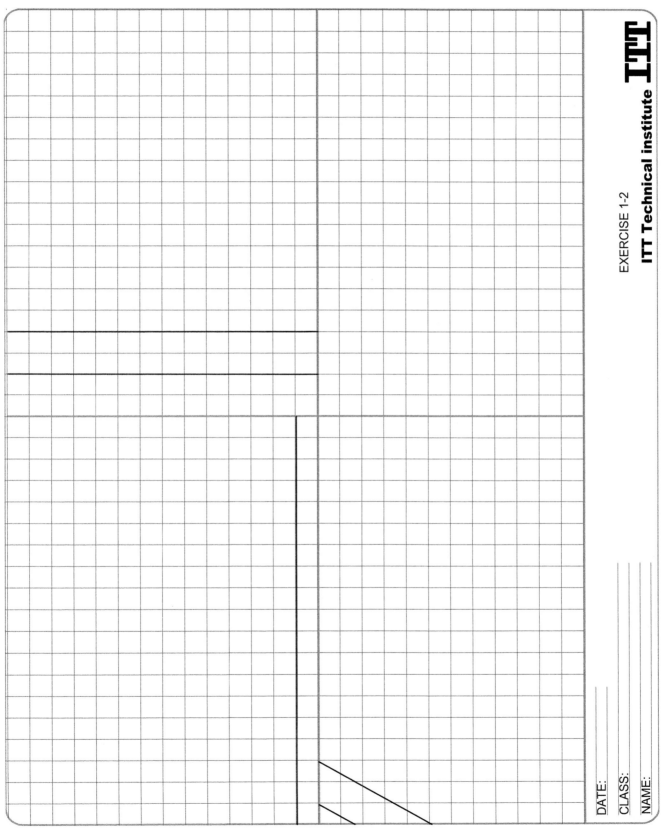

DATE:

CLASS:

NAME:

DATE:

CLASS:

NAME:

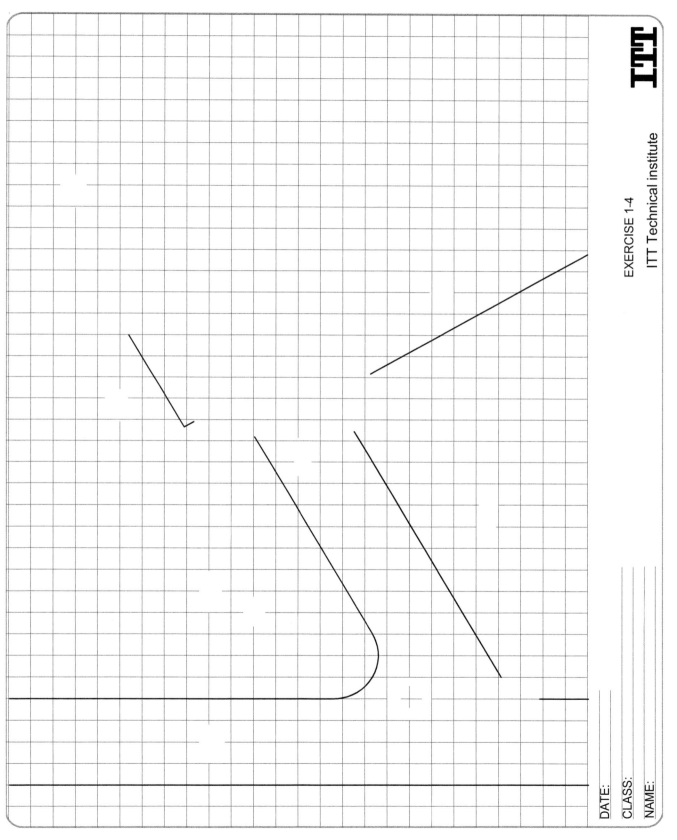

EXERCISE 1-4

ITT Technical institute

DATE:

CLASS:

NAME:

ITT

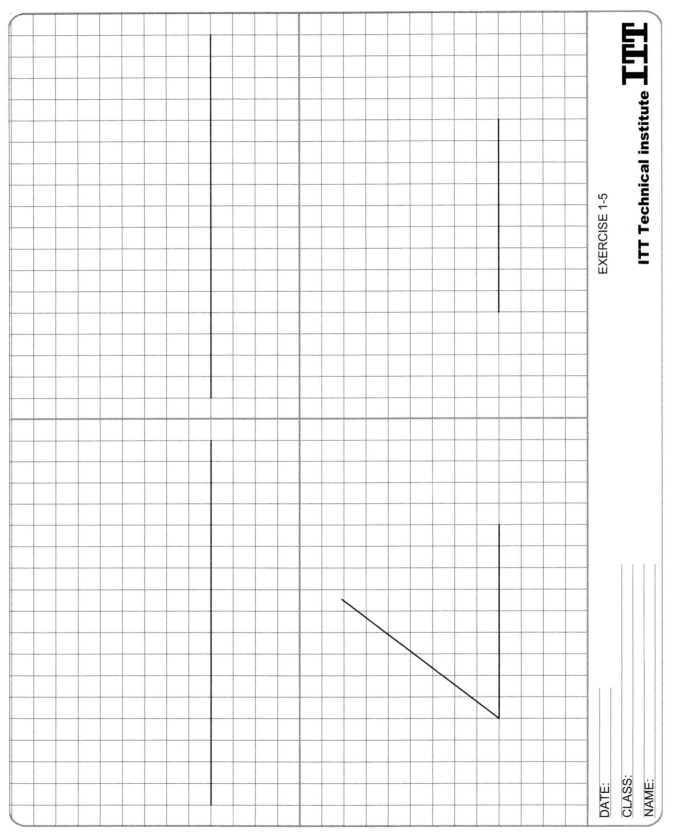

ITT Technical institute **ITT**

DATE: _____

CLASS: _____

NAME: _____

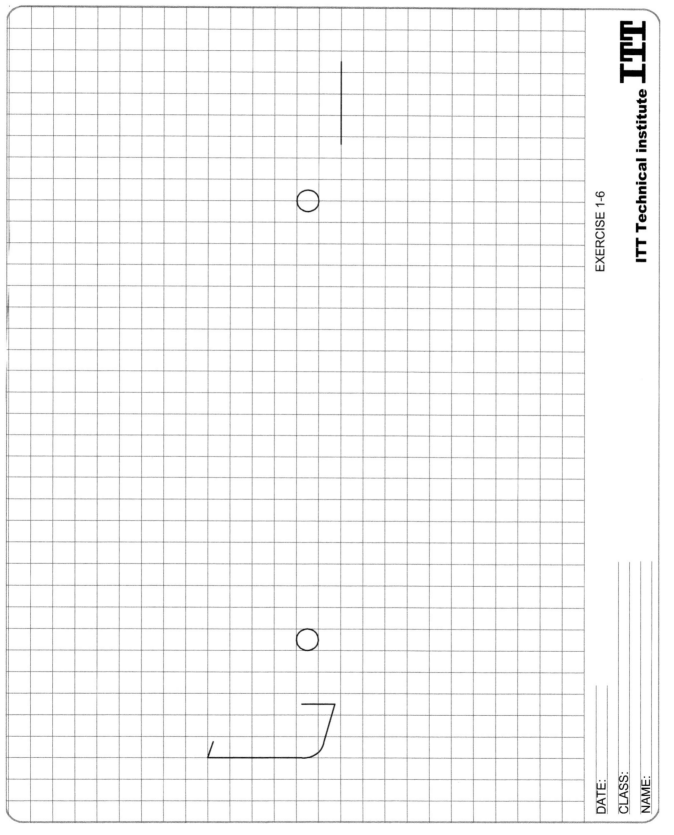

EXERCISE 1-6

ITT Technical institute

ITT

DATE:

CLASS:

NAME:

DRAW LETTERS AND NUMBERS 7 TIMES

A		B	
C		D	
E		F	
G		H	
I		J	
K		L	
M		N	
O		P	
Q		R	
S		T	
U		V	
W		X	
Y		Z	
1		2	
3		4	
5		6	
7		8	
9		0	

$1\frac{1}{2}$" $2\frac{3}{4}$"

5 TIMES   5 TIMES

GOOD LETTERING MAKES A GOOD SKETCH BETTER

G

G

G

G

5 TIMES

DATE: EXERCISE 2-1

CLASS:

NAME: **ITT Technical institute ITT**

DRAW LETTERS AND NUMBERS 7 TIMES

A	B
C	D
E	F
G	H
I	J
K	L
M	N
O	P
Q	R
S	T
U	V
W	X
Y	Z
1	2
3	4
5	6
7	8
9	0

$1\frac{1}{2}$" 5 TIMES

$2\frac{3}{4}$" 5 TIMES

GOOD LETTERING MAKES A GOOD SKETCH BETTER

G

G

G

G

5 TIMES

DATE:

CLASS:

NAME:

EXERCISE 2-2

ITT Technical institute ITT

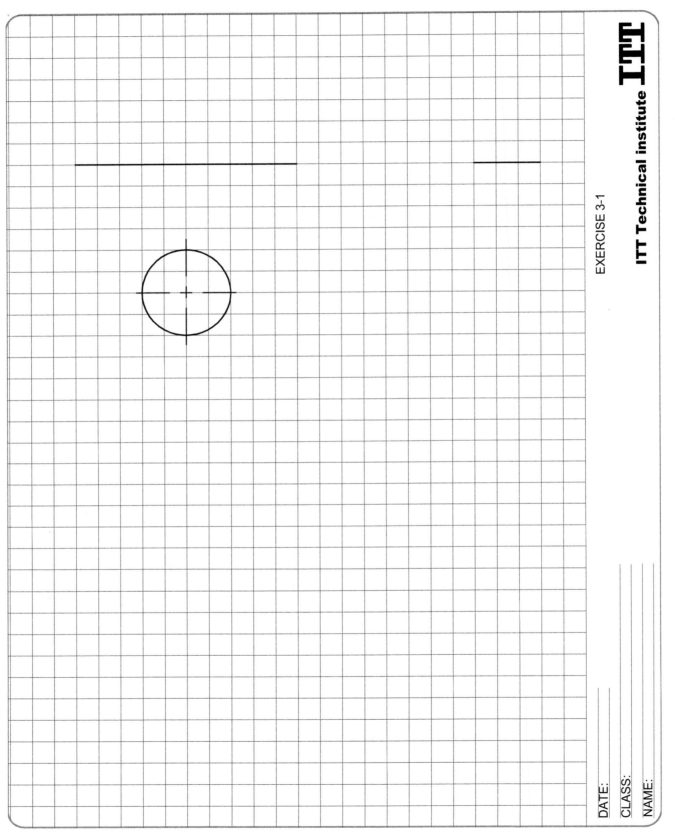

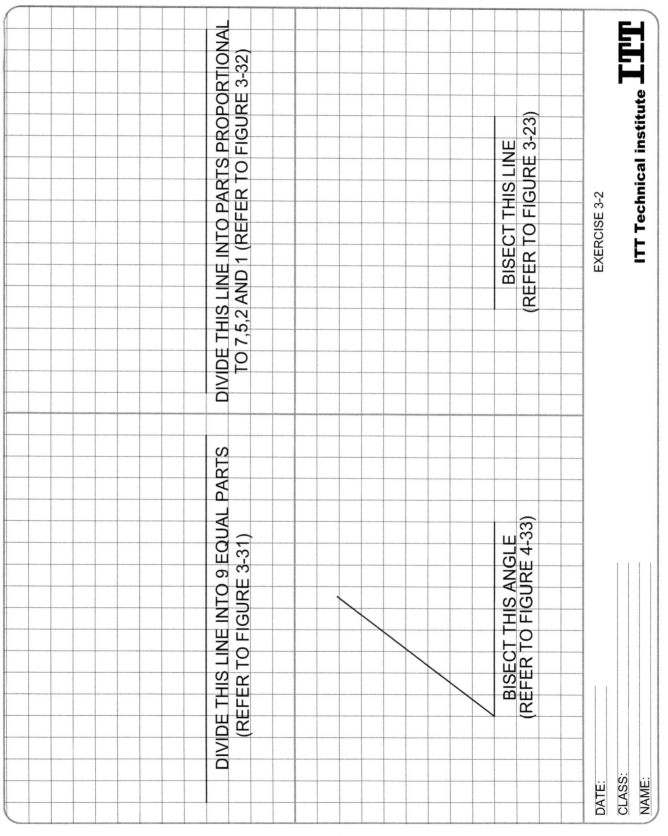

DIVIDE THIS LINE INTO PARTS PROPORTIONAL
TO 7,5,2 AND 1 (REFER TO FIGURE 3-32)

BISECT THIS LINE
(REFER TO FIGURE 3-23)

DIVIDE THIS LINE INTO 9 EQUAL PARTS
(REFER TO FIGURE 3-31)

BISECT THIS ANGLE
(REFER TO FIGURE 4-33)

EXERCISE 3-2

ITT Technical institute

DATE:

CLASS:

NAME:

A–15

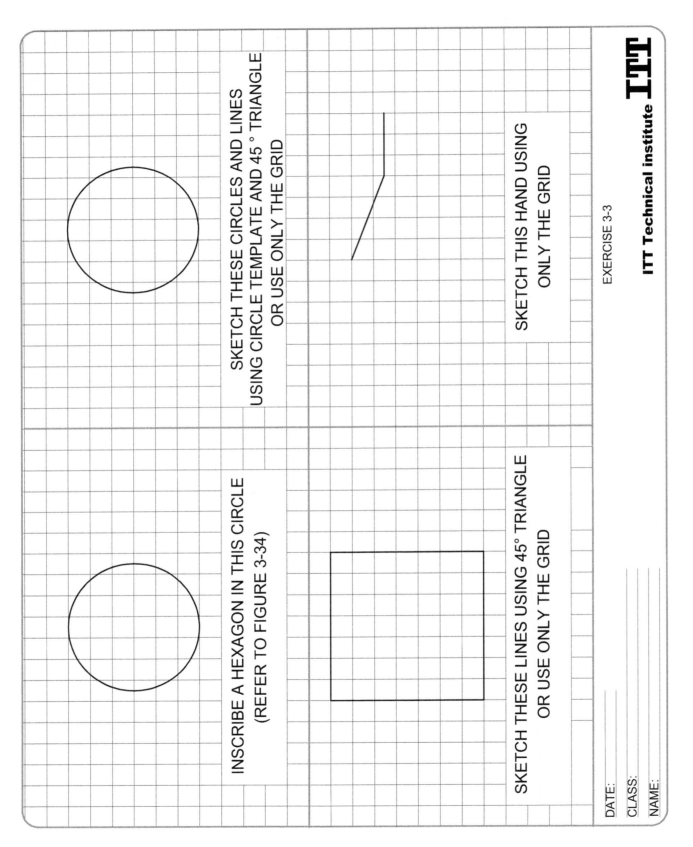

SKETCH THESE CIRCLES AND LINES
USING CIRCLE TEMPLATE AND 45° TRIANGLE
OR USE ONLY THE GRID

INSCRIBE A HEXAGON IN THIS CIRCLE
(REFER TO FIGURE 3-34)

SKETCH THIS HAND USING
ONLY THE GRID

SKETCH THESE LINES USING 45° TRIANGLE
OR USE ONLY THE GRID

EXERCISE 3-3

ITT Technical institute

DATE:
CLASS:
NAME:

A–16

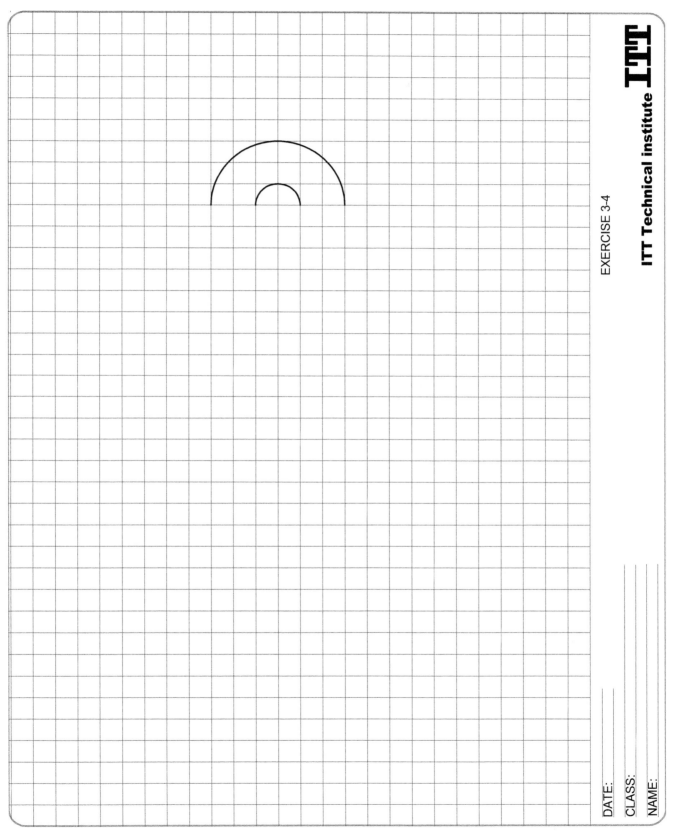

ITT Technical institute

ITT

DATE:

CLASS:

NAME:

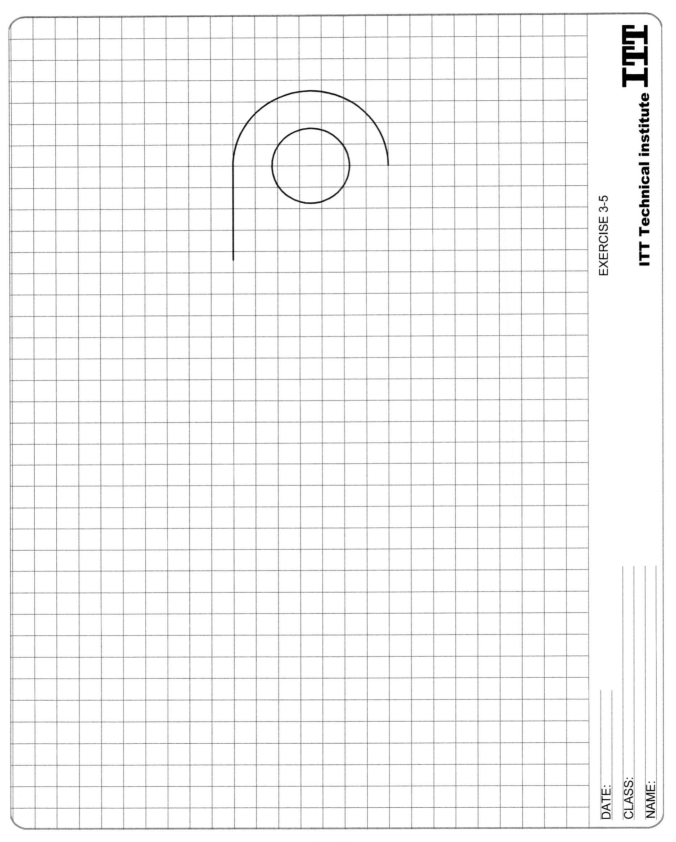

EXERCISE 3-5

ITT Technical institute

ITT

DATE:

CLASS:

NAME:

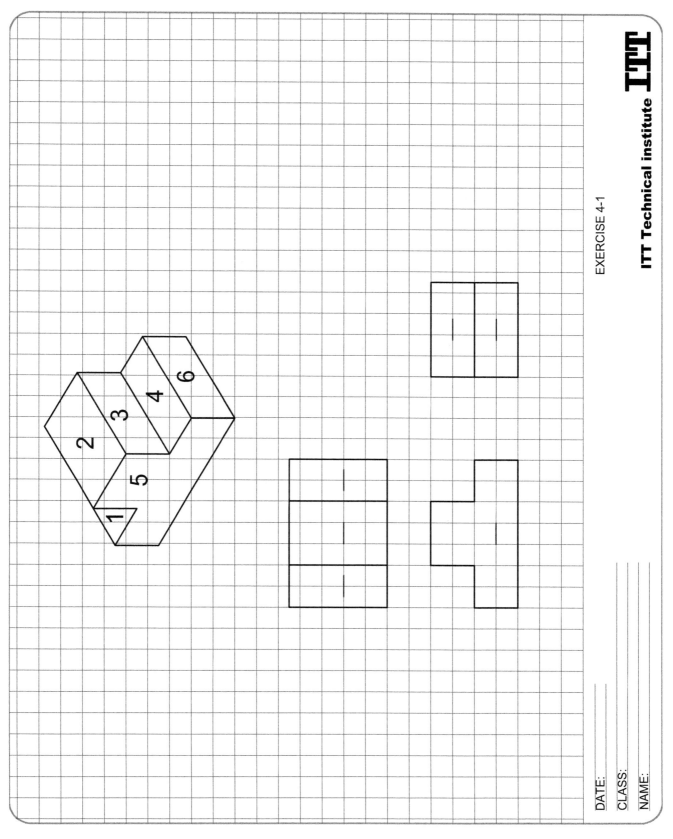

DATE:
CLASS:
NAME:

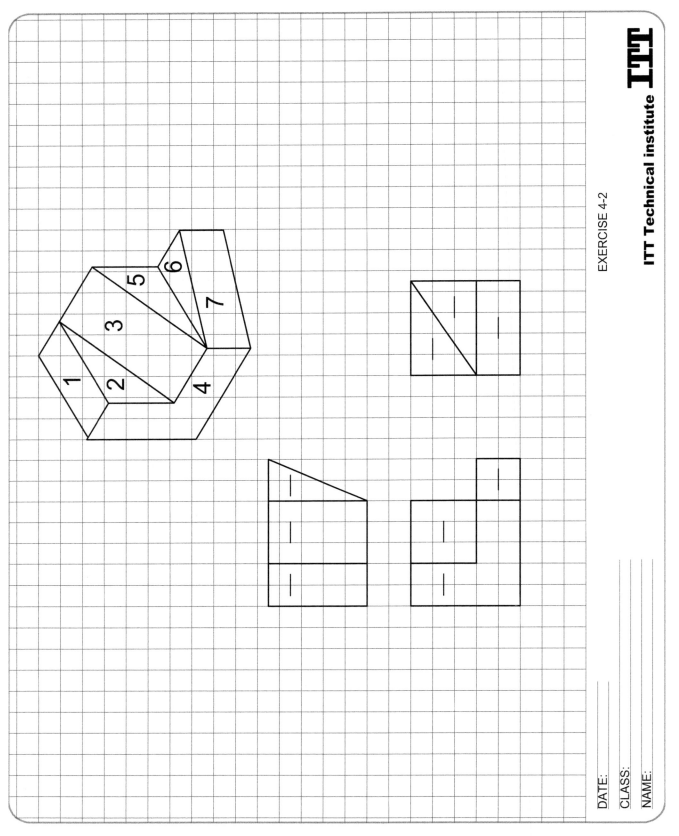

ITT Technical institute

ITT

DATE:

CLASS:

NAME:

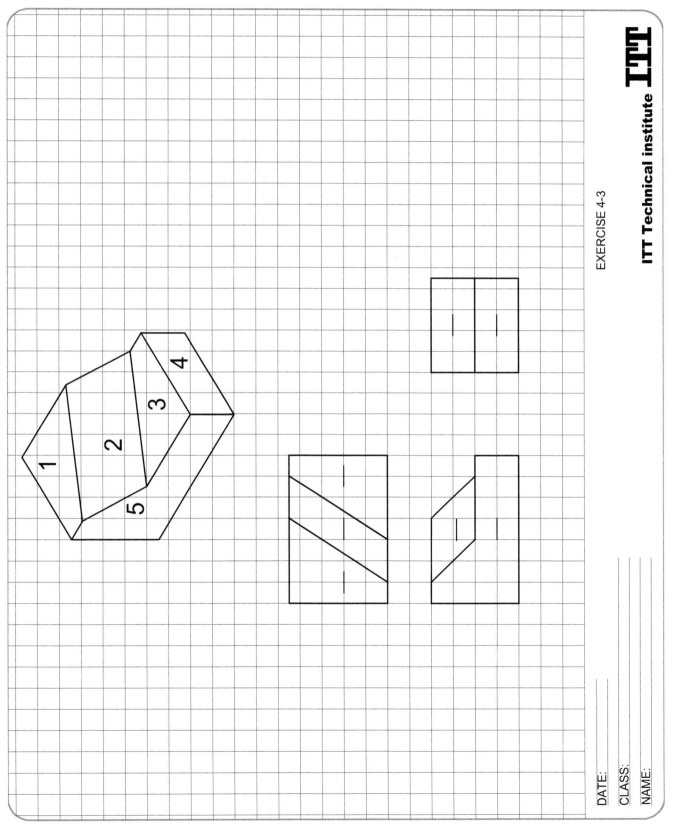

EXERCISE 4-3

ITT ITT Technical institute

DATE: _____

CLASS: _____

NAME: _____

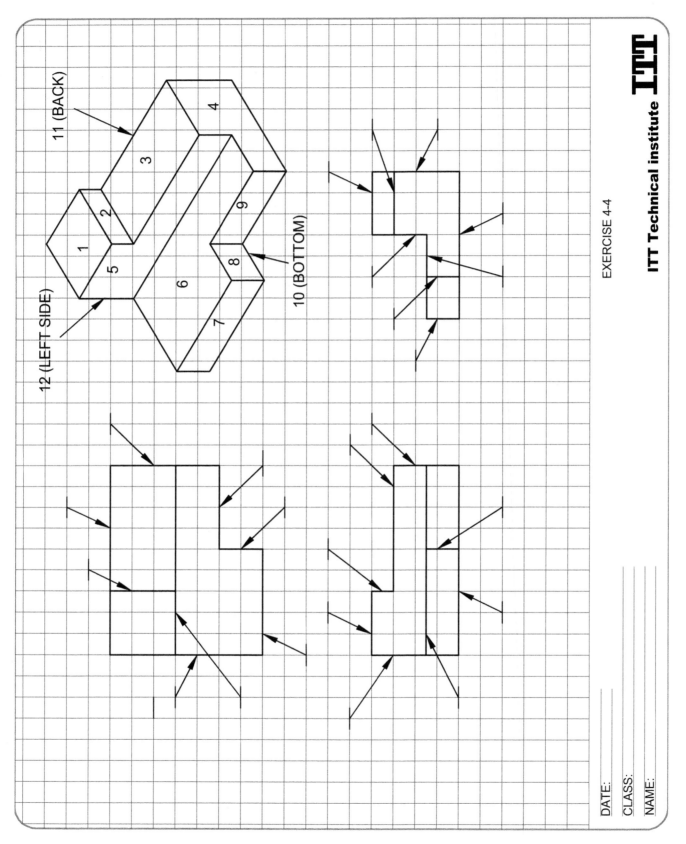

11 (BACK)

12 (LEFT SIDE)

10 (BOTTOM)

1
2
3
4
5
6
7
8
9

EXERCISE 4-4

ITT Technical institute

ITT

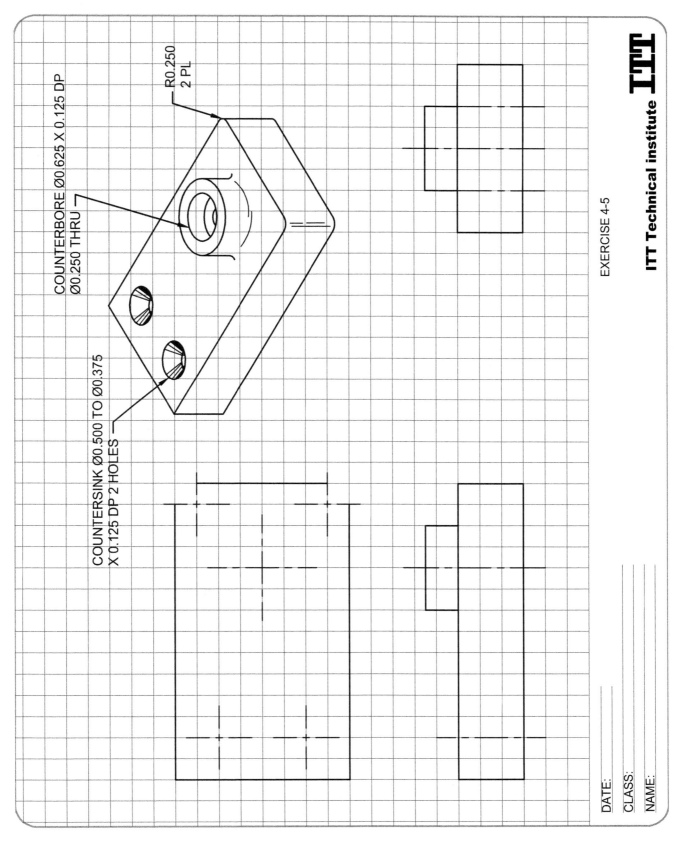

COUNTERBORE Ø0.625 X 0.125 DP
Ø0.250 THRU

R0.250
2 PL

COUNTERSINK Ø0.500 TO Ø0.375
X 0.125 DP 2 HOLES

EXERCISE 4-5

DATE:

CLASS:

NAME:

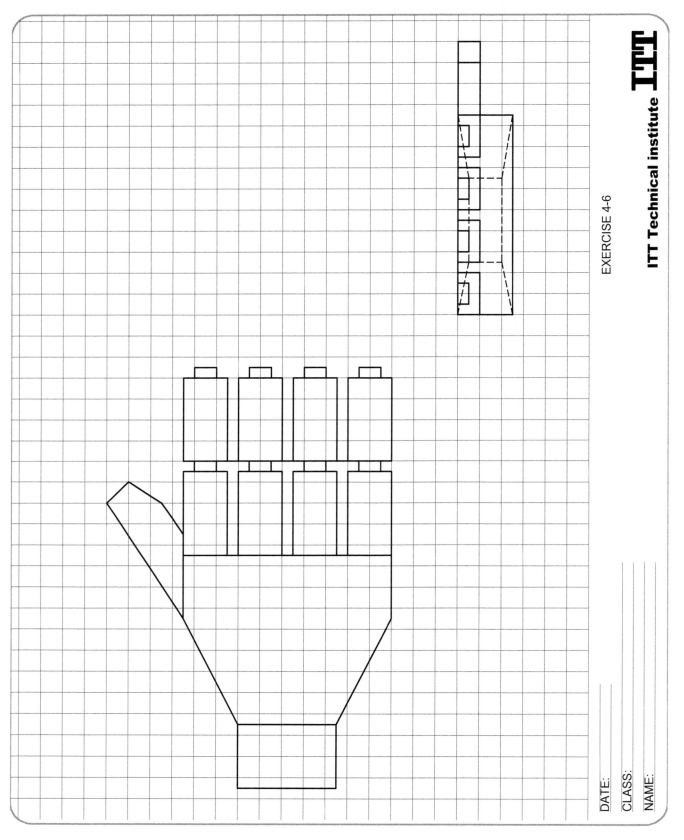

EXERCISE 4-6

ITT Technical institute

ITT

DATE:

CLASS:

NAME:

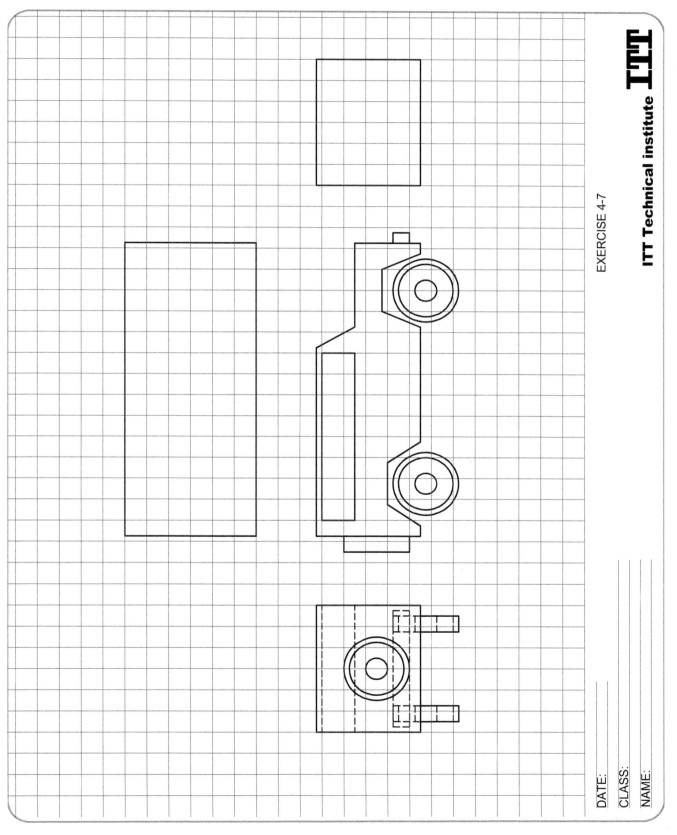

EXERCISE 4-7

ITT Technical institute

ITT

DATE:

CLASS:

NAME:

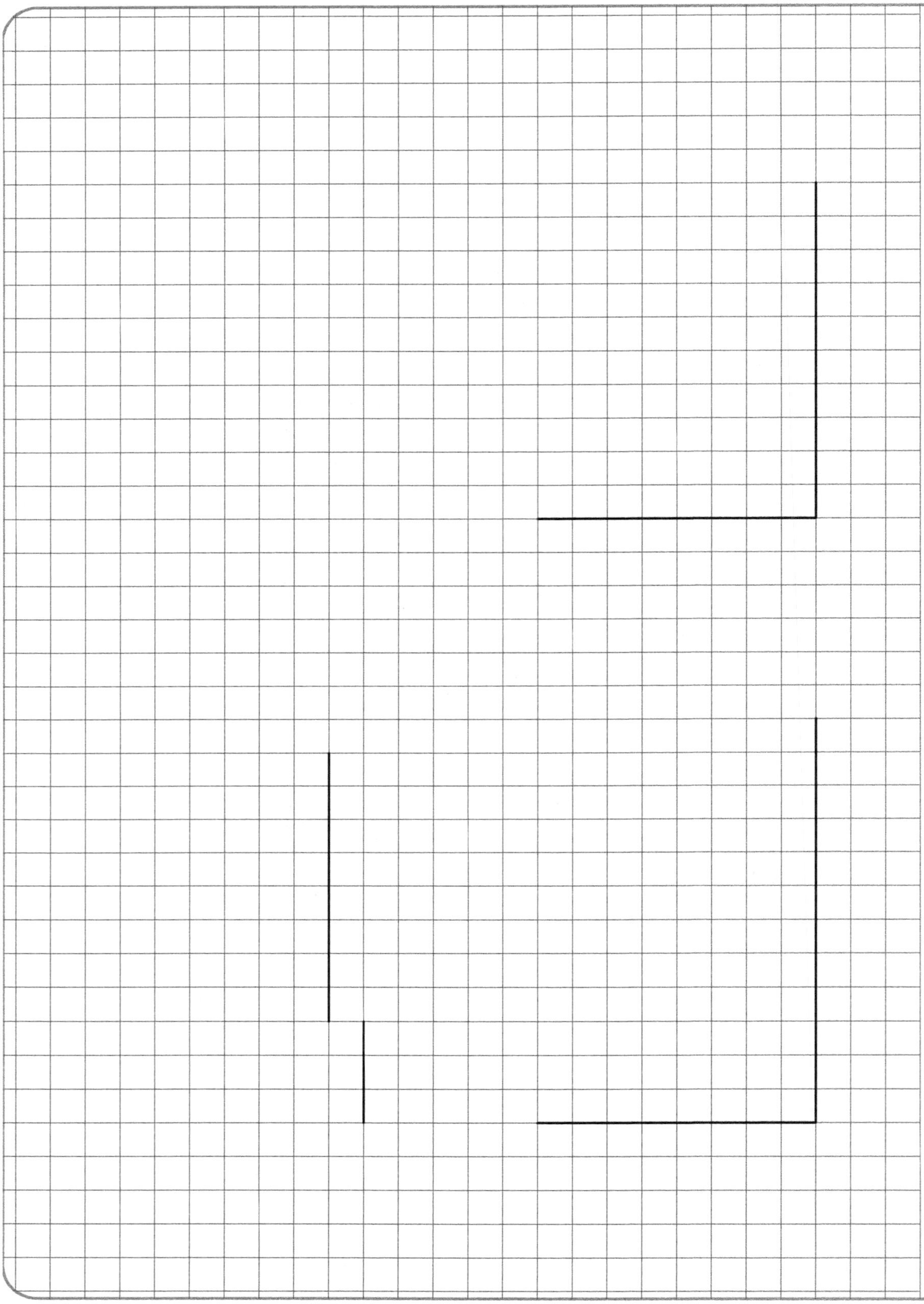

EXERCISE 4-8

ITT Technical institute

DATE: ________

CLASS: ________

NAME: ________

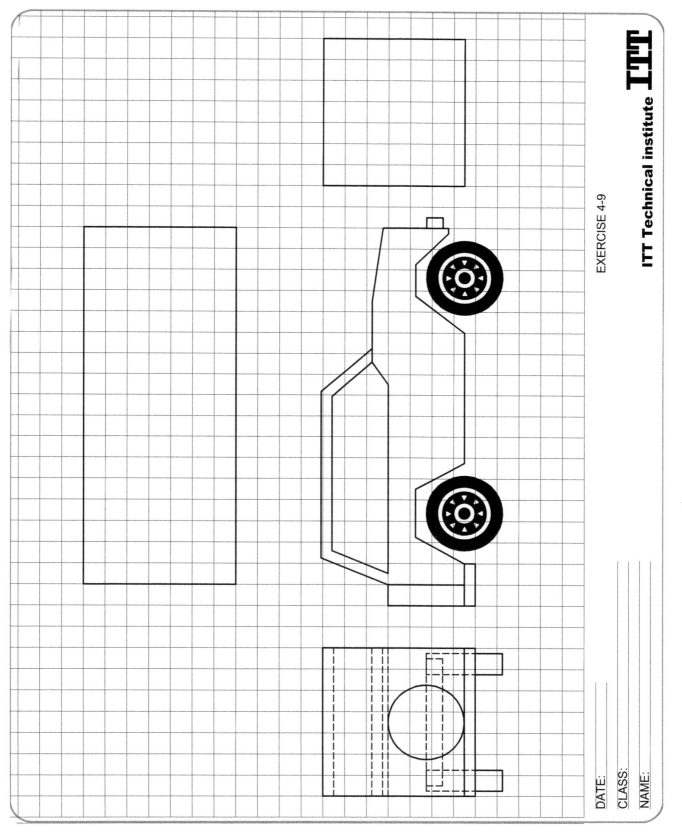

ITT Technical institute

ITT

DATE:

CLASS:

NAME:

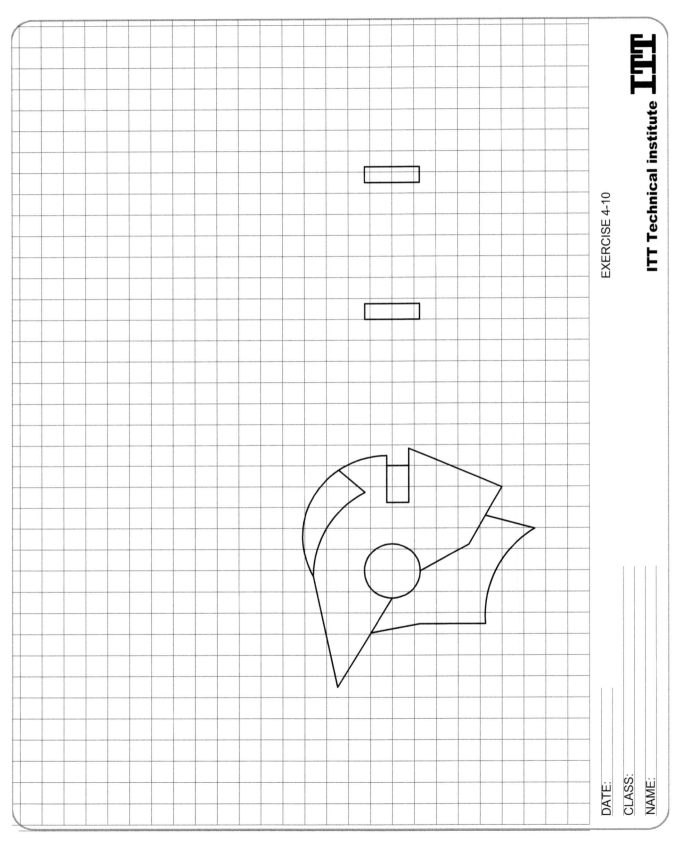

EXERCISE 4-10

ITT Technical institute **ITT**

DATE: _____

CLASS: _____

NAME: _____

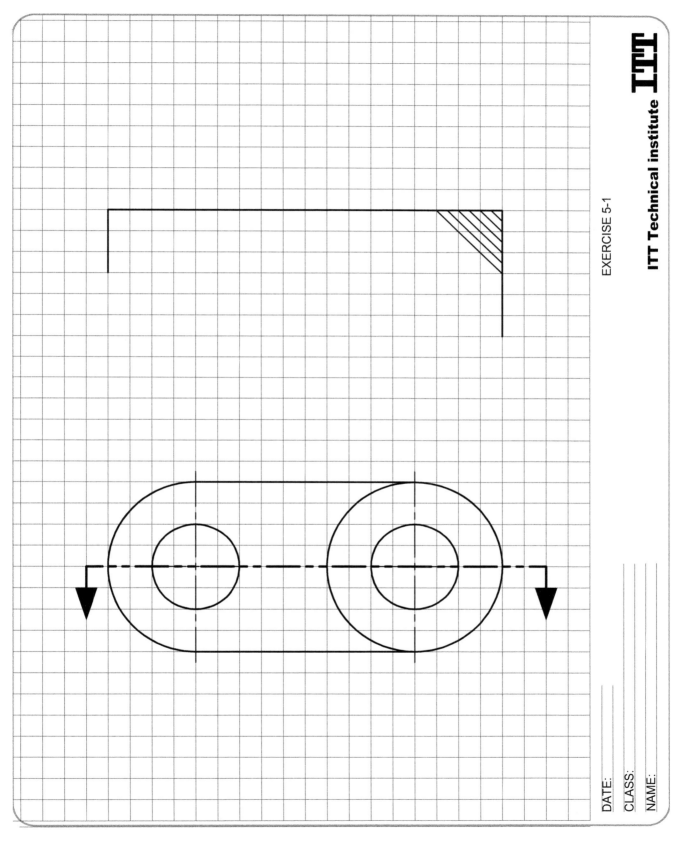

ITT Technical institute

ITT

DATE:

CLASS:

NAME:

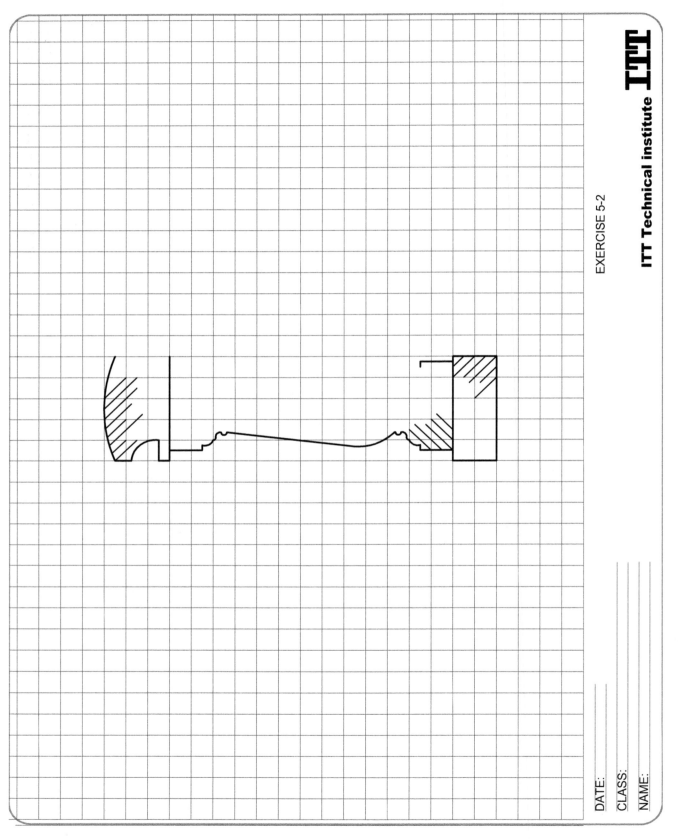

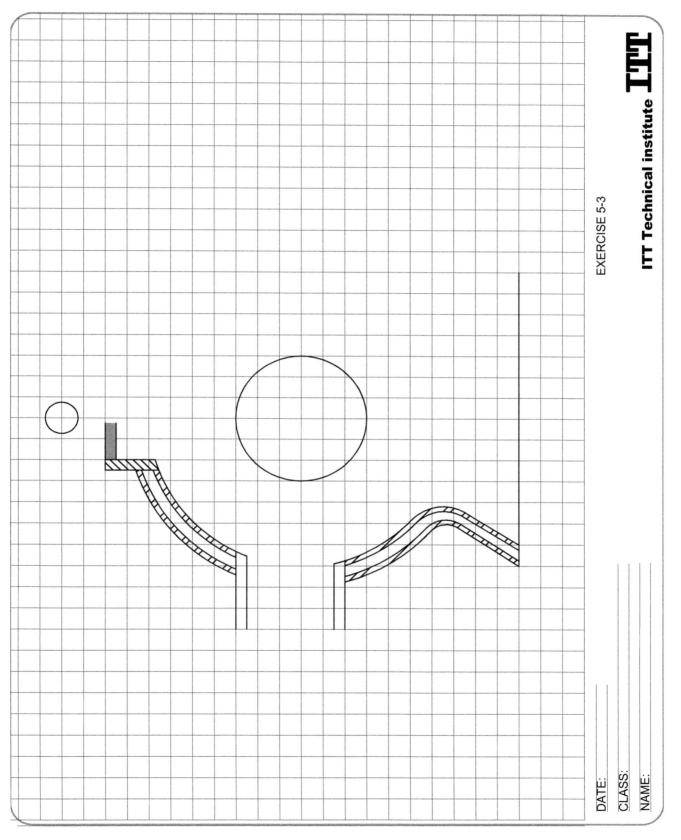

EXERCISE 5-3

ITT Technical institute

DATE:

CLASS:

NAME:

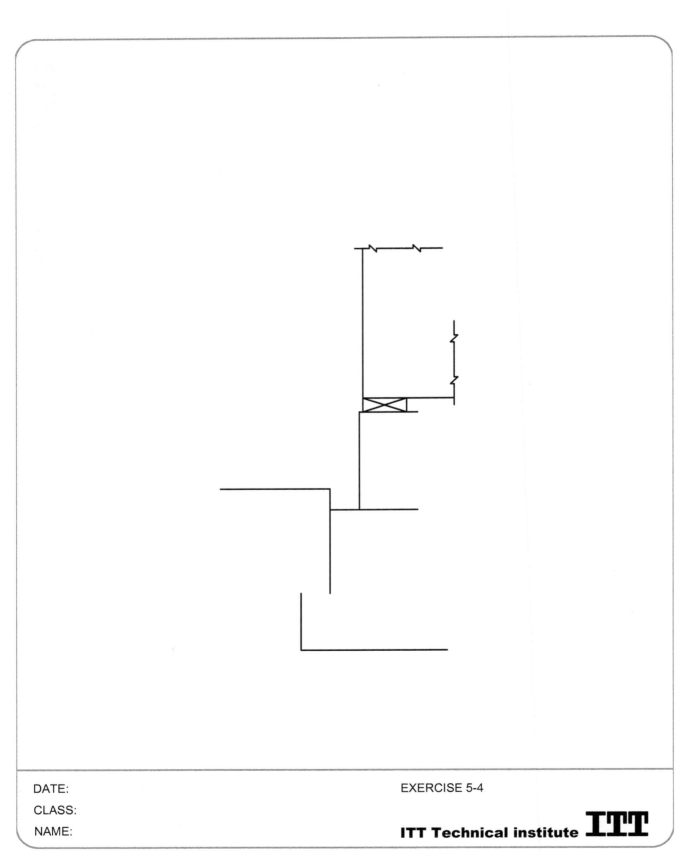

DATE:

CLASS:

NAME:

EXERCISE 5-4

ITT Technical institute **ITT**

A–32

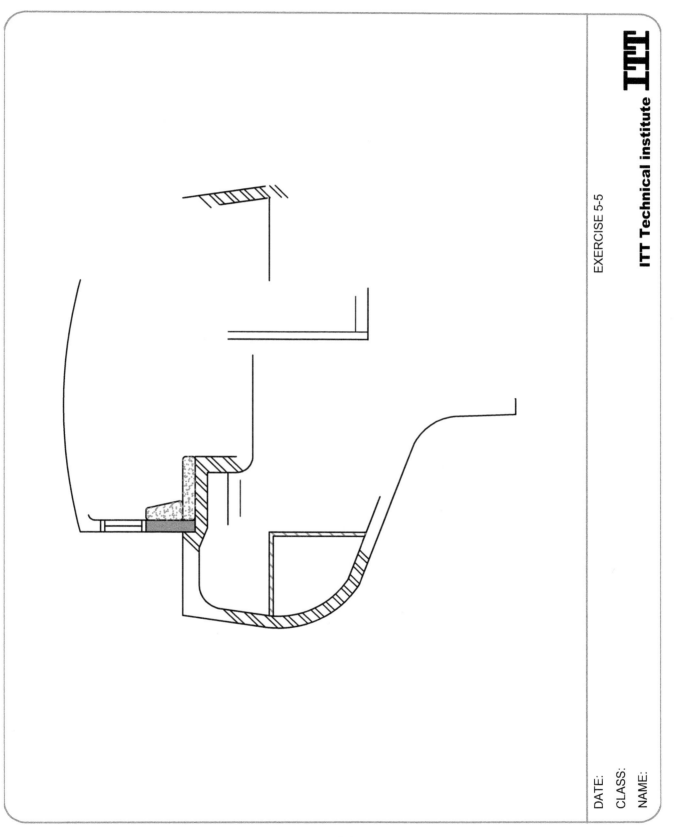

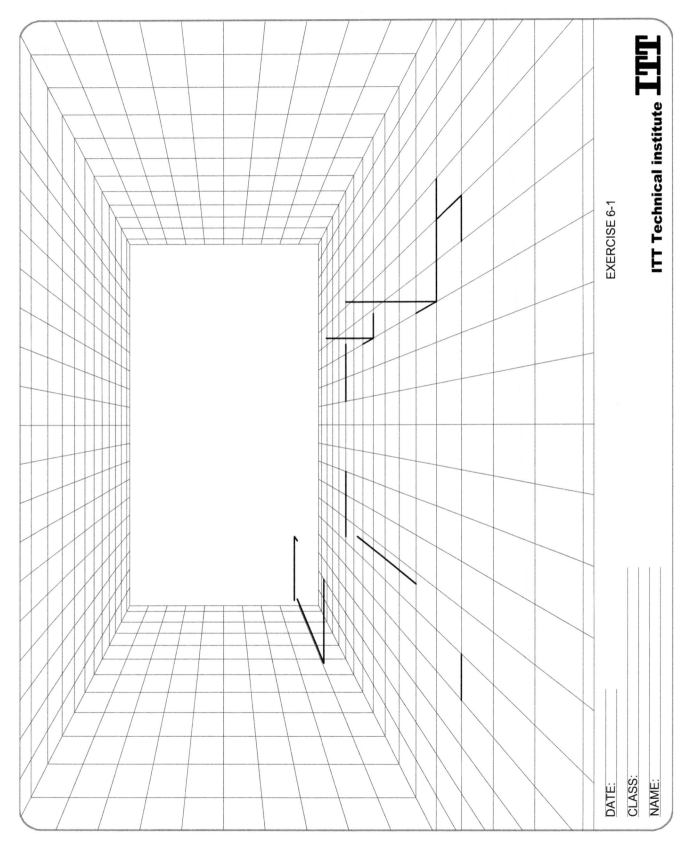

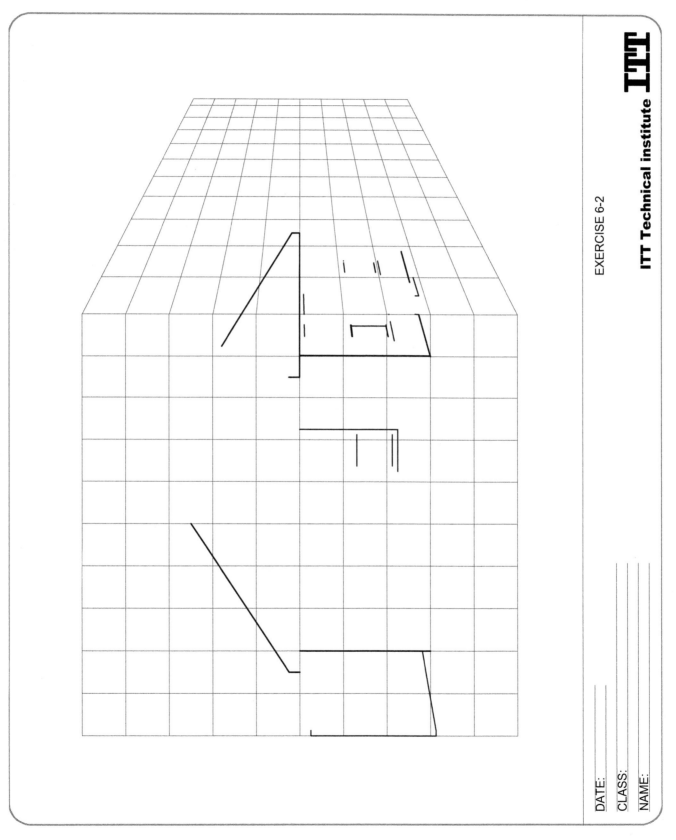

ITT Technical institute

ITT

DATE: _____

CLASS: _____

NAME: _____

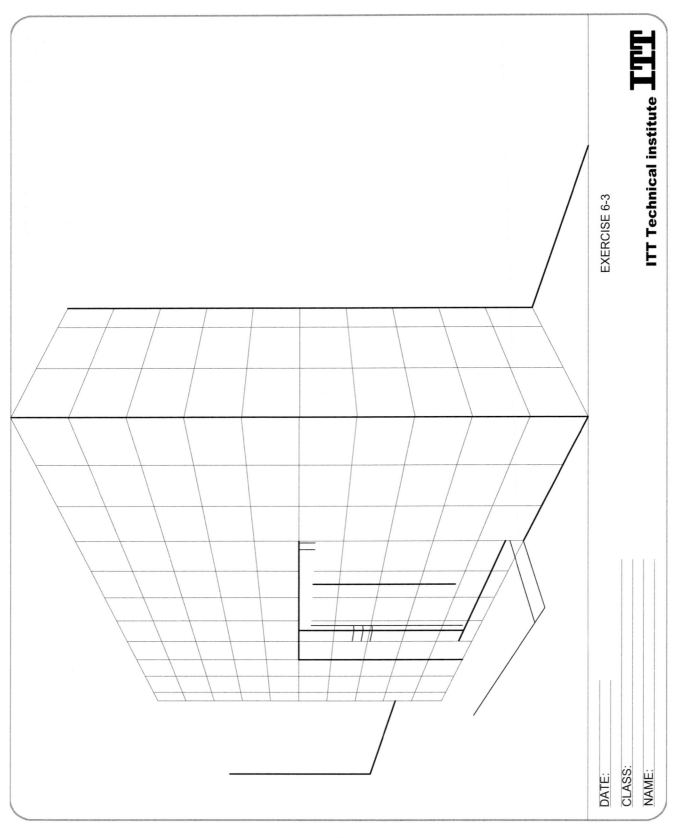

ITT Technical institute

ITT

DATE:

CLASS:

NAME:

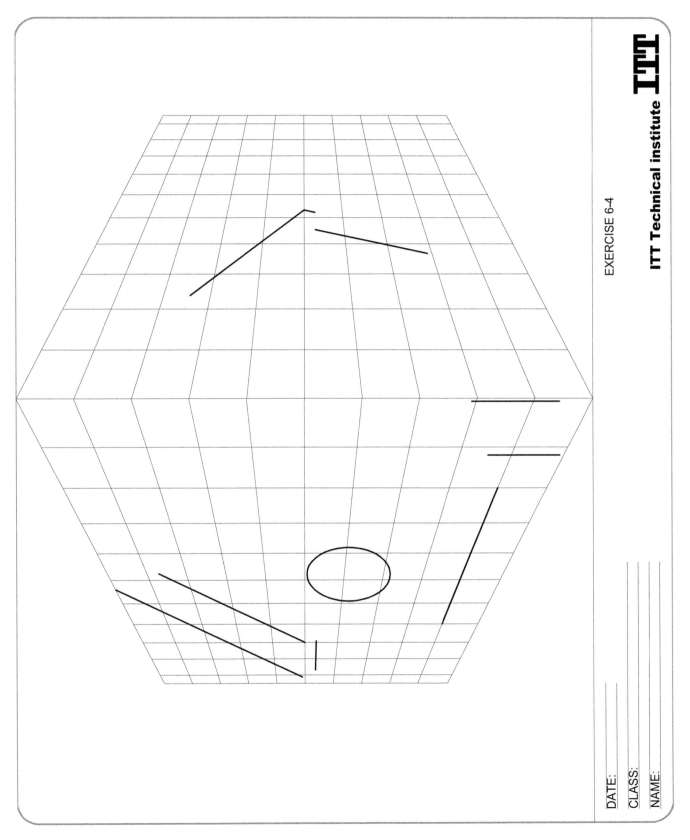

DATE:

CLASS:

NAME:

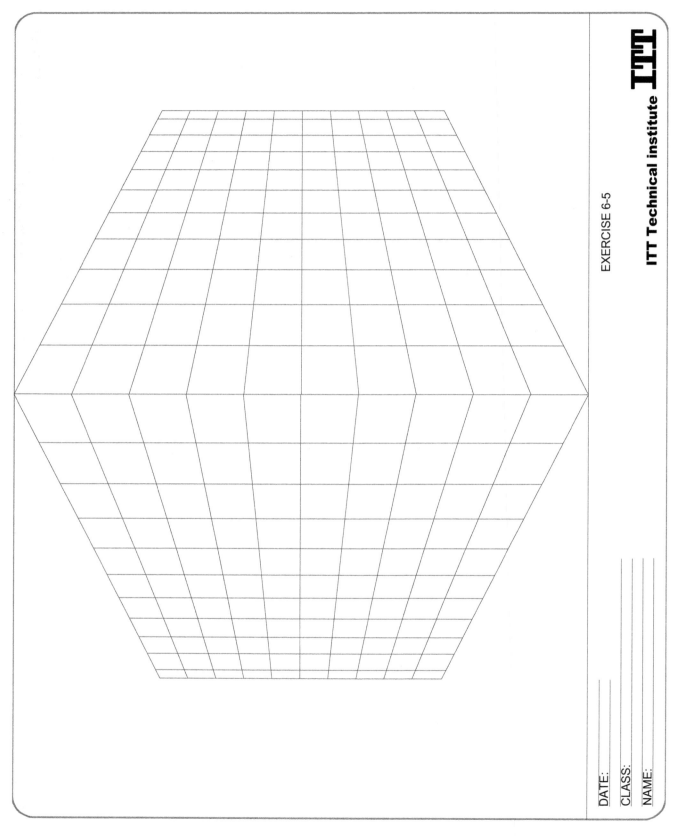

ITT Technical Institute

ITT

DATE:

CLASS:

NAME:

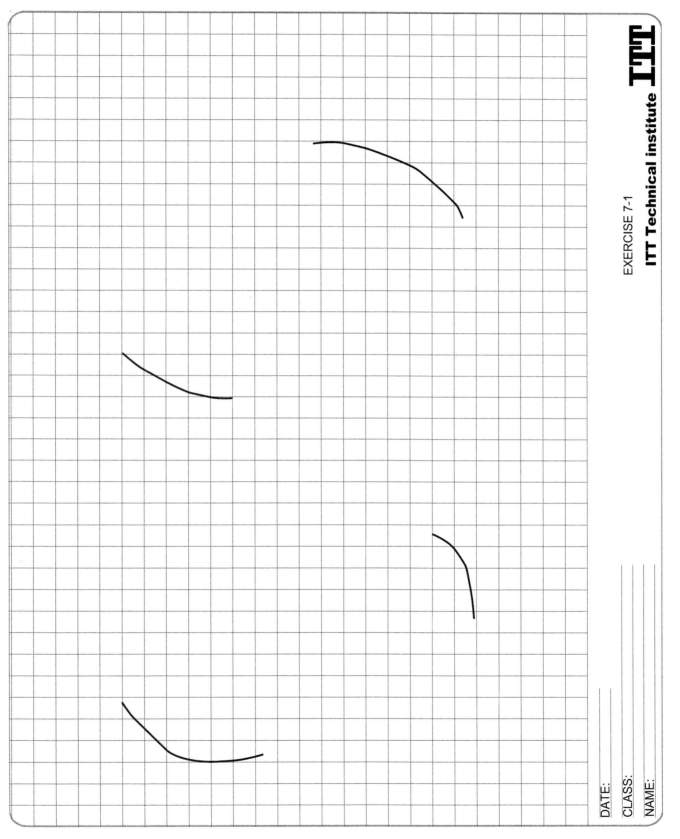

DATE:

CLASS:

NAME:

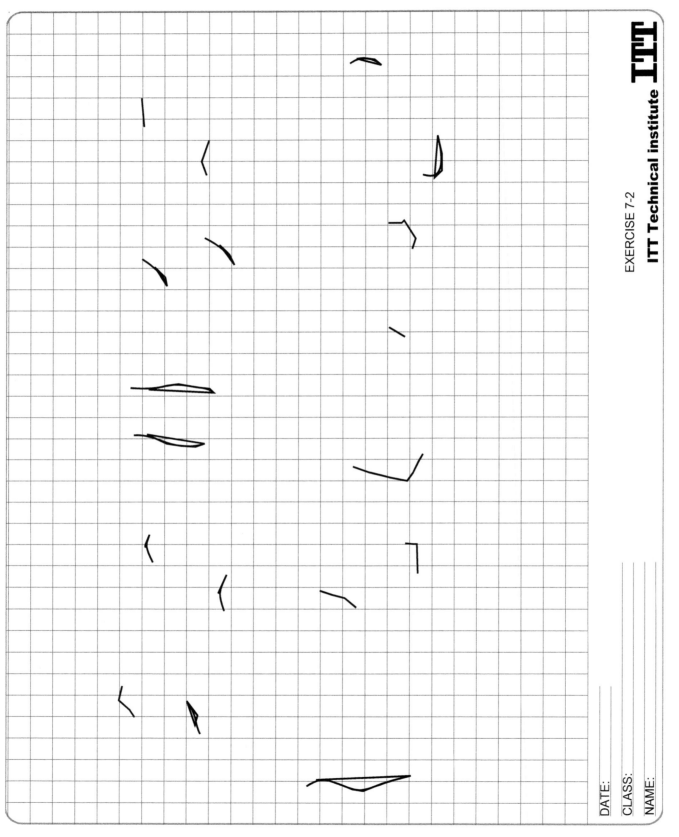

DATE:

CLASS:

NAME:

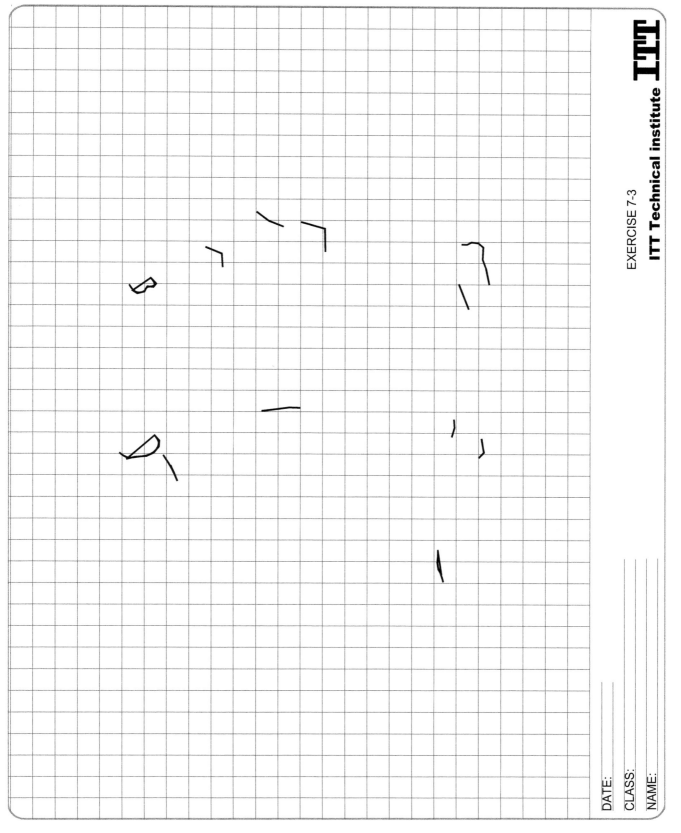

DATE:

CLASS:

NAME:

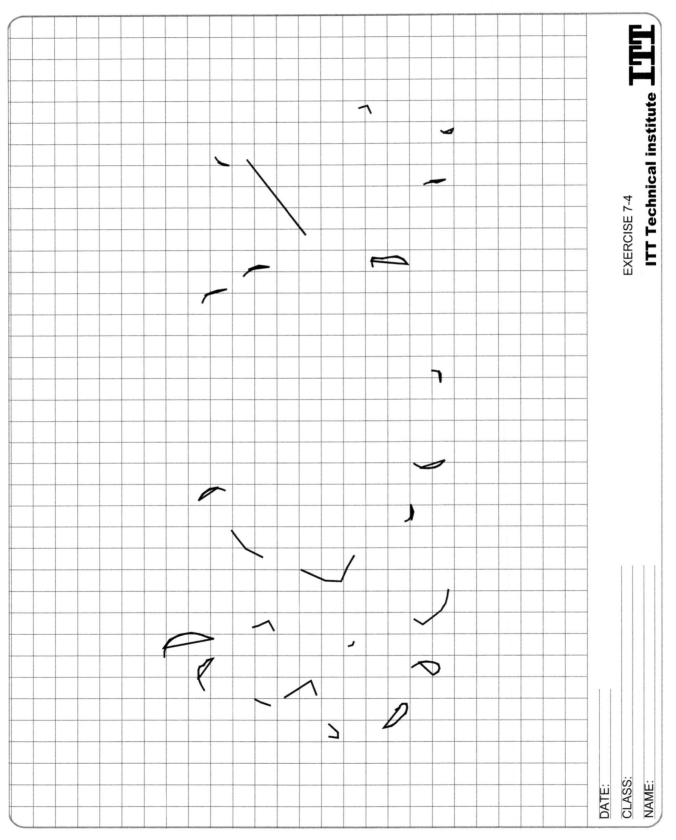

DATE:

CLASS:

NAME:

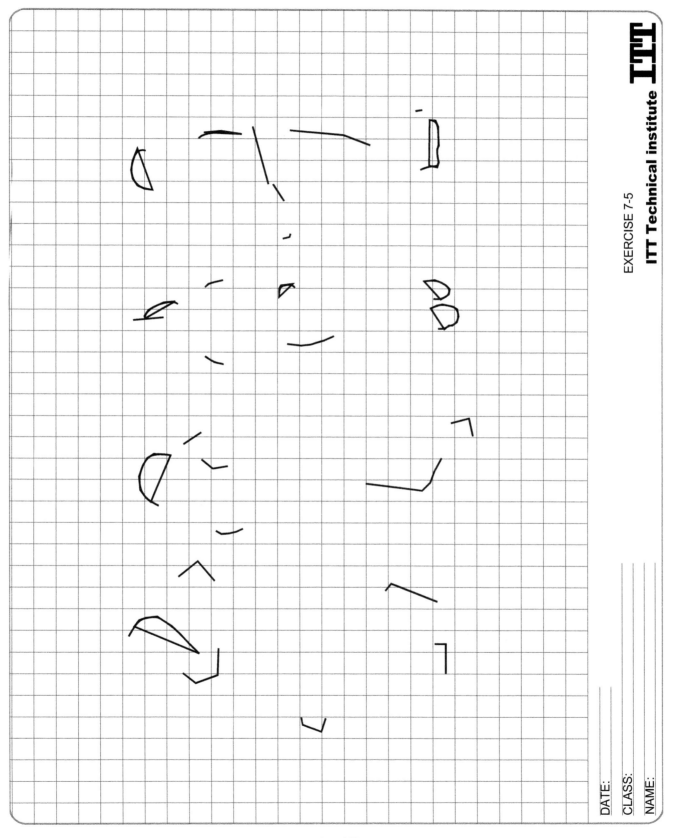

A–43

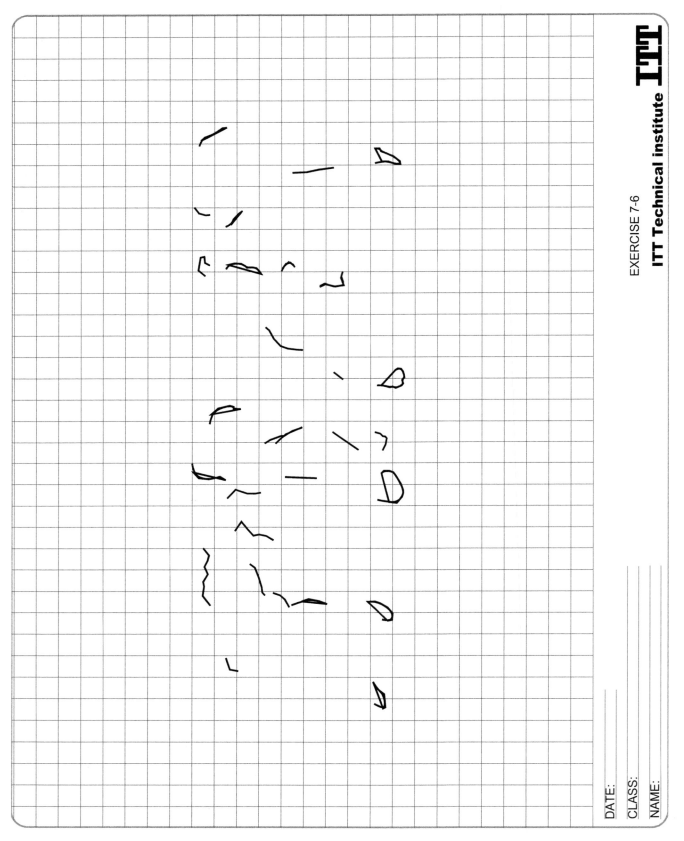

A–44

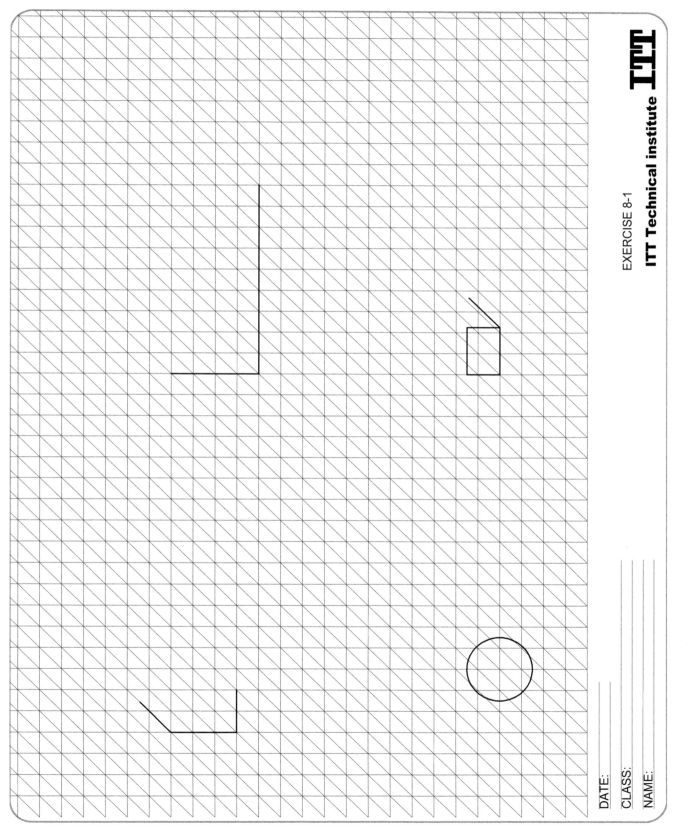

DATE: _____

CLASS: _____

NAME: _____

ITT Technical institute

DATE:

CLASS:

NAME:

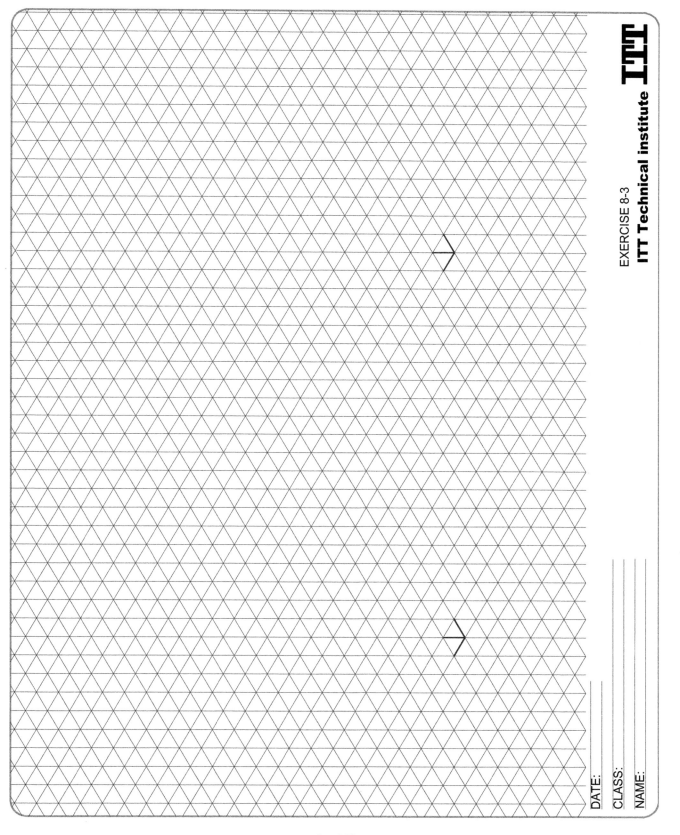

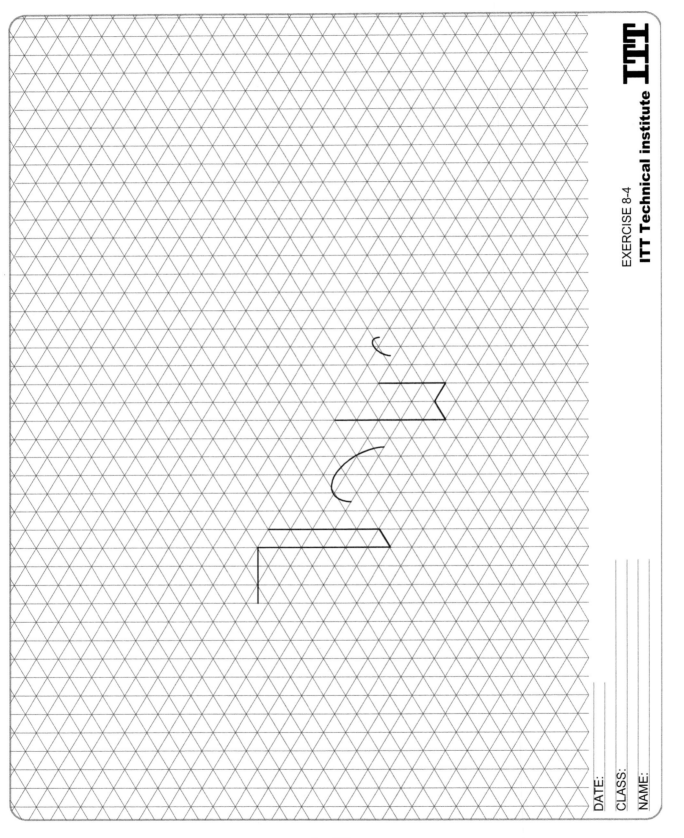

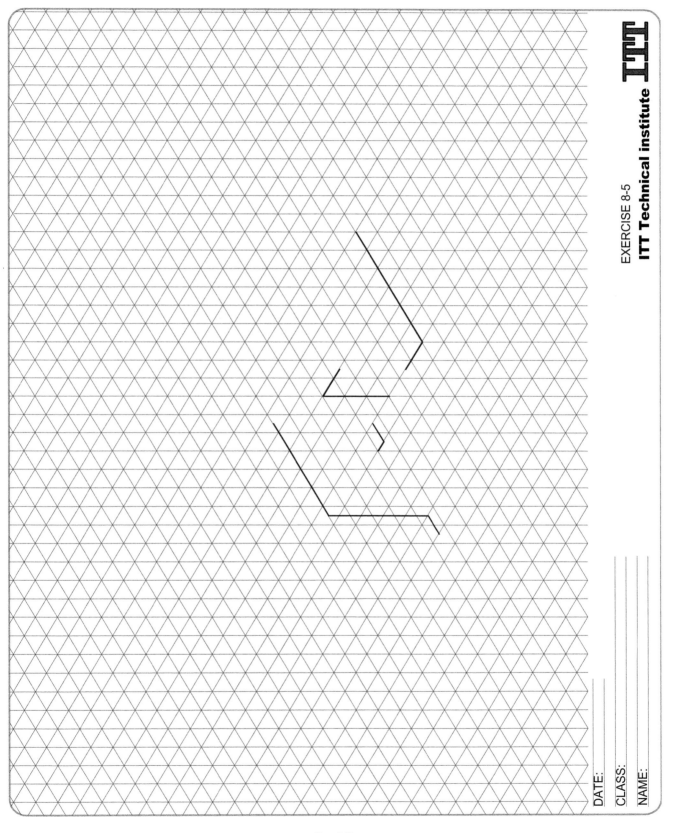

DATE:

CLASS:

NAME:

A–49

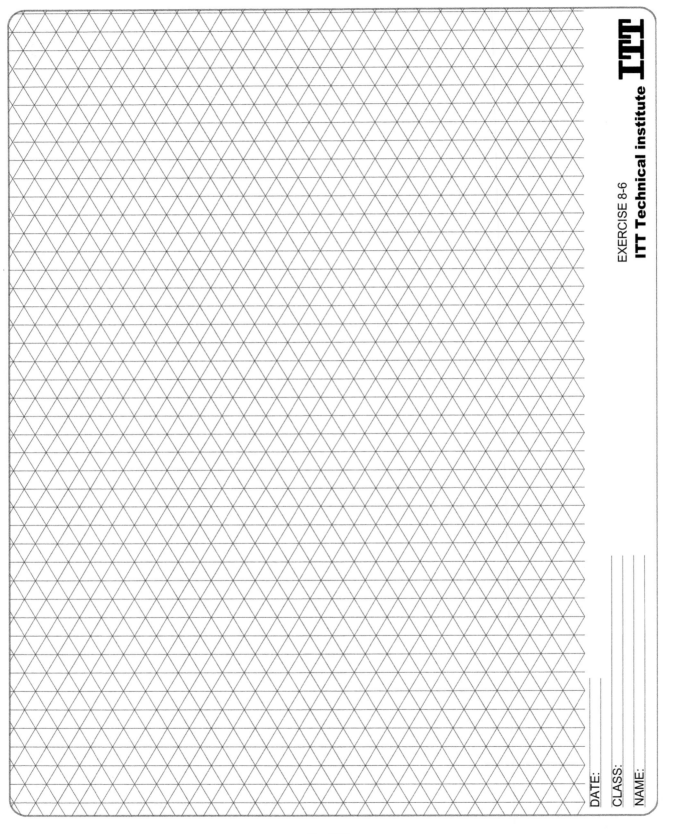

DATE:

CLASS:

NAME:

EXERCISE 8-7

ITT Technical institute

ITT

DATE:

CLASS:

NAME:

A–51

DATE:

CLASS:

NAME:

DATE:

CLASS:

NAME:

EXERCISE 8-12
ITT Technical institute

DATE:

CLASS:

NAME:

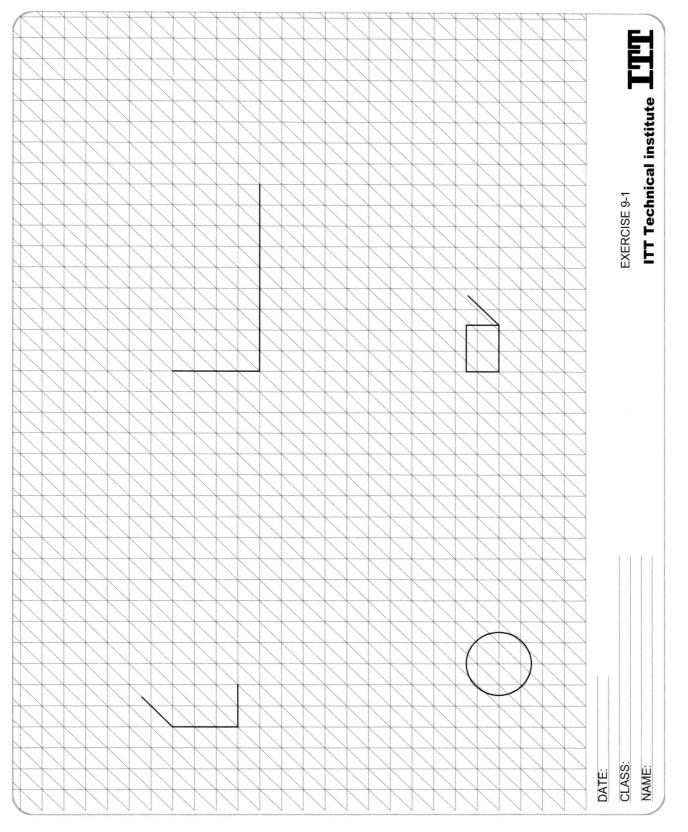

ITT Technical institute

ITT

DATE:

CLASS:

NAME:

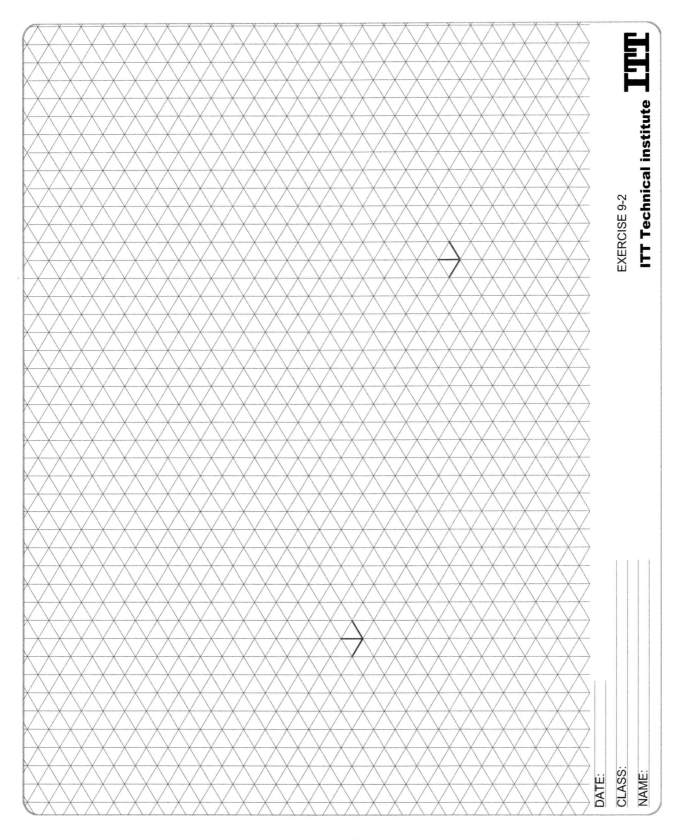

EXERCISE 9-2

ITT Technical institute

DATE:

CLASS:

NAME:

EXERCISE 9-3

ITT Technical institute

ITT

DATE: _____

CLASS: _____

NAME: _____

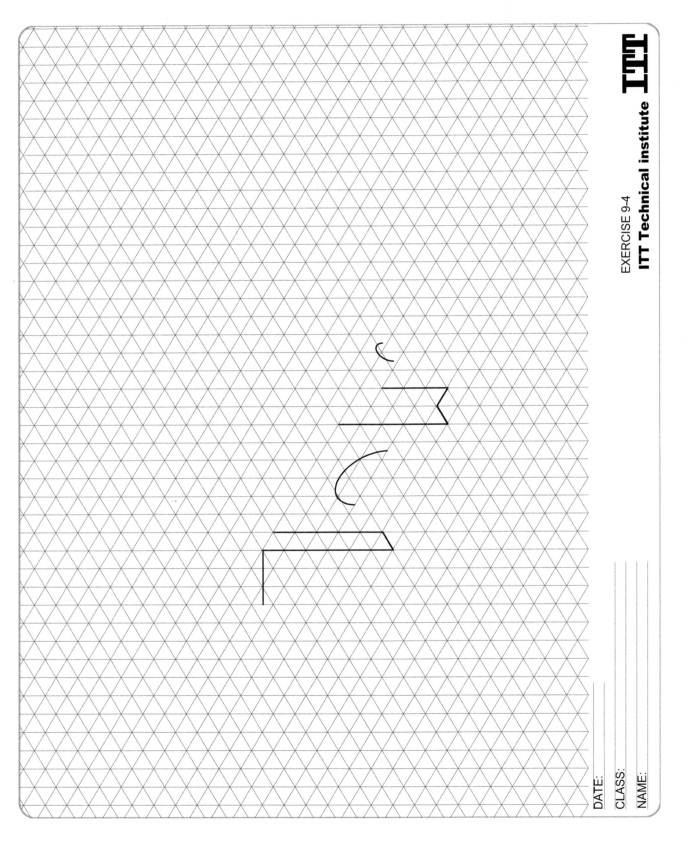

DATE: _____

CLASS: _____

NAME: _____

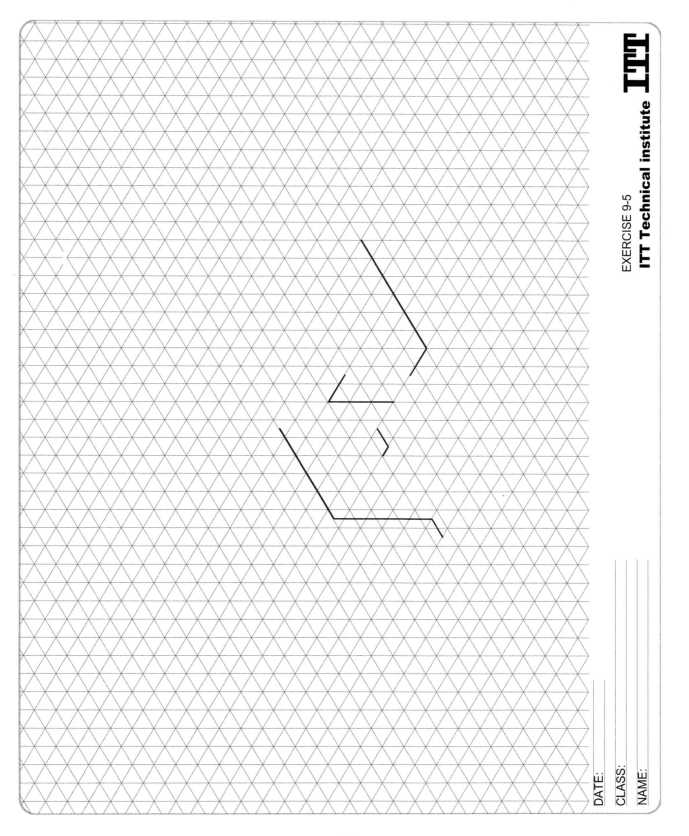

DATE:

CLASS:

NAME:

DATE:

CLASS:

NAME:

EXERCISE 9-7

ITT Technical institute

ITT

DATE: _____

CLASS: _____

NAME: _____

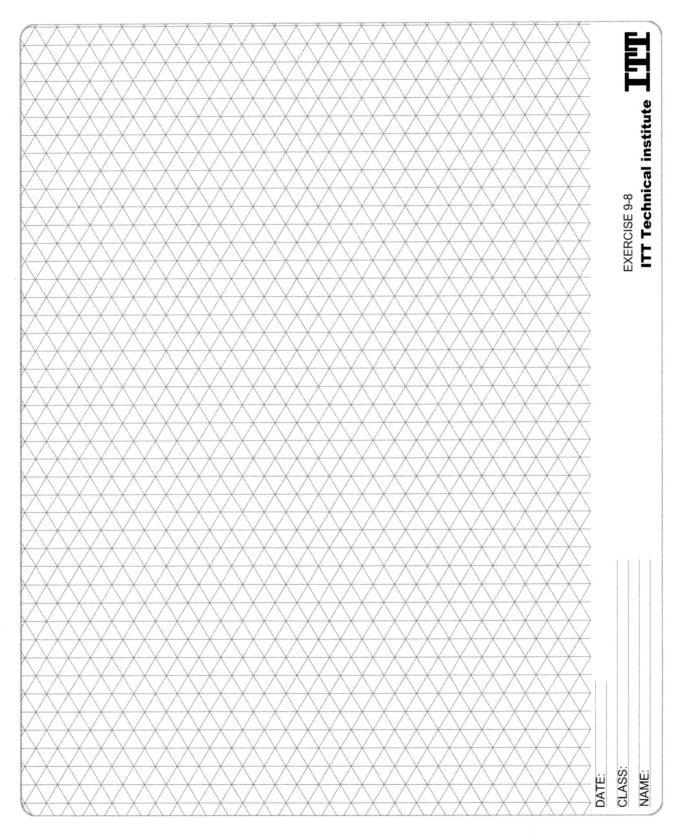

EXERCISE 9-9
ITT Technical institute

DATE:
CLASS:
NAME:

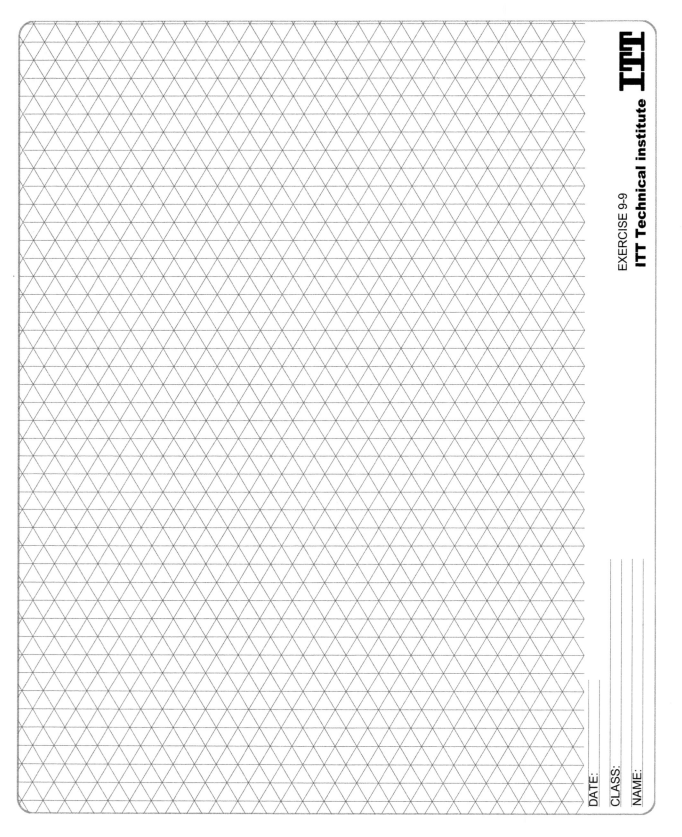

DATE:

CLASS:

NAME:

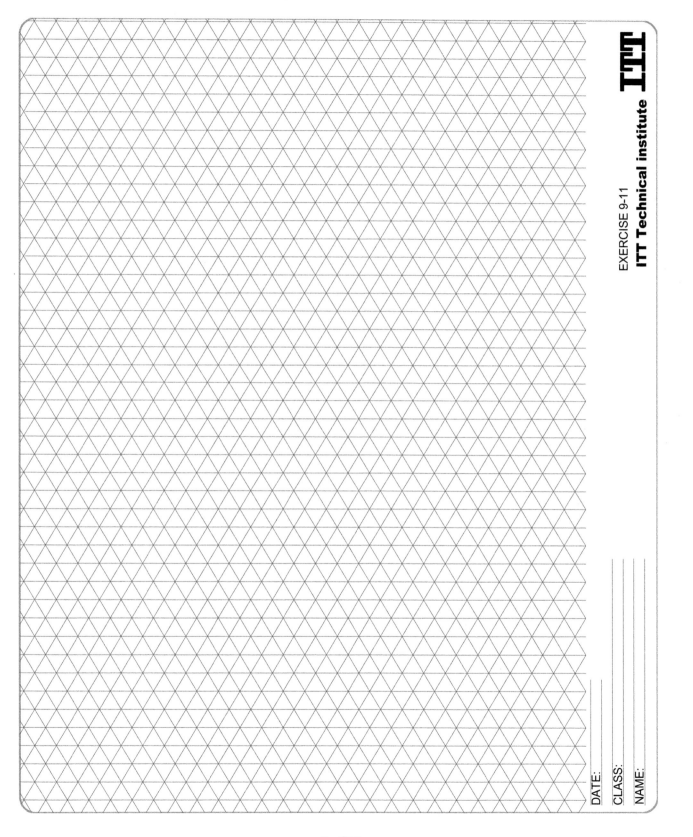

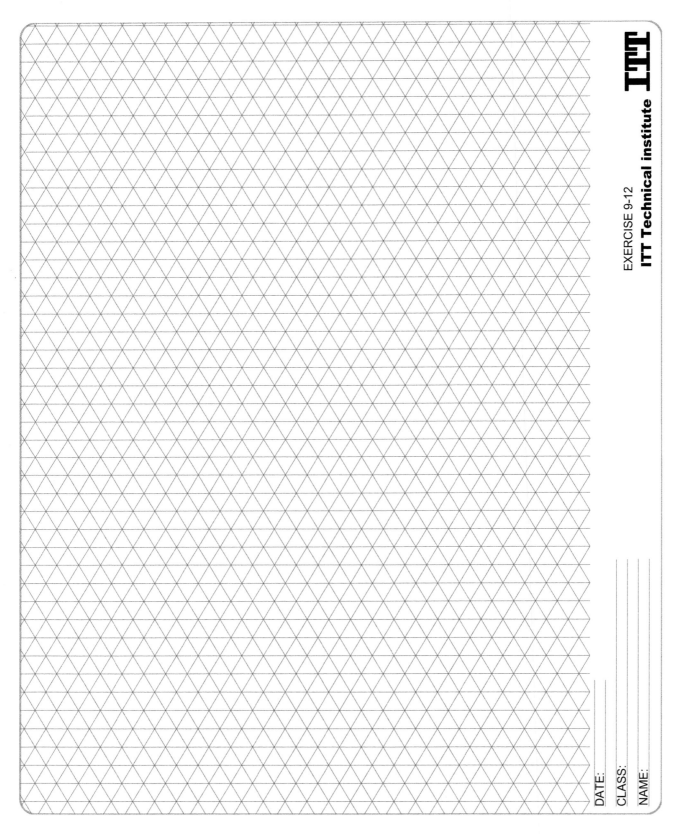

EXERCISE 9-12

ITT Technical institute

ITT

DATE:

CLASS:

NAME:

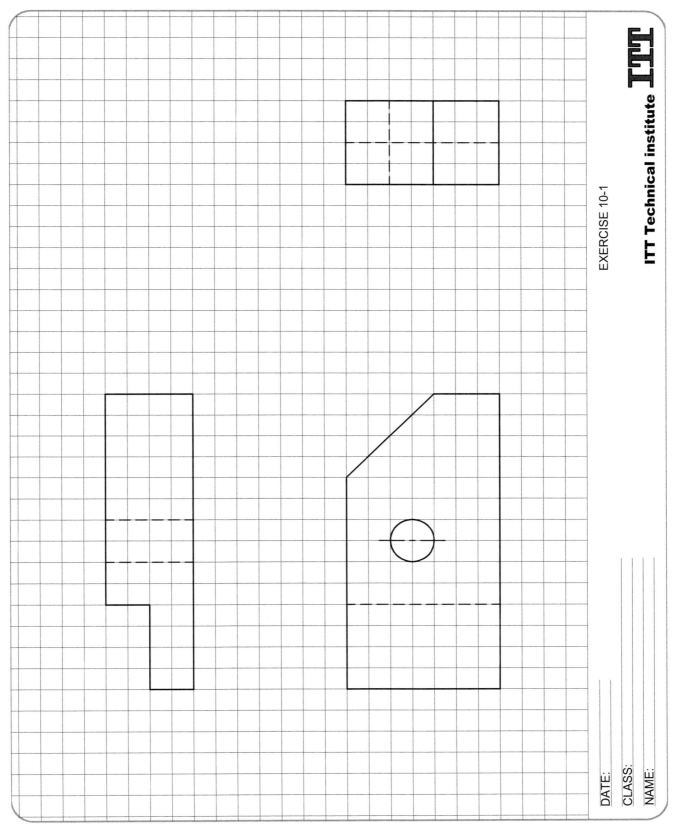

ITT Technical institute

ITT

DATE: _____

CLASS: _____

NAME: _____

A–69

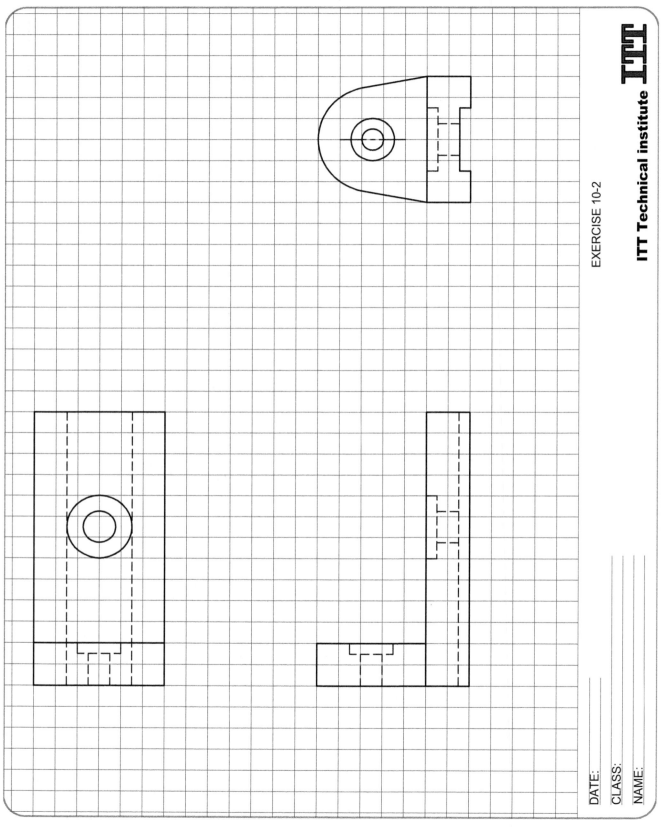

DATE:

CLASS:

NAME:

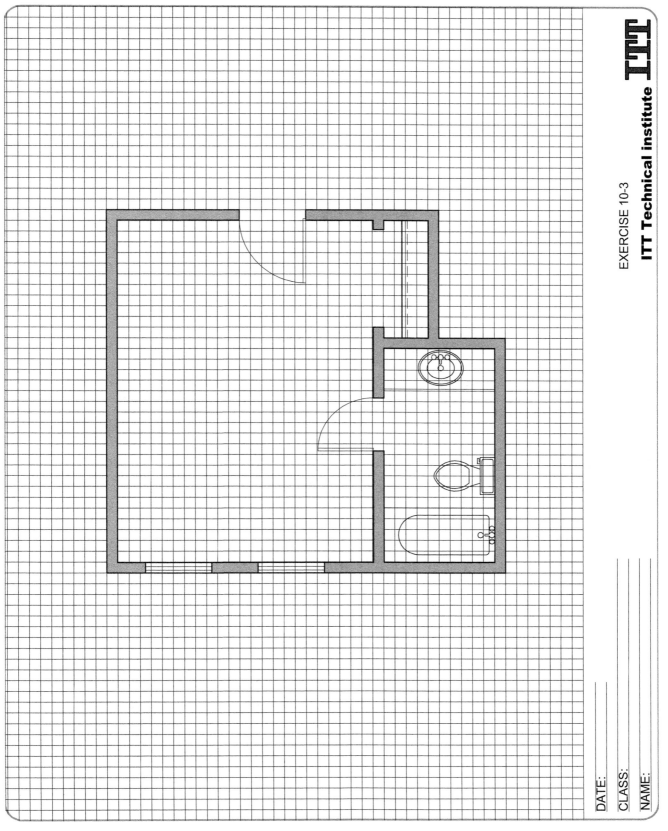

DATE:

CLASS:

NAME:

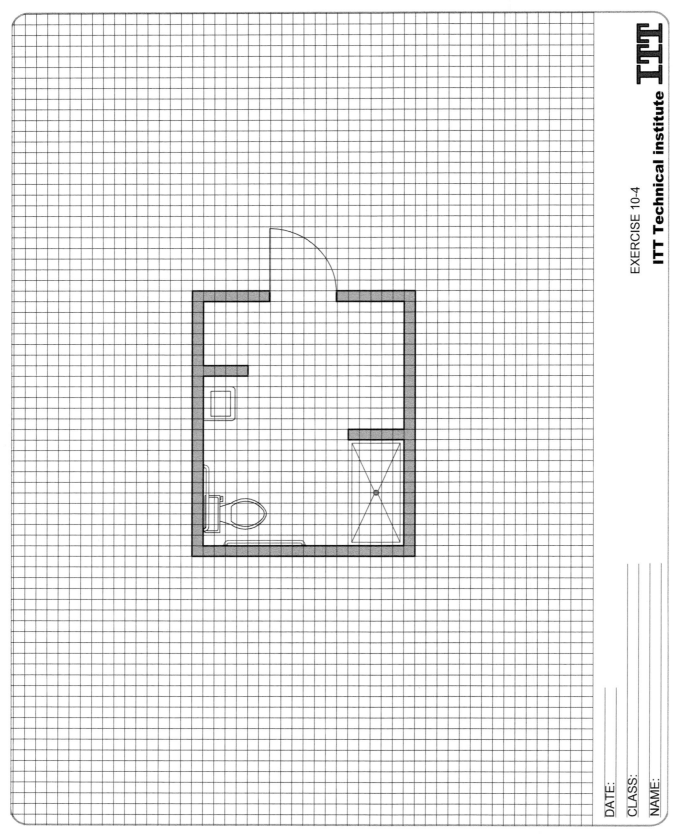

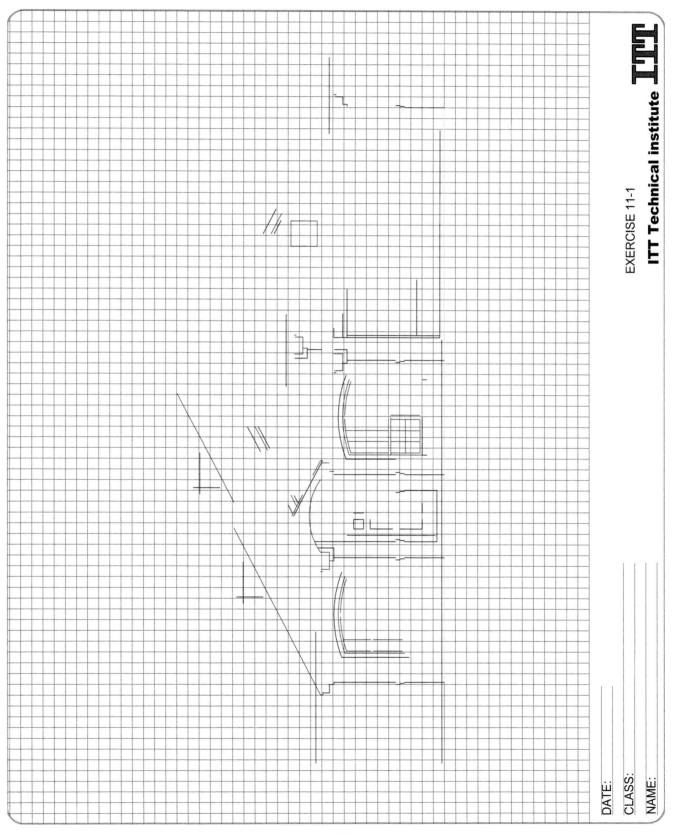

DATE:

CLASS:

NAME:

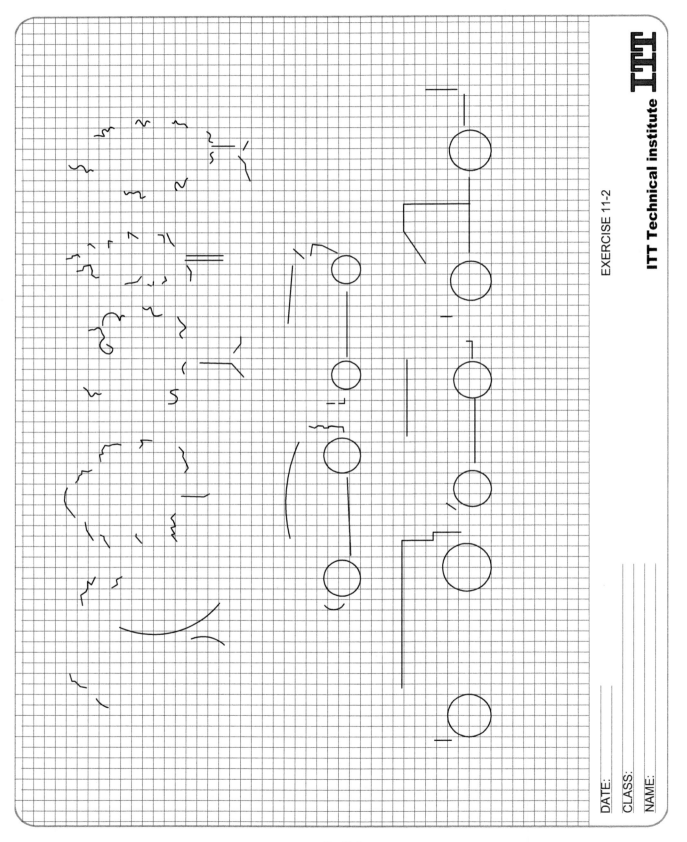

EXERCISE 11-2

ITT Technical institute

DATE: _____

CLASS: _____

NAME: _____

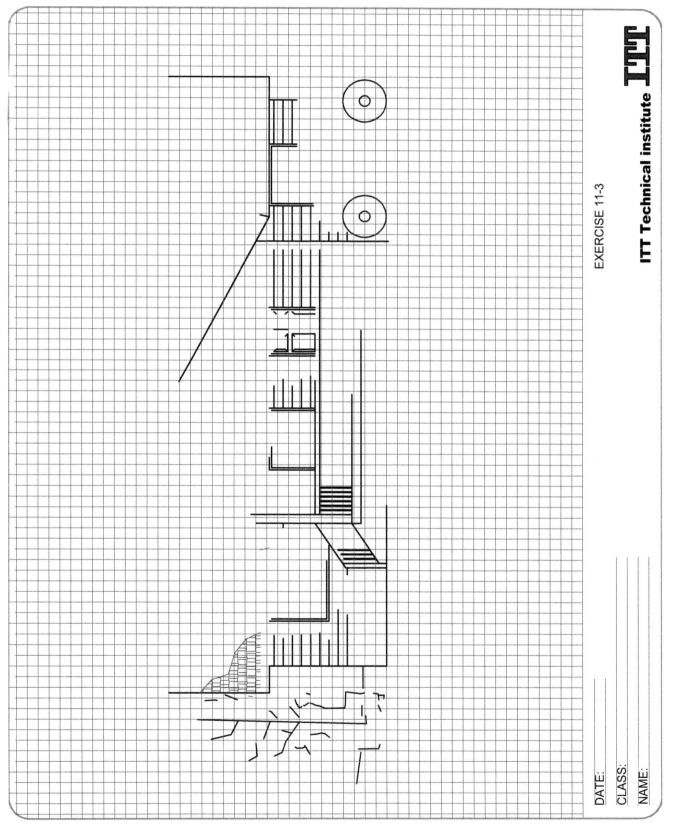

ITT Technical institute

ITT

DATE:

CLASS:

NAME:

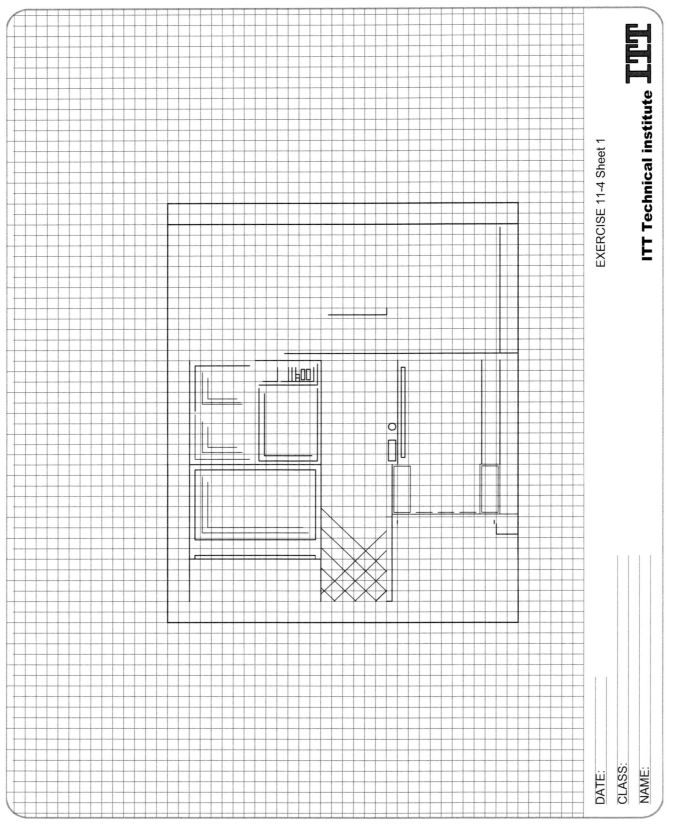

DATE:

CLASS:

NAME:

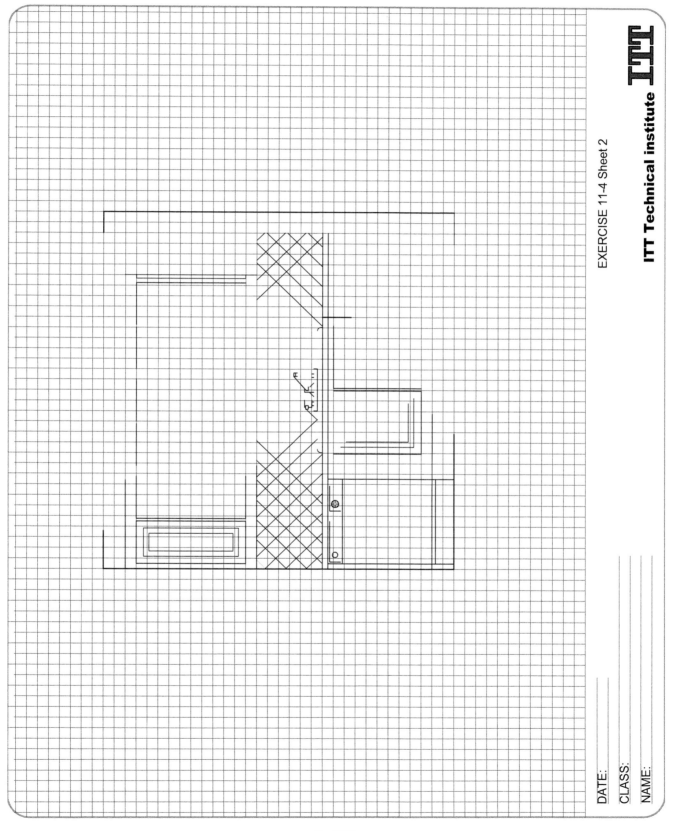

DATE: _____

CLASS: _____

NAME: _____

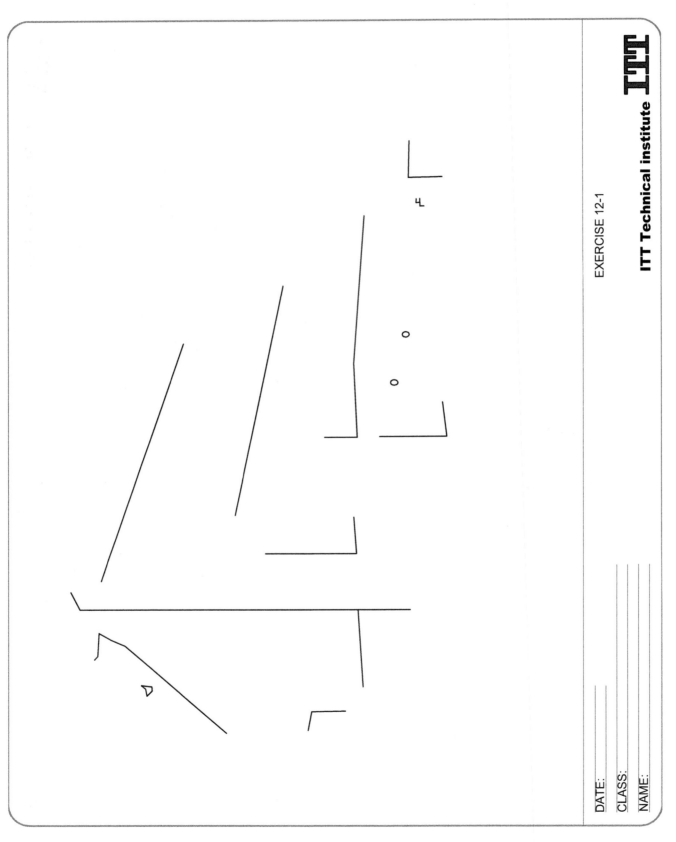

ITT Technical institute

DATE:
CLASS:
NAME:

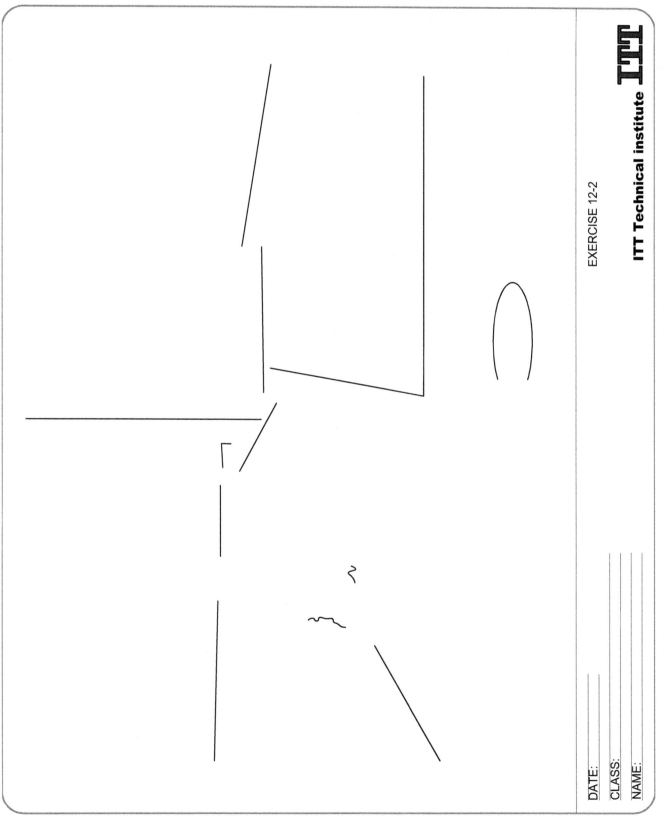

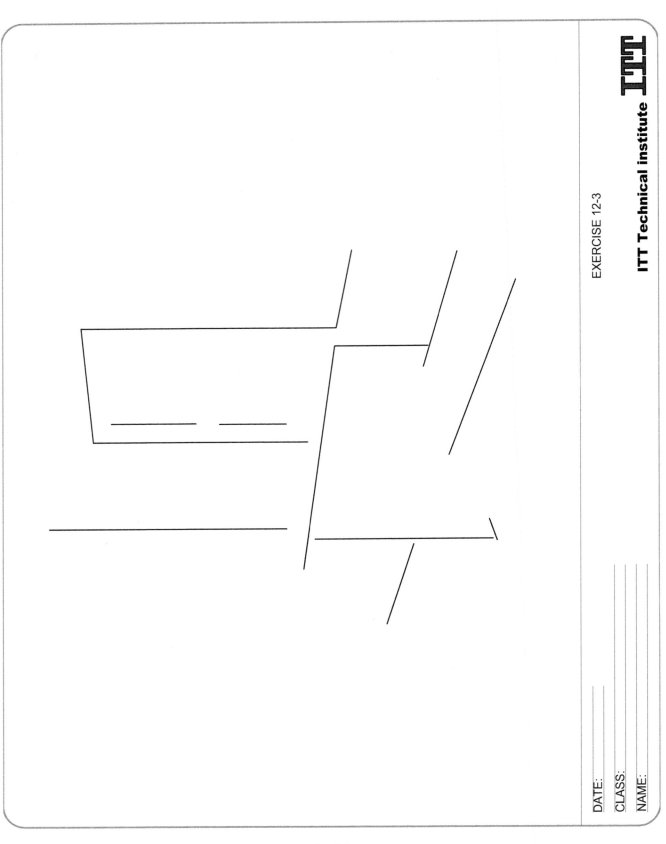

ITT Technical institute

DATE: _____

CLASS: _____

NAME: _____

EXERCISE 12-4

ITT Technical institute

ITT

DATE:

CLASS:

NAME:

EXERCISE 12-5

ITT Technical institute

ITT

DATE: _____

CLASS: _____

NAME: _____

ITT Technical Institute

DATE: _____

CLASS: _____

NAME: _____

ITT Technical institute

DATE: _____

CLASS: _____

NAME: _____

ITT Technical institute

DATE: _____

CLASS: _____

NAME: _____

ITT Technical institute

DATE:

CLASS:

NAME:

ITT Technical institute

ITT

DATE: _____

CLASS: _____

NAME: _____